LADY
UNDER FIRE

LADY UNDER FIRE

THE WARTIME LETTERS OF
LADY DOROTHIE FEILDING MM
1914–1917

EDITED BY
ANDREW AND NICOLA HALLAM

Pen & Sword
MILITARY

First published in Great Britain in 2010 by
Pen & Sword Military
An imprint of
Pen & Sword Books Ltd
47 Church Street
Barnsley
South Yorkshire
S70 2AS

ISBN 978 1 84884 322 6

A CIP catalogue record for this book is
available from the British Library

Typeset by Acredula

Printed and bound in England
By CPI Books

Pen & Sword Books Ltd incorporates the Imprints of Pen & Sword Aviation,
Pen & Sword Family History, Pen & Sword Maritime, Pen & Sword Military,
Wharncliffe Local History, Pen & Sword Select, Pen & Sword Military Classics,
Leo Cooper, Remember When, Seaforth Publishing and Frontline Publishing

For a complete list of Pen & Sword titles please contact
PEN & SWORD BOOKS LIMITED
47 Church Street, Barnsley, South Yorkshire, S70 2AS, England
E-mail: enquiries@pen-and-sword.co.uk
Website: www.pen-and-sword.co.uk

Contents

Preface

'I was sitting at an open window [in Calais] … when I saw a lady's face in the street. The last time I had seen it was in an old English mansion, filled with many gallant and gentle ghosts of history, and with laughing girls who went scampering out to a game of tennis on the lawn below the terrace from which a scent of roses and climbing plants was wafted up on the drowsy air of an English summer. It was strange to see one of those girls in Calais, where such a different game was being played. She had a gravity in her eyes which I had not seen before in England, and yet, afterwards, I heard her laughter ring out within a little distance of bursting shells.'

Philip Gibbs, *Soul of War*, 1915

The lady that Gibbs describes meeting was Lady Dorothie Feilding, the daughter of the 9th Earl of Denbigh. Only twenty-four years old when the First World War broke out, and with three brothers already in the services, she had seized the opportunity to be useful. After a short training course at St Cross Hospital in Rugby, she joined the Munro Ambulance Corps to drive ambulances in Belgium. She would go on to be the first woman to be awarded the Military Medal for bravery in the field, in addition to receiving two further medals from Belgium and France.

Dorothie was born on 6 October 1889 at Newnham Paddox, in Warwickshire, the ancestral home of the Feilding family since 1433. In her letters the affection between the Feildings is obvious and this manifests itself in a proliferation of nicknames; so the Earl and Countess of Denbigh and their children – Rudolph, Hugh, Mary, Dorothie, Agnes, Marjorie, Henry, Clare, Elizabeth and Victoria – become Da, Ma, Rollo/Tubby, Hughie/Neb, Moll, Diddles/Dodo, Agger, Marjie, Peter, Squeaker, Betty and Taffy. In fact, Dorothie had nicknames for most things including her hot water bottle (Jim), her ambulance (Daniel) and even for period pain (Tonks).

She spent almost three years at the Belgian front, with periods of leave ranging from a few days to several weeks. Warwickshire County Record Office holds some

400 letters, postcards and telegrams that she sent home during this period. She wrote almost daily, especially early in the war, from short notes to long epistles. All her letters were handwritten – she sometimes wrote on any bits of paper that came to hand and with whatever writing instrument she could find: pens of varying quality that she sometimes curses in her writing, but most often in pencil, which means, sadly, the letters are slowly fading with time. Along with photographs and other reminiscences by Dorothie, these make up a small part of the vast Feilding collection.

Once our transcription of her correspondence was complete, it became apparent that we would have to make some changes for the collection to be more readable.

We have edited the collection down and, although some letters are here in their entirety, others, such as short telegrams detailing arrival and departure times, and duplicate letters to both mother and father, have been removed altogether.

The dates of her letters are occasionally a bit vague, understandably so considering that she was so busy and working at night a lot of the time. We have arranged the letters in the most sensible order and clarified the dates where necessary.

We have corrected her erratic spelling and punctuation but have left the words that she has purposefully misspelled, for example, 'diskivered' and 'anyfink'. She was a fluent French speaker and often lapsed into that language. We have translated the larger paragraphs but have left the single words such as *blessé* for wounded and *obus* for shell.

Her letters are largely uncensored as she often either sent them via people she knew were heading back to England, or through friends she made amongst the officer class. Occasionally, though, some were censored and large chunks cut out, much to her indignation.

Also, we believe that Dorothie censored her own letters after the war, or when home on leave. Some bear her writing in pencil with amended dates, often incorrect, others refer to letters in which she had been angry or rude to her mother and, while these were clearly received at Newnham, they were not amongst the letters that remain. There are no letters in the collection between February and April 1916. Although she did have a period of leave it is not clear what has happened to these letters, if even there ever were any. It seems unlikely that Dorothie would have gone for such a long period without writing.

Dorothie's letters provide a fascinating insight into life at the front line, right at the 'heart and pulse of things': dodging shells and misogynist officers; healing the sick and easing the passing of the dying; driving ambulances in the dark with no lights; dealing with fleas and marriage proposals; and just living from one moment to the next. While she downplayed her experiences and her role, it is clear that she must have had not only some terrifying moments but also, especially at the beginning, lived in some uncomfortable circumstances. We have included excerpts from other sources – official newspaper reporters such as Philip Gibbs and fellow ambulance workers such as Mr Gleason – to illustrate more fully some of the events.

Her early letters are full of wonder and excitement, and packed with detail. This enthusiasm inevitably fades over time and the details of what is happening lessen. Sometimes she only makes passing mention of the war and describes such jolly times that it is easy to forget that this was going on against a backdrop of artillery bombardments and the daily horrors of looking for wounded.

Excerpts from letters by and about Dorothie Feilding and related photographs reproduced by kind permission of the Warwickshire County Record Office.

Dramatis Personae

DOROTHIE'S PARENTS:

Mrs Ma/Commandant	Cecilia Mary Feilding (née Clifford), Countess of Denbigh
Mr Da	Rudolph Robert Basil Aloysius Feilding, 9th Earl of Denbigh

SIBLINGS (IN ORDER OF AGE):

Rollo/Tubby	Rudolph Edmund Aloysius Feilding, Viscount Feilding, DSO, Lieutenant later Captain, Coldstream Guards
Hughie/Neb	Lieutenant Commander Hugh Cecil Robert Feilding
Moll	Mary Feilding
Agger	Agnes Feilding
Marjie	Marjorie Feilding
Peter	Henry Simon Feilding, Lieutenant later Captain, Coldstream Guards
Squeaker	Clare Feilding
Bettie	Elizabeth Feilding
Taffy	Victoria Feilding

OTHER RELATIONS:

Dudley	Captain Edward Dudley Hanly, Royal Inniskilling Fusiliers
Evy	Francis Henry Everard Joseph Feilding, Dorothie's uncle
Geoffrey	Major General Geoffrey Percy Thynne Feilding, GOC Guards Division

Gladys/Boo	Gladys Hanly, sister of Edward Dudley Hanly
Mellins	Agnes Imelda Feilding (née Harding) married to Rollo

FRIENDS AND COLLEAGUES:

Burbidge	Lieutenant Arthur William Lancelot Brewill, Royal Navy
Deb	Lieutenant Arthur Henry Seymour Casswell, Royal Navy
Field	Archibald William Field, RNVR/RFC, Lieutenant, later Captain
Ginger	Lieutenant Desmond Nevill Cooper Tufnell, Royal Navy
Hélene	Hélene Van der Wende, Belgian refugee
Jelly	Dr Henry Jellett MD, Dublin gynaecologist
Johnie Baird	John Lawrence Baird, Intelligence Corps. Conservative member for Rugby 1910–1922, Dorothie's godfather
Mairi	Mairi Chisholm
Mrs K	Elsie Knocker, later Baroness de T'Serclaes
Munro	Dr Hector Munro, founder of the Munro Ambulance Corps
Ommanney	Captain Rupert Ommanney, Royal Engineers, attached to GSO3 2nd Division Staff
Papa Broqueville	Charles de Broqueville, Prime Minister of Belgium 1911–1918. He had five sons: Pierre, John, André, Robert, Jacques.
Robert de Broqueville	Son of the above. Given military command of the Munro Ambulance Corps, later Captain in Artillery. He was married to Théresé.
Peter Chalmers	Lieutenant William Scott Chalmers, Royal Navy
Ronarc'h	Admiral Pierre-Alexis Ronarc'h, 1914 Marie Fusilier Brigade, 4th Cavalry Division, French VIII Army
Shoppee	Lieutenant Denys Gerald Charles Shoppee, Royal Navy

Teck/Algy	Major General His Serene Highness Prince Alexander of Teck, brother to Queen Mary
The Bloke/Halahan	Commander Henry Crosby Halahan, Royal Navy, naval guns in Flanders
The Gen/Roger	General Roger Hély d'Oissel, 1914 commander of 7th Cavalry Division, French VIII Army
Winkie	Winkie Speight

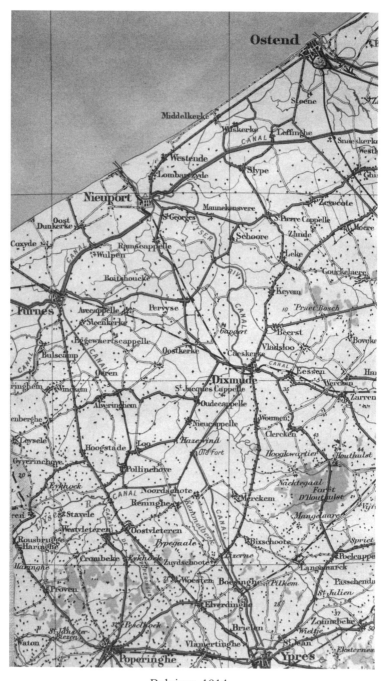

Belgium, 1914.

CHAPTER 1

August–September 1914

Dorothie trained at Rugby St Cross Hospital in preparation for service overseas. Even though she was not far from home, she still wrote regularly to her mother. Her first letter from the hospital was dated 24 August 1914 – as war had only been declared on the 5th, she had obviously not wasted any time.

She confessed that she was impatient with herself for not picking things up quickly: 'I'm getting on well here but wish one didn't take so long getting a grasp of new things. It's a bit despairing sometimes but I s'pose no one yet learnt a lot about anything in a week.' Later, she tells her father: 'I felt terribly clumsy the first days, but am much more use now.'

She was already keeping a close eye on events:

> I saw McKinnie today who proudly told me they had roped in 240 recruits by that meeting & that 40 more joined yesterday. Rather splendid for podgy Rugby inhabitants. I didn't think they had the spunk … Dudley will be home very soon. I wonder if it's possible that they will put him straight back into his regiment or into the Reserve … What ghastly news this is of our losses. It makes one sick with anxiety. Mellins tells me Rollo nearly went yesterday & his C.O. [Commanding Officer] says he is sure to go. Poor little Mellins.

She was quite pragmatic at the idea of working with wounded men – as part of her training she was required to work in the men's wards at St Cross.

> I'd much rather, & you know in the men's wards they don't make you do any more terrible things than in the women's, in fact they say are far less trouble as they don't go in for dozens of minor diseases like us poor women. Please write me about this, not the matron as she hasn't said anything to me. After all if we are wanted to help the tommies we must be a bit in the men's wards to be any good.

Dorothie calls all Allied soldiers Tommies.

She already had realistic expectations of what was to come, thanks to her contacts in the military:

Had a long letter from Ommanney who is at the front on Headquarters staff of General Communications. He went over in the 1st boatload to see to getting troops across. He was on French's staff for several years you know at the W.O. [War Office] He says there a[re] bound [to] be gigantic casualties & they hope people in England won't be frightened by them, but it's impossible it should be otherwise. [19 September]

With two brothers in the Army and another in the Navy she was also anxious about the potential impact on her family:

I have been thinking so much of you all yesterday & today, it must be like dragging off a large piece of your heart to see Rollo go, but I am so glad you had time to go down there. I know & feel God will bring him safe back again & it is so splendid to feel one can be proud of them wanting to go off isn't it? But it's awful for the poor mothers. This awful war just swallows up everyone's happiness in the most limitless way, & I have been aching for you for what you have been going through.

Dorothie and her mother made enquiries with the War Office about who she should work with and she eventually joined the Munro Motor Ambulance Corps.
Dr Hector Munro had advertised for adventurous young women to equip an ambulance unit for service in Belgium. He received around 200 applications and accepted four: Dorothie, Mairi Chisholm, Mrs Elsie Knocker and Helen Gleason. In addition, Miss May Sinclair came along in an administrative role. Mrs Knocker described Munro as 'an eccentric Scottish specialist ... whose primary objects seem to be leadership of a feminist crusade, he was far keener on women's rights than most of the women he recruited. He was a likeable man ... but wonderfully vague in matters of detail.'
Dorothie wrote on the night before she left for Belgium, obviously nervous at what was to come:

Thurs night [24 September]

Mother darling
As I told you we flit from Victoria at 10 Friday morning. I saw Munro last night & he was much more coherent & businesslike & told me more details. It appears all the equipment is already waiting us at Ostend. The four doctors are all going with us tomorrow – not half following as they thought might happen. We will go on to Ghent & put up (we women) in good rooms in the big hotel now a hospital. The men may be billeted out in town if space limited. We will work the ambulance scouting business & also be prepared to help in any way in the hospital itself if required. Cable communications can be sent from Ghent ok for 1/6 & thus you can be informed of any

change of plans or address. Letters & parcels also delivered & to be addressed to

Dr Munro's British Red Cross Motor Ambulance Corps

Hopital militaire no2

Ghent – Belgium

Will cable you from the other side how we get on, but it's sure to [be] alright.

I felt ever so seedy today after typhoid bugs so had to stay in bed till the afternoon.

I will phone you tonight so as just to say goodbye. It's more real than writing to hear your voices again.

Goodbye & God bless you all

Yr loving Diddles.

In train to Folkestone [25 September]

Mother darling – I tried & tried to phone you this morning just to say goodbye only had rotten luck & couldn't get on. They kept cutting off & then number was engagement. How splendid to get that letter from Rollo, but it's awful reading about Brigham & others who have since gone. I feel Rollo just will come home to us all right.

We are a dozen going today. 4 women, 4 doctors, 1 Red Cross parson & 2 motor men owners & mechanics. Mrs Knocker, the leading lady & trained nurse, inspires me with great confidence & seems most capable. I was very relieved to find someone of that kind of stuff in the contingent as I was rather doubting the capabilities of Miss Sinclair. But it's Mrs Knocker I see will run the show. Dr Head dined John St last night & told me about Munro. Said he was thoroughly trustworthy & a good sort & I would be quite ok with him. The only fault he had was vagueness & he told me to follow my own judgement in matters of prudence & initiative rather than leave all to the boss. But if I did, that would be all right. I was afraid he might crab him but he didn't which was reassuring ...

The typhoid has worn off now. I made my soul with a dirty old pig of a German padre at Farm St yesterday who was furious at being asked for when I hadn't even a mortal sin for him. He was such a pig I nearly turned mahomadan [sic] on the spot & that prayer meeting was OK.

Goodbye darling – God bless you all & don't worry about me. I'll turn up all right & if I find one is useless there or things badly run I can so easily come home with my funds. Much love Diddles.

A quickly scrawled note on a scrap of paper: 'Alive – boat off – Diddles.'

3

CHAPTER 2

September–October 1914

Belgium had been invaded by the German Army on 4 August 1914. The Belgian Army had fought gallantly but were slowly being pushed back and morale was suffering. The Munro Corps arrived in the country at the end of September into the midst of the chaotic retreat of the Belgian, French and British armies as the seemingly unstoppable German war machine swept across Flanders and northern France.

Sat morn [26 September]

Mother darling – We got here about 7pm all right & put up in the hotel for the night as you can't motor after dark. Great flutter in Ostend because a zeppelin had dropped 5 bombs the night before & they were all convinced they were going to be blown up. Miss Sinclair (who may be brainy but is a perfect ass on this kind of an expedish) was in a panic & said it wasn't safe, & the Germans would come again & being in the station hotel & they trying for the station etc etc etc. But we had a very peaceful night.

All sorts of trouble today because unable [to] get petrol without endless formalities thro' the militaries which delays our start. Hope to get off soon though & muddle through in the true British way & once in Ghent we will be quite all right.

The Red X [Red Cross] president from Ghent came to meet us here & is making the arrangements. We are all being put up free in Ghent too, & boarded and lodged. We have two vast motor ambulances. Old pattern Daimler & Fiat & two chauffeurs & a light Ford to follow us today. Saw some Red X people tho' from Antwerp today who say they have 11,000 beds prepared & no wounded & nothing on earth for Mrs Stobart's people to do. So I'm jolly glad we didn't go with them and are much more likely to be useful. Our party is a dozen: Mrs Knocker A1 thank God, Miss Chisholm a strong buxom colonial wench pal of hers & capable, an American lady hanger on & quite useless tho' most obliging, Miss Sinclair ditto & Mr Wakefield ditto, two young doctors – sports & good souls & will get a move on, a Mr Gurney an engineer & car mechanic – not a gentleman but a good soul & knows his job. Then a boy scout parson about 35 (not a child) a well meaning ass.

I will be able to tell you more on arriving at Ghent.

Everything here most peaceful & not a bit war-like. The sea full of submarines yesterday. Looked chilly work – poor beggars. Anchored just on watch like that.

Don't worry about me. No kind of danger. These Red X men we met here have been doing our work for 6 weeks & told us a lot about it – you aren't allowed any where near the actual fighting line & there are no Germans at Ghent tho' they can come if they want. It's not under German control as I imagined which is splendid.

Goodbye vile pen.

Bless you all – yr loving Diddles

Hopital militaire no 2, Ghent

Sunday 27th? [27 September]

Mother darling –

Well here we are & post going so I must write as long as I have time. We got here last night. Ghent is now entirely under Belgian & military control & no kind of danger. Only being an open town ie unfortified anyone can come in as likes. This is a huge hotel turned into hospital & run by Red X nurses – Belgian ladies & thundering good too for amateurs – organisation A1 & beat English Red X into fits.

We were met by a huge crowd of Ghentites who loved us on the spot because we are English & ditto here. Everyone looks after us & is too kind – no sort of roughing as we [are] in the hotel rooms & it's hard to believe war is going on. Skirmishes all the time from 12 – 30 miles away & today we saw 8 or 9 wounded brought in. We couldn't do anything today as had to go thro' endless red tapes as to passports & everything which is at last done & one of our ambulances was called up just now in the middle of lunch & has gone off with two doctors of the party. We had begun to think red tape was so endless the war would be over before we got a job – only this is splendid & they will use us now. Another doctor from England joined our party today, a Dr Renton. Jolly glad too he's a good man & we badly need 'heads' to organise this party which is sadly sloppy. But we are trying to kick ourselves into shape & get things going.

Our job is to [go] up 3 to 5 miles from the firing line, or as near as the military authorities will let us, & pick up wounded (brought us by the soldiers) & take them in our ambulance to the hospital here.

5

Very little dressing apparently done on the field – just iodine & a dry dressing & all dirt left on for luck.

But they don't seem to mind. Great fun this morning. Their armoured mitrailleuse car here had captured a 2 seater German car by ambushing it & captured the 2 officers. The Belgian shooting was A1, they stopped the engine with 5 shots slap thro' the radiator & wounded both Germans. The prisoners were gone when we saw it but the car with pots of gore – the screen bashed to smithereens & we amused ourselves picking bullets out of the bodywork. Miss Sinclair in a fuss because she thought you had made her responsible for me – so I told her I took all responsibility on myself – would use my own brains as to prudence & be responsible for myself. She is utterly useless for practical things. Thank God I can look after myself & am now under Mrs Knocker's jurisdiction. She is a capable woman & fit to give orders & I am safe as houses with her.

We don't run any danger so don't worry. If anyone goes actually in firing line it's the doctors who bring people to us a little way back. Now we are authorised to work under the military I hope we will be useful. Only it took 12 hrs work interviewing every damned official in Ghent.

No time for more –

Write more later

Much love Diddles

PS. We have 100 wounded in this place & 100 in the other – lots of indoor staff – it's for outdoor work they want us.

D

Ghent 28 [September]

Mother darling –

This to say I am very well & most happy having just come in from my 1st job on the ambulances. Frightfully exciting & we brought back five wounded. One, a German shot thro' the head who won't recover we are afraid poor devil. It's most impressive being outside there & seeing all the troops & being in the midst of things. It's hard to realise the war in the town itself tho' all this happens a few miles out. Perpetual skirmishes & dribbles of wounded all the time. Everyone here mad over us & England & we have the time of our lives. Am very empty it's 5pm & I haven't fed yet today and the bearer of this is going now. Much love & I'm as safe as houses you know.

Diddles

Ghent
October 2nd

Thanks for yours got today. I want very much to see Rollo's last letter. Mother promised me it but I never got it. Not much doing here these 3 days – fighting stopped everywhere more or less. The descriptions in English Papers of Alost fight much exaggerated – we were thereabouts so know. But reporters are only allowed with Belgium army so they have to make the most of it. We have no sort of hardships as yet being lodged in a very comfortable ex hotel & today our ambulances haven't even been out everything is so peaceful. Refugees stopped pouring in too for the moment. We fed 6,000 2 days ago from noon to 4.30 – poor beggars

Have written Mother a diary with further news. Got some quite good photos at Termonde yesterday – love Diddles

Oct 7th 1914

In a convent hospital. Waiting for orders.

Well, life has been a hustle these last 2 days & I've had precious little time for letter writing. The last 3 nights have been very busy for us as some of our detachment have been up all night each time to help bring in wounded from the station to the hospital that were being sent into Ghent from Antwerp as they don't want any wounded to be left there in case the Germans should collar it, which means they'd all be made prisoners of war. So 300 came in one night & 500 the other & going the other way are trainloads & trainloads of British Tommies. It's rather awful to see the two trains meeting & thinking how little the reinforcements know what they are in for. I am afraid Antwerp is very serious because tho' the allies have come up strongly at last they have no guns big enough to be able to get at the German siege ones. Yesterday the blighters drove our allies back 7 miles nearer the town. I wonder what on earth will happen there now.

I have lots of news since I wrote last. Yesterday we got our 1st bit of fieldwork – real fieldwork – we have been able to get yet. We are generally put under the command of a military doctor who suffers from severe funk & won't let us really get hold of people that otherwise just die in the trenches for want of being fetched.

There was pretty heavy skirmishing & shelling going on around Termonde yesterday, as the Germans were, as usual, trying to build a pontoon bridge over the Sheldt there & the Belgians lining the river & putting a spoke in their wheel. The Germans turned their artillery onto the Belgian river trenches with the result they had to retire, but kept the

Germans off building pontoons by shelling the shore whenever they got really going.

Well when we got up to where guns were popping, the old Belgian doctor got such a funk he just threw himself out of our bus & refused to go on, so we blew kisses to him & left. A sentry told us of where some wounded men were lying up in the trenches close to the river, so we left the car & carried our stretchers to go & look for them. We found most of them were men well enough to work their way back further so they had gone, but there were 2 others – an officer & a tommy very bad indeed lying right up by the river. It was five kilometres to walk each way carrying stretchers & taking cover & walking over slippery banks the last bit. Also coming back was pitch dark & it was 8.30 by the time we got them to the ambulance. As we lost our way in the dark & the ambulance couldn't light up on account of Germans (a bullet buzzed by the driver while he was waiting & made him sit up!). The poor beggars had been lying there since 8am that morning & would have died if they had had the night out as well, which would have been the case if it hadn't been for us. The car couldn't get closer as there was no road – it being dyke country. The Tommy had had his foot blown right away by a shell & a bullet in his back as well. He was amputated as soon as we got back & I hope will live, but it is still touch & go. The officer shot through the right leg. Both being soaked & nearly dead already from exposure, but so pathetically grateful to us for getting them out of it. They hardly ever do much shooting at night here so we weren't in danger really getting back. Just as we had got the commander we looked over the river bank trench & saw a couple of German patrols, so we hurried 'some'. Luckily we met some tommies who helped with the stretchers or we couldn't have got them all that way.

This morning grand tableau! Our doctor funk pal we had thrown out, went to the military authorities & said we disobeyed his orders & in fact raised Hell generally & today we have [been] put right back & not allowed to go anywhere near anything & that is what happens every time we break out a bit & try & do what really is needed. Because at present the military won't send their ambulances nearer than 5 kilometres to the firing line which means that men are just dying there, as Rollo says, for want of immediate help & because the doctors funk it – so now we are arranging a new scheme – that we women of the party run the 2 large ambulances which are kept behind – our men are procuring light cars & necessary passes to enable them to go right up & get people to fetch back to us – we are going to do that tomorrow, see how it works & if so adopt it definitely. We will work these light cars entirely on our own as 'civilians' & keep the big ambulances under Red X. Civilian passes can be had, as these bally reporters have them and are always around the firing line. Some of them are really rather sports & one Englishman, Dugmore by name, is a cinema man

& perfectly killing. I am told he sits in the trenches with his cinema last week the draught from a shell going four feet over his head blew down his camera. But Dugmore quite unmoved grabbed the concern & went on turning the handle ... quite calmly so as to get a good picture of the smoke! The soldiers just love him. The man that took those photos in Alost was dragged out, last man, hanging onto a cavalry officer's stirrup. Last night when we were getting those men in they turned up & were awfully good lending us a hand with the stretchers & things. The worst is tho' Belgium is getting overrun with reporters & one can't move I foresee without being placarded. It's pretty sickening & takes away all the good feeling one has of being able to help.

As for writing a chatty letter to The Tablet – tell Marjie to inform him to go to Hades and to add any further remark she thinks suitable.

Oct 8th

Am sending this letter thro' someone going to England so you'll get it sooner. Bad news from Antwerp today, still our guns aren't big enough – we are told they are landing big guns off the Dreadnoughts there as their range is bigger. I hope it's true. I s'pose that's why the marines went to Antwerp thro' here & today I have seen some naval guns in an armoured train in the station here which bears out the statement. I think things will be moving soon. Tommies are some of them camping here, it's good to see them – we must have a huge lot of our troops in Antwerp now & I hear we have already a lot of casualties as our men just have to stand the shellfire without being able to get in range. No doubt about it – the German artillery is damned good & marvellously accurate. From 3 miles back they can shoot 5 & 100 yds over their men's heads at Termonde so as to get the Belgians who are only separated by the river from their own men.

I am not going out with the ambulances today. It's not my turn so am waiting here. Alas I don't think we women will be allowed to do much actual fieldwork. We will have to be behind most of the time if not all & certainly if there is big fighting wouldn't be allowed in it. But there's going to be heaps to do though, it's topping being up near things & so jolly interesting. About 300 French marched thro' the town today. No new English troops as I know of. But the numbers are as elastic as for 10,000 to 40,000! Everyone says a new figure & as they run many trains straight through & at night it's impossible to say.

Goodbye – must take this now to be posted by the kind bearer.

Love to you all.

Yr loving Diddles

Lots of days you know very little to do. Things come in rushes. We have had 3 days 3 nights on the move. Some of the people & cars out for something all the time.

Melle/nr Ghent
Sitting in the car
Oct 10th

Well dears – Events have been moving so damn quick lately there hasn't been any time for writing. Thank God we really have been of vast use this last week & have done a lot to save lives & wounded. We have had two more ambulances sent out to us & have been using all four all the time. What was just Belgian skirmishing before is rapidly turning into big fighting & entirely undertaken by the British + French troops. The Belgian troops have retired from the firing line all round & are leaving it to the allies – most of the French troops are marines. A fine lot of men. The Belgian troops have just lost their heads now & refuse even to meet the Germans. They just retreat the moment there is a question of a fight. They are utterly worn out at having had to stand the brunt of it all these months & now are in a pure state of funk & run like hares. But it does one good to see all these British soldiers about & you know you won't go under with them about.

Well I'd better begin & tell you back history – 2 days ago there was quite heavy fighting other side of Zelle about 100 wounded that day – our ambulance was working hard as now we are allowed to work on our own – of course the Belgian medical doctors & their ambulances were 6 kilometres back in a café drinking beer. As our ambulance passed them I got out with another of our women, & we hauled them out & said we were going to show them where the wounded were. So when we climbed in their car to pilot them they couldn't in decency refuse to go where women went, so we got them to go & help at last. The limit was too that that time there was no sign of a bullet where the men were lying round. The military ambulances here make one just sick. The Red X voluntary people are ok & full of pluck.

Well, all the wounded were being poured into a convent at Zelle & our ambulance took the last load it could carry back 20 miles to Ghent. So much help was needed, some of us, including me stayed at the convent to help during the night & our ambulance to fetch us 1st thing in the morning. I was up all night as they kept bringing in wounded & I would help a lot with the dressings as there was only 1 nurse & military doctors (one fat pig half tight). At 3am in prances a Capt informs us the Germans are advancing & all the village to be evacuated by 5am & wounded men sent to Ghent. So we had to hustle & pack them all in the ambulances & it was awful having to move practically dying men who it was imperative to keep perfectly still. But it had to be done & by 5 the whole place & village was evacuated, soldiers & all & just us left. We phoned for our ambulance & were told it had started at four am so wasn't worrying. But there was a mistake in the message & it only arrived at 9.30 & saved us by 10 minutes about from the Germans. Fighting was already going on the other side of the village & we went there & picked 3 wounded men, & as we came back down our street where we had been waiting for the ambulance they were already shooting down it & a man on all fours scooting up a drain out of the way. But we got our men through to Ghent all right & were picking people up all the rest of the day that were straggling about on the high roads with broken limbs, quite unattended & of course no Belgian ambulances in their minds.

Then Antwerp is in an awful way & burning in lots of places. All the British hospitals have been cleared out, we have a lot of English wounded in our hospital now & a lot of English infantry sent back from Antwerp to us here as more numbers were useless there. It is big guns they want not men at all. All this help is just 8 days too late. That much sooner & the Germans would never have got past 1st line of forts.

Oh I forgot to tell you how the day at Zelle an American, Mr Gleason, his wife is in our party, went into Zelle to see if I had been left there, or any wounded. Pretty splendid of them. He is a real plucked 'un & has been captured already once by Germans, but they are wonderfully good to Yanks so Mr Gleason the brick went right into the town to the house where we had been & found we had gone ok but he was collared by 20 Uhlans who marched him out of the town, with revolvers up, but they let him go quite alright. He is such a cool beggar he'd get through anywhere.

Then yesterday quite hot fighting outside here at Melle about 4 miles from Ghent. It was French marines who just arrived, went straight into position & were under fire about 28 hrs & we worked with them all the time. They lost about 10 men killed & about 30 or 40 wounded which we took back into the hospital for them. Their ambulance work splendidly organised & we never had to go to their trenches, as with each regiment they have a lot of Red X people who bring them back to the ambulances, so we stayed in a village about 300 yds from the trenches & they brought their people to us there & we looked after them & took them home. They are a fine lot these French sailors – pots better than the Belgians. One of our ambulances with Dr Renton (such a nice man & 2nd in command as cool as blazes & plucky & jolly good doctor) was shot at yesterday & jolly near got hit too.

Today Saturday, a quiet day & nothing doing except picking up German wounded. They were driven back some miles yesterday & we went on to yesterday's battlefield to get their wounded. They lost very many more than the French dead & there were masses of dead lying around – a ghastly sight.

These Germans too, you never know they might fire on you as you pick 'em up with the result the men do most of that work, & I for one don't hold with being potted by a German. I don't mind running risks for our men or the French but I'm blithered if I'm going to have hole put in me by a bally Teuton while I pick up their men. I frankly am not taking any.

Dr Renton today was fired on by the Germans while getting in some of their men. Yesterday near us they put civilians in front of the troops again & they were shot by the Belgian firing. 2 days ago the Germans near here got 15 of Belgians wounded & knocked their heads in.

Lots of cases brought in have evidence conclusive of explosive bullets, worse than dum dum being used. They are devils.

Such haste much love

Diddles

Rollo's letters are extraordinary. Poor boy I'm glad he's alright they've had an awful time.

An eyewitness in War Illustrated *was just outside Furnes in November 1914: 'One afternoon, however, I saw no less than fifteen hundred men sent out at once in different companies for Dixmude. "There are 37,000 German dead lying outside that town," one Belgian officer told me. "They are in rows, in stacks, in heaps. We must bury them or there will be an epidemic."'*

CHAPTER 3

October–November 1914

Ghent as an open town offered no resistance to the German Army. In the early hours of 12 October a party of German cyclists, infantry and Uhlans entered the town, and, after conferring with city officials, the German flag was raised over the town hall.

Hotel Belle Vue
Dunkerque

Oct 17th

Mother darling
Such a life! We had to clear out of Ghent in the middle of the night & since then everything has been chaos & I have had to run the whole damn show. I wish there was a man with a head in charge. As soon as I get back I shall settle down & marry a big strong man who will bully me. I'm sick to death of trying to run other people. Well at Ostend I ran into Thérésé de Broqueville & she & her pa-in-law [Charles de Broqueville, Prime Minister of Belgium] have taken us under their wing which has given our party a new lease of life & we hope to able to go on working here. Tho' for a day or two we must just sit tight & wait. Munro goes home today to settle up muddle with Red X & arrange funds. It was too sad to have to leave Ghent. We were doing heaps of work there & were really useful. It's disgusting having to leave like that & we hated being shovelled out and made to bunk – we had to evacuate all the wounded too. Lord it was a night! Will write you more later – no time now. We hope to get attached to a British Red X field hospital which is coming out here shortly under an A.1 man Dr Beavis. I hope it will work as he's a ripper. He had his hospital at Antwerp & was burned out.
Lv ever Diddles

Dunkirk
Oct 18th
To my family in general
Life since we left Ghent having been such a muddle. I will begin a summary

of events from then. When Antwerp fell on the 9th it became evident that all the English & French troops the far side of Ghent would have to retreat to prevent them being cut up on the flank. It was a bit 'ard, because at Melle the Germans had been driven back by the French marines & English troops (the latter some 8,000 strong roundabouts) & were very bucked & not at all wanting to retreat. Also it was awful for the poor Belgians, mad with joy when the English arrived to see them beating a retreat after 2 days, & leaving poor little Ghent to its fate without so much as firing another shot to keep them back. Well all the troops had left by the evening of the 11th, a Sunday, & at 1am on Monday morning we were told the Teutons were at the gates & all the wounded had to be evacuated at once. This was done by train to Ostend, except just the English Tommies we were told to take in our ambulances as they were to be kept separate. What a night it was having to dress them all & pack them & our belongings up. Some of the latter we had to leave behind & trust to getting them after the war. We got the wounded into a convent at Eekloo by about 5am & left them to sleep a bit, while we lay on the parlour floor of a neighbouring Englishman's villa & slept like pigs for an hour or two, looking like nothing on Earth sprawling on the carpet. Then on to Bruges & Ostend – having to keep on returning for evacuating troops on the way. I was miserable at leaving Ghent like that in the middle of the night & being obliged to bunk after all the Ghent people had done for us – but our ambulances would have been begged & our work over so we had to lump it. But I mean to get back into Ghent with the English army or die in the effort from wrath & indignation if nothing else.

Arrived at Ostend no one knew what to do – all the party were squabbling. Munro losing his silly head & running round in circles & there seemed nothing to be done but trek home & try & get out to France – a doubtful event. When I suddenly ran into Thérésé de Broqueville in the street by the purest luck and they were most awfully kind to me & helped me get the ambulance to Dunkerque with the ministry whom leaving next morning. Such a job as I had to get my coven under way. None of them up – half of them lost & Munro insisting on picking up futile lady pals of his all along the beach & affixing them to our ambulance when we have already 3 times as many awful females as we can digest or need. He's a well meaning & enthusiastic little man, but as to being in charge of anything or anyone let alone himself, it's a jest. He has to be looked after just like a good natured biddie.

Broqueville has been our guardian angel all along the line & I can't imagine what we would do without him. He & I have just settled things up & this is how the situation stands:

Dr Beavis field hospital, late of Antwerp is being attached to Furnes, now Belgian headquarters & is a movable affair.

Our Ambulance column now consisting of 6 ambulances, 4 limousines & 2 open cars is under the command of Robert de Broqueville & attached to the cavalry division. We are 2 in each ambulance with a change of clo' [clothes] and a toothbrush & no fixed abode & fed with army rations, in fact like soldiers. Our wounded we take to Beavis field hospital & run in conjunction with him, though he is bound to get other wounded from round about besides what we bring him

We have got funds between us to look after the wounded from the moment they come into our hands, to when we land them in London, having made arrangements with London hospital to take them in.

It's such a joy to be really organised at last – I've got them off now & under military orders & they will just have to be in order & run.

Thank God –

Much love dears – yrs Diddles

Sunday Oct 25th 1914 [actually 18 October 1914]

We are off now & properly organised ...

I've had to work like a nigger to arrange all the details & interview everyone & haven't had a moment to write though I've lots to tell you.

Am writing in the car at Calais where I came for the day to arrange about cars – have just met Philip Gibbs in the street in tears at not being able to get a journalist's pass so am going to get him one through Broqueville & he is very pleased. I am running a sort of Bureau at present. Anyone in difficulties comes & bothers me.

I am so glad now our show is on a sound & recognised footing as regards organisation and funds. The latter point has been settled by the Red Cross London who give us a quid a week to keep ourselves, so far I have had practically no expenses to pay.

I wonder if you ever got half my letters from Ghent? Munro found the people in London had not got hardly any of his, & I am wondering if much of my diary to you got waylaid. Had fun at Zelle that night & missed being a German prisoner by 10 minutes.

Must go now

Love Diddles

The Belgian Army was frantically engaged in what would become known as the First Yser Battle which would only end when the Belgians took the drastic step of opening the sluices and flooding the land in front of the advancing German Army and creating impassable flooded marshland.

Did you recognise me tending a wounded civilian in a stretcher some days ago in Daily Mail back page?? No name but it was me at Melle near Ghent.

Oct 22nd
Dunkerque

Mother dear – Just back in Dunkerque for one night & so will send this off by English bearer if one's going home for a day.

It's 1am & I am very sleepy having slept in my clothes all last night & not washed more than half my neck for a day or two. Just had a bath. Thank God for our good soap.

We are quartered at Furnes for the moment as very heavy work round there. [The Munro Corps was stationed in an old convent in Furnes. Philip Gibbs describes the scene: 'One could not deafen one's ears against that note of human agony. It pierced into one's soul. One could only stand gripping one's hands in this torture chamber, with darkness between high walls and with shadows making awful noises out of the gulfs of blackness ...The smell of wet and muddy clothes, coagulated blood and gangrened limbs, of iodine and chloroform, sickness and sweat of agony made a stench which struck one's senses with a foul blow.']

All English troops in Belgium now. None in France – but Gen French won't advance his army which he meant to do 2 days ago which leaves all the hard work for the poor little Belgian army now about 80,000 strong. All the reservists having been disbanded on Calais.

Belgians done very well – 500 Germans crossed river this morning near Nieuport but were all shot & prisoned & Belgians now in strong position on far side of river. French Army rotten. Artillery not come up & when it does has no ammunition – at least I am speaking for this division. Lots of French marines though who are fighting on land & perfect rippers. Belgian army taken new lease of life & fighting like fun again. Ghastly bombardment of Dixmude by quick German guns yesterday & our people (me not there absolutely) had the hell of a time getting wounded out. Shrapnel on ambulances & all around. Robert de Broqueville got left behind by mistake & we didn't know till 10pm he was safe, after having become convinced he was killed. It was awful. It's much worse being frightened for someone else than being in it yourself. I was in a car just outside & couldn't get in. The whole town was blazing & looked horrible in the night. The road up to it had been shelled all day – you never saw such holes as those big shells made in the boggy ground each side – when they land a column of mud as high as a house goes up. One fell on ammunitions wagon yesterday & reduced horses men & all to jam and powder. It was almost incredible – poor devils. [Gibbs again: *'In front of us on the road lay a dreadful barrier, which brought us to a halt. An enemy shell had fallen right on top of an ammunition convoy. Four horses had been blown to pieces, and lay strewn across the road. The ammunition wagon had been broken into fragments, and smashed and burnt to cinders by the explosion of its own shells. A Belgian soldier lay dead, cut in half by a great fragment of steel. Further along the road were two other dead horses in pools of blood ... But we had to pass after some of this dead flesh had been dragged away.']*

Such an awful lot of wounded these 2 days & such awful serious cases too. Quantities of German prisoners today. One man talked to left Berlin 5 days ago & was taken prisoner today without firing a shot. Another was from Ghent & one of the blighters chased us away. Please God we will soon be back.

English troops south of our line, but I hope to meet some of them & get news of him [Rollo]. Our luck is immense. I'd go mad if I met them just.

Goodbye dears. War is an utterly incomprehensible horror & how we should want to bring it on ourselves I can't conceive. But it's worse far from a distance, than actually near it. Somehow it doesn't frighten me so much when you understand it a bit – I was far more miserable over people in it when I was at home.

Much love Diddles

Oct 25th 1914

PRIVATE

Sunday night 1pm

Mother darling
Have heard through the ministry the Coldstream are in Belgium now not at the Aisne anymore. Whereabouts I don't know but I know what it will mean to you & Mellins to know he is out of that living hell there. It's very different warfare in Belgium where every man stands a chance & gets some of his own back. That Aisne trench business was ghastly & this is Heaven by comparison. This is private & news will be published – I promised not to say but must break my word for you – just off Dieppe at 8 tomorrow & hope to get this posted somewhere.
Love Diddles

Furnes Monday [26 October]

Mother darling
My soul is OK – Don't worry – it's often odd times & weekdays instead of Sundays but I trust the Almighty makes allowances, & as to Fridays I got dispensed by a horrid fat German padre at Farm Street. We are still at

Furnes & working awful hard. Day before yesterday, 5 of our ambulances only brought in 157 people & those the other direction ditto. It's awful – the desperate cases we have at the hospital here and all possible we send on by train. 2 days ago 4,500 wounded passed through Furnes. This war is a nightmare just – I can't see when it is to end. We may have to evacuate this place today so don't worry if you see the Germans have it as it means we have moved the hospital further back.

I now drive a limousine in our ambulance column, as the chauffeur, a Belgian, has cold feet & funks. So when it gets exciting he gets down at the roadside – I drive on & collect the 'blessés' [wounded] & then pick up my chauffeur on the way home. It's killing & makes everyone die with laughter. Thank you so much for my little parcel & all the letters. You are an Angel about writing. I have been getting letters nearly every day from you through Broqueville. Thérésé still with her Ma at Dinaid – Robert runs us – a nice lad.

Poor Mother it's awful for you having everyone gone & not even seeing Hughie – poor darling – I will pray so hard all your people come home. Don't worry over me I'm as right as rain. Saw Johnie Baird yesterday in a staff car! Very few English troops nearer than Ypres where I believe the Coldstreams are – DoDo

Arthur Gleason, describes Dorothie's driving skills in his book The Golden Lads:

One day, as we were on the road to the dressing stations, the noise of guns broke out. The young Belgian soldier who was driving her stopped his motor and jumped out.
'I do not care to go farther,' he said.
Lady ——, who is a skilful driver, climbed to the front seat, drove the car to the dressing station and brought back the wounded. I have seen her drive a touring car, carrying six wounded men, from Nieuport to Furnes at eight o'clock on a pitch-dark night, no lights allowed, over a narrow, muddy road on which the car skidded. She had to thread her way through silent marching troops, turn out for artillery wagons, follow after tired horses.

Tuesday, Oct 27 1914

Mother darling
I am simply crying with rage – Beavis & Munro will take tame correspondents about with them – at present Ashmead Bartlett & Philip Gibbs are glued onto us & I have just been making the hell of a row as having got the old Chronicle with Gibbs' account of Dixmude & dragging me into it all. I think Gibbs was more of a gentleman than to make a fool of me like that, & it makes the whole thing so sordid to look as if we had pet

reporters to advertise us. [The *New York Times* and several British newspapers of 26 October ran an article by Philip Gibbs which describes the events of 21 October when Dorothie and the corps went to Dixmude and Robert de Broqueville was left behind.] Robert & I have been so mad. This morning we have just stuck our toes in & say we leave the damn show as soon as a reporter comes near us, & in fact have kicked up such a stink since this Chronicle slush this morning that I think that will now will be a thing of the past.

It is such a shame using me as a lever in this disgusting way.

We would like the ambulance very much – but better still an open car with driver only – a good make & quick. Not too huge & not Johnie Morgan's as I couldn't bear him.

If the lady's car isn't already fitted as an ambulance perhaps we could have it as it is.

Oh Mother I am sick over this reporter business – I do hate it so – it's so cheap & undoes all the nice feeling one has inside of being able to do something. Our hospital has been evacuated to Poperinghe where our headquarters will be. As the Germans aren't here yet, we are hanging on with half our ambulances & no cook & not much food!

The Germans have crossed the Yser between Dixmude & Nieuport in the centre of the line & one will have to fall back soon to a second line of defence a little way back. There are so few reinforcements to back up the Belgians.

Fighting has been awful here & in a week 9,000 wounded Belgians have been through Furnes. I hear Rollo is south of Ypres so may see him. They have been having a tough time but English fighting awfully well there.

Much love darling. Write me c/o Broqueville always DoDo

A year later, in October 1915, Dorothie looked back on the events of this time, and the 1st Yser battle:

We had barely reached Furnes, & the hospital had not had time to even unpack their beds etc, before the German push began & the wounded came streaming in. For about ten days the average number wounded from the Belgian front (between Dixmude & the sea) was a thousand a day. The Belgian RAMC was disorganised after its hurried flight from one big town after another. They had a fair number of ambulances considering, but nothing to be able to cope with such a gigantic stress of work & ours just went & worked wherever the push was hardest. At 3 places in particular the Germans tried to break the line: at Dixmude, at Pervyse & Nieuport. It was not until after they had succeeded in advancing badly in the two latter places, that the Belgians inundated the country alongside the Yser.

We did most of our work those days in the neighbourhood of Dixmude where the fighting was appalling. The Belgians were being driven back & back & would have had to abandon the position if it had not been for the Fusilier Marins (French sailors) under Admiral Ronarc'h who came in support & from then on stood all the brunt of the heavy attack through the town itself.

At first they were in shallow, hastily dug trenches on the far side of the town & then for many days fierce fighting went on in the streets. One day the Germans would gain a footing & the next the Marins would drive them out. During that awful week Ronarc'h lost 8 tenths of his effective & he himself was always in the thick of it & shelled out of one cottage after another.

Our cars were going day & night, the last 2 miles into Dixmude was down an open dead straight road, raked by shell as soon as anything living showed down it. Many is the race we have had down there with our scout cars with stretchers laid on. The ambulances were cumbersome to move & turn & the wounded stood a far better chance being fetched in the open cars & put in the ambulances a few miles back.

All day & all night the town & villages & farms around were burning. The glare helped you to see at night but sometimes it looked like hell, with the flames curling & leaping up in the darkness & the crash as the houses fell in had something awful about it.

Driving through the streets of Dixmude one night, it was so hot, with the houses on each side burning, I just had to drive through as quick as I could & how the tyres didn't get cut to blazes by glass or burnt by embers oftener than they did I cannot understand.

The awful thing about the fighting all that time was that when you had got your wounded away from the lines, there was nowhere to take them. The numbers made it possible for the hospital at Furnes only to take in the practically dying men. All the rest had to go on by train & what trains. Not well arrayed Red X trains as they have now but goods trains & even cattle trucks with a little dirty straw & no light or water or any doctoring to speak of. As soon as a train was full, it would be shunted out, but perhaps only to remain on the sidings for many hours. It took as a rule 3 to 4 days before the men got to a hospital at Calais some mere 40 miles back.

You can imagine the poor souls in those awful ghastly trains by the time they reached the base. Men with fractured legs racked by the jolting, without a stretcher to lie on, or a rug to cover them & shivering with cold in their mud & rain & blood soaked uniform.

Please God – I shall never see men suffer in conditions like that again. It was too awful. If one hadn't just been working day & night & knew everyone was doing all they could to stop matters being even worse, it couldn't have been borne.

The hospital staff were superhuman – both doctors & nurses – I don't think they can have ever slept or rested & I never once saw one of them, but that didn't tend each new patient with the same individual tenderness & care that they had given the first one that passed through their hands.

There too everything was of the most primitive – no sheets or luxuries & most of the medical etceteras had got hung up & never arrived. Wounded men were everywhere. The beds in the wards were full, every available stretcher was laid on the floor & held some poor suffering soul.

Many were just propped against the wall on straw as best one could & even then hundreds had to be turned away & sent on in those ghastly cattle trains.

And nightwork now is nothing to what it was then with the cars – no lights of course near the lines & only room on the pavé for one vehicle at a time. At each side deep, slimy mud, in pot holes. To get your wheel off the edge of the pavé meant untold suffering & jolting to the men on the stretchers within & yet this had to be done each time anything was to be passed & in the dark it was a nightmare.

The tide of battle rocked to & fro all that ghastly week. The Germans took Pervyse & Ramscapelle & were driven out again, they advanced to the edge of Nieuport & it looked touch & go. Then the inundations were let out & that eased the pressure & forced the German artillery in many places to retire or to risk being bogged & cut off. Gradually the fighting lessened & the German offensive became a little weaker, but still countless wounded men passed through our hands each day & the price had been a heavy one.

They had all fought magnificently, but best of all the little French sailors, though but few of them came out of it unhurt – it was to them the honour fell of having prevented the enemy breaking the line at its most critical point – Dixmude.

The whole country round was one vast smoking battered ruin & only here & there a few stubborn peasants had stayed on in the ruins of their homes.

It was never hoped at the beginning to hold Furnes – it seemed certain the line must break somewhere under the awful strain & most of the inhabitants had fled, although most of them returned some weeks later. We of the Munro Corps had been given an empty house to occupy. The owner a doctor had disappeared. We were some 16 to 18 people & there were 3 beds! The way in to the house (the keys were lost) was through a back door & then through a broken window. You never saw such a piggery. Beds, stretchers, mattresses & sleeping bags on the floor of the rooms & passages in all directions. I was lucky to have a wee room 10 ft by 5ft about with a mattress on the floor & just room to lie down. The 1st night we had no blankets to speak of & Helen Gleason & I slept in our clothes & hugged each other like babies for warmth & slept like that! I remember thinking how funny it was when I woke up & found we were still tightly locked together in the morning!

We used to feed at the hospital mess & just stagger up the dark muddy lane to our house & roll into bed. No fire anywhere in the house of course & only ice cold water & no drains!

Later on when we had time we got very comfortable there & lived & messed in the house like human beings for some months. But during the Yser fight things were primitive to a degree.

Robert de Broqueville was splendid all during that battle & always seemed to have the cars at the right places when required. He was absolutely fearless & always perfectly simple about it all. He & Gurney many a time went reconnoitring on ahead in the scout cars looking for wounded & got into some very nasty corners indeed. But Robert's luck was uncanny & always got him out of it. Since he left us he has had his horse killed under him by a shell & was untouched.

I used to share a car with him most of the time. Often I have driven down that long Dixmude road with Robert, all out, while the Germans followed us down the road with shells some short, some long & one just wondered where the next one would be. It's extraordinary the way as long as one has speed and action, one does not feel frightened. It's sitting still that is so unpleasant.

R & I were coming up that road in the Rolls scout car one day & we had a man on a stretcher from Dixmude when we had a very lucky shave. A shell was chasing us from behind, coming up on our left. You could hear it shrieking after you & coming closer & closer. It eventually burst the far side of the road on our right, but in the mud so the pieces didn't travel but to have burst where it did it must have crossed right over our bows & at just about the height of the car & have missed our bonnet by practically nothing.

Had we been travelling a few yards faster we must have met it. Really the way Providence has kept a personal eye on all our crowd is nothing short of marvellous.

Oct 29th, Furnes

Mother darling

Mr Johnyson, who is a land agent at Dunchurch, has been driving one of our ambulances, but has been seedy & obliged to go home. Also, he loses his head in an emergency. We want a chauffeur we know to take his place & I am longing to have little Smee unless you have found him a job or can't spare him.

He could be taken on & paid by the Red Cross & it would be ripping having him. Anyway if you can't spare him for good do let me have him for a few weeks temporarily – the expense is very small as you can get a free passage – do let me have him at once. Mr Johnyson is seeing about all the particulars & if Smee goes to him in London he will see him through – so do send him me there's a dear, & warn him I hope he doesn't mind being shot at, as he is pretty certain to be! If he thinks he would mind going into a tight corner now & then it's no earthly use his coming – but I think his heart's alright & he is such a hard working little devil he'd be a treasure.

We are still at Furnes – the position has improve[d] since I wrote last – Rollo is somewhere near & I mean going to look see as soon as I get a chance.

Prince Alexander of Teck is here now, I dined with him last night. The kind man has allowed me to use his hot bath & it's weeks since I had one.

We camp out in a deserted house here, & get in through the window. The only drawback is that while we are out in the ambulances, the French soldiers come in through the window & spend the day in our little beds! – OO – ER! – We found it out by their leaving a revolver & a grease mark on the sheets.

Such a lot of black Senegal troops here at Dixmude. As black as ink & on mules with the weirdest eastern effect. They give one no end of a turn in the dark as they creep by.

Much love darling
DoDo

Furnes Friday [30 October]

Mother darling – I wonder if Smee is coming out to be shot with me or not? It struck me you wouldn't be wanting him if things were being shut down & he could be taken on by the Red X & paid by them. It seemed an excellent solution & we would much rather have him than a shady man sent out & of our men we have had to change – two couldn't stand shells – it's odd how the mere sound of one crumples men up. It was that way with Johnyson of Dunchurch – the moment there was a black maria in sight he got in a sort of faint & utterly collapsed & one of the other chauffeurs the same way. We have got some rippers among our chauffeurs – one of old man Horlicks' chauffeurs, Tom is a great sport & bears anything with a smile & a dirty cigarette end hanging out of one side of his mouth & uttering waggish remarks the while the Teutons take pots at him.

We have about a dozen cars now half ambulances, half limousines & light cars. The ambulances go up as near as is safe & then the light cars run on to see where the wounded are, fill up with 'sitting' cases & come back to say whether the ambulance is required up or not for stretcher cases. This we find works much best as ambulances are cumbersome things to move in a tight corner & so it's no good bringing them up until it's necessary.

Then if things are really too hot – we women have to look after the ambulances & the men go on the scout cars. They look after us very awfully & we need never go where we don't want to so don't worry at all.

As a matter of fact shells & shrapnel don't alarm me half as much as a bullet. They make an unpleasant little flip & you feel they are steered your way. While with shells things are such a huge element of luck that they won't fall just where one is standing. At least they haven't yet thanks to the kind way the Almighty looks after us.

This last 2 days Broqueville, Gleason & Gurney have all had some real near shaves. In one case, a shell stove in a door 20 yards away from the ambulance but luckily burst inside the house. Gleason is real plucked 'un ever since he came into the German lines that day at Zelle to look for me. I have a great opinion of him! It was a jolly plucky thing to have done, but the ambulance by mere luck had got me off just 5 minutes before the Germans came down the street. It was a near thing that day – & my birthday – a birthday present I shan't forget in a hurry!

Yesterday, Robert & Gurney had run up to a house near the trenches to get some wounded men. A little place we have been working to & fro lately. Only yesterday it was hotter than ever & while they were turning the car, five huge black shells fell each side of them, luckily again on houses, which saved them & they got away with a fat head & earth on the car.

Last night we turned in at 11pm & turned out at 11.10pm! Some wounded out Nieuport way in a village called Ramscapelle which was burning & the Germans & Belgians & Spahis & black men were having a house to house fight. The Germans eventually driven back. The wounded were carried back to a little farm & kept pouring in. The military doctor was a fool & Munro & I had to dress several very bad fractures by the light of one candle as no big light was allowed & we had to bring ambulances up in the dark as we always do at night for the last 5 miles or so. It was an extraordinary sight in there in the half light, black men & white men & tired out soldiers all lying about on the straw poor devils. They are all so plucky, & one boy who was in awful pain with a fractured knee was so touchingly grateful when we looked after him decently & brought him back to our hospital. We got back about 2am. It is now Saturday & I am writing this sitting on an anvil in a forge while they are soldering a spare part onto my car. Trouble being they will fire their big guns on the high road & each time they are fired the recoil makes a vast hole, so that the roads end in being a perfect nightmare & everyday we have one car crocked up nearly – it's just awful – I can't think what the roads will be like in another month also when the real bad weather sets in – oo-er! A real hot bit of horseshoe just flown off the other anvil & missed by mebby [*sic*] an inch. I shall move further.

Damn – this box is covered in nails & most uncomfortable to the sit upon.

Sunday.

Just been to confess & com & mass – all on the same day – quite an occasion.

I went to Ypres yesterday, Rollo's brigade was in the trenches 4 miles away & I couldn't find him but hope to some other day all the same. Maybe I can get there today. I went to his headquarters of 2nd div (Ommanney is on it) Rollo's boss for news, which was at a chateau at Hooge, but a shell has blown the side of the house out an hour before & the staff skedaddled & I couldn't pick them up again in the time as we were carrying English wounded all day. They have had a tremendous lot of casualties these days & German shells were bursting on the edge of Ypres yesterday. As usual no ambulances near the places wanted & they loved us simply – one little sergeant nearly hugged me with excitement because ours was the only bus that went up the road to that chateau to get the people from a cottage near by where they were pouring in wounded.

Tubby was seen by a soldier Coldstream I met, 2 days ago, so he is ok & I'm dying to see him. The Tommy in question had been with him in Egypt I was so sad not to see him but may do so yet. The Nieuport line is quiet these 2 days & Ypres busy so we help there – much love DoDo

Much love darling God bless you all – excuse messy paper DoDo

Dorothie describes her long night in Ramscapelle in more detail in the following 'reminiscence':

Ramscapelle – Autumn 1914

Of what was once a prosperous little country village there remain roofless homesteads & desolate gardens, with personal treasures & children's toys trampled under foot. Artillery fire had set the village alight. It was dark & the flames were shooting up into the night, licking & fondling the crumbling ruins. The place was in the hands of the Germans & the Tirailleurs [Riflemen] Algerians had orders to take it before daylight. It was a case of attacking house by house, yard by yard & five lives for one.

From where we were in a farm little way back during the fight, you could hear the patter patter of the bullets as they struck the houses, the incessant crack of the rifles & that wicked merciless little toc-toc of the machine guns, which always gives me a chill feeling of fear whenever I hear it in action, & to which I shall never get accustomed.

The village was lit up almost like day, each roof detached against the glare. I could see the whole thing imprinted on my mind as vividly as if I had been a silent witness of the attack. The medley of shouting men, or rather savages, with their fezs & blue tunics, charging like wild beasts, their bayonets running with blood & glinting in the flame light ...

Next morning, as I was coming home, having slipped out to mass early, I saw the Grande Place, here at Furnes packed with people & the King of the Belgians passing in review the remains of the blue tuniced Algerians who had so gallantly stormed Ramscapelle the night before – another Regiment had relieved them & they were off to be used for another similar attack Dixmude way in 48hrs. They stood there in the dull grey morning light, so spick & span & still while the King walked down the lines. Every face was so grave & quiet it made the night's work seem very far away now & I passed on my way, wondering.

Dorothie added a poignant footnote: 'This regiment left in Autumn 1915 for the Eastern Theatre of war. The transport was torpedoed & sunk with all hands in the Mediterranean.'

Furnes Monday [2 November]

Mother darling
Our line from Nieuport to Dixmude quiet these 3 days – no casualties. I went near Ypres yesterday but couldn't get near Rollo – I'm afraid I won't either as English authorities won't let me near on account of being female – I hide in the car & put on a khaki coat now and then & get close enough for news.

The 4th Brigade is still the other side of Ypres on the Hooge road & I am pretty sure Tubby is ok. I never see English papers hardly here.

Yr Dorothie

Furnes Nov 4th (Wed)

PRIVATE

Little Mother – it's awful, poor Ommanney has been killed last Saturday, & it simply haunts me. He was on the headquarters staff of the 2nd Division that were quartered in that chateau on the far road of Hooge by Ypres, that was blown up by a shell last Sat. They were all standing on the steps discussing maps when two big shells landed right on them & made perfect havoc & killed about 6 & wounded some 10.

I arrived there at the chateau an hour afterwards & saw all the place blown out, I had gone to find out where Rollo's regiment was. The bystanders told me people had been wounded but not killed & I went to the different hospitals in the town to see if I could get news of Ommanney but came to the conclusion he was ok. It was so hard to find out as the H[ead] quarters had been moved in such a hurry.

Only next day on going there again & getting hold of all sorts of staff people did I eventually find he had been killed. It was so awful having been there only an hour afterwards & not realising. Then tonight I got a long letter from him poor kid – so glad to be at the front, longing to see me, & telling me all about things & the chateau too & so sorry he couldn't say where he was. Little thinking I had found out quite by chance through a sailor in an armoured car here that told me where the staff were.

It was horrible getting that letter after he was killed & I can't believe it. Pray for him poor kid Mother darling – I know you never quite approved of him but I did & he was one of my best friends. I have felt so much not being able to see him this year past.

Yr
Diddles

Captain Rupert Ommanney was attached to General Staff, 2nd Division. On 31 October 1914, the chateau where he was stationed suffered a direct hit by German shells. One of the generals was mortally wounded and seven senior officers, including Ommanney, were killed. He is buried in Ypres Town cemetery.

Furnes Nov 4th

To my family at large
1stly a description of the photos – The 1st ones are of French sailors who we 1st worked for at Melle near Ghent when they were in action there & that we have now met again at Dixmude all these last weeks. Whenever they see us they dash for us & give us coffee & food & letters to post for them & whenever they are in trouble with wounded & no one will take an ambulance up to them, they always come for us & we give them a hand. They fight like little lions & are such nice simple souls & so grateful & nice mannered. In that they resemble the Belgian Tommies. The French Tommies (not the Marins) are an odious bunch – rude & unobliging.

The other photos of artillery were taken at Termonde & I am sorry to say that very battery was destroyed that very day or the next morning. It's awful this war – every day one hears of all one's pals of the day before that have gone. At times when one was standing alongside them perhaps only a few hours or minutes before – it seems hard to believe the appalling rapidity with which one can be moved off the face of the earth.

No 14 & 15 are of a German prisoner who came through Ghent & gave us news of the place.

No 16 is left to right Mrs Knocker, Lady Dorothie Feilding & Mairi Chisholm.

The latter a great dear – only 18 but as brave as can be & most refreshingly calm & good tempered under all circumstances.

Mrs Knocker is a capable lady but a little trying at times when she over does things & gets on the party's nerves – but given lots of hard work to do she A1.

The remaining photos are of me in my breeks & a jersey Evy sent me which saves my life. As a rule I wear an overcoat khaki item – over this to my knees & am more decent, but when bored with excess of clothes run round in the jersey which is most comfortable.

I have been to Ypres 3 times to look for Rollo but have never been able to get to him. 1st day we carried so many wounded & their headquarters being blown up I couldn't [get] the information I wanted as to their whereabouts.

The second day we carried wounded all the time again & I made an assignation with an RAMC man who was going to take Robert de Broqueville & I up to the Coldstream trenches in the dark when they went up for the wounded. His regiment were then the other side of Hooge in a wood, having a hot time & they wouldn't have allowed a woman up in the daylight but wouldn't have known my sex at night! It would have been just splendid to have had a chinwag with Tubby & was maddening to get within a mile of him as I was & not be able to work it. The reason of the frustration of plans was as follows.

After our cars had been getting in masses and masses of wounded from far up while all the army ambulances stayed in the Grande Place at Ypres, a Captain Fitzpatrick dashed up, was frightfully rude to us & Broqueville & tried to arrest us for working in the English lines without being 'army'. He turned us out of Ypres before I could meet my doctor & go up to Tubby. It was disgusting too because we were doing work that no one else was. Gleason got some people off up by Rollo's people that had been there 2 days & all the men & officers just implored us to come back. I & Robert got a lot of Irish Guards in from a cottage near their trenches, in the dark, dodging caverns in roads made by shells that evening. We got two loads away & had promised to come back for the others when Fitzpatrick refused to let us go on working & we had to go knowing the poor devils would probably be left there for hours until they were brought off on an old horse cart that jolted like mad & lucky if they were fetched at all.

The RAMC have crowds of lovely ambulances that are too 'precious' to go near the firing.

MUST OFF

DoDo

Furnes.
Oct 7th [7 November]

Mother Darling

Thank you so much for the jersey you sent me, but as I have plenty of them with me I expect I shall return it you in a day or two as soon as I get my coat which I am waiting for – meanwhile Johnie Baird has leant me his as he is now quartered at Furnes. They still now and then try & shell this dear old town. They had a shot at it last night but as usual I never woke up, & at breakfast discovered the rest of the population had spent the night in the cellars! & me never woke up! It's a great thing to sleep heavy. Spares a lot of useless anxiety.

Four new ambulances turned up & Evy's committee sent us eleven people with them which gave us fits! However Miss Fife, a very nice lady, kindly left all her unnecessary nurses & co behind in a hospital at Dunkirk – I write being now 26!

You know I got within a mile of Rollo the other day & then the English boss wouldn't let our cars work any more in the English lines & we were sent off. A bit 'ard as I was going up with Robert de Broqueville & some RAMC men to look for Tubby's lot in the dark.

However I saw a tommy of his who told me he was well & that he had held his horse that morning.

I was in Ypres on the quiet next day to try and find Tubby & came in for the big shells at Ypres between 5 & 6 pm & jolly near got snookered too. The Almighty looks after us very nicely, I had left the car along side a building, then saw the English officer coming who had been so rude to us the day before, so hurriedly took the car & hid round the corner. Just after the first big shell came phut exactly where our car had been & so I am rather grateful to that officer for having made a nuisance of himself the day before. [Arthur Gleason wrote: *'At Ypres she [Dorothie] dodged round the corner because she saw a captain who doesn't believe in women at the front. A shell fell in the place where she had been standing a moment before. It blew the arm from a soldier. Her nerve was unbroken, and she continued her work through the morning.'*]

We picked up some men that were wounded by that shell & were running them round to a hospital when another came & dropped between our car & Dr Munro who was following us on the pavement. It knocked him down but luckily didn't hurt him.

Then we had some more exciting moments as, having mislaid Dr Munro, we couldn't leave our post till he turned up & our pew happened to be the cathedral at which they were aiming!

Much love DoDo

Furnes
Nov 11th

Father darling –
Thank you so much for your dear letter. It is most nice of you to say nice things about me, but I feel am awful fraud & much exaggerated & don't think I shall ever dare come home.

I wish you weren't going you know & can't quite make out if you have left or not. If you come by Dunkirk mind you come over in a car and see me. It's only 15 miles & I should have a fit if I knew you had been about & I hadn't known it.

A lot of English new recruits were landed there 4 days ago – some 40,000 the yarn goes so I don't see why you shouldn't come here. The Belgian line – Nieuport to Dixmude is very quiet now – stalemate – each holding the other without attempting to attack & hardly a shot fired. French artillery here pretty busy but very little German answering – they have taken all theirs & their spare men down to Ypres way & that's where the big struggle is now – I wish to God it were over.

I am so miserable over Ommanney. It just haunts me – the whole thing arriving at the place an hour afterwards & getting a long letter from him that night so full of life & everything. Poor soul – he was a brick & one of the best.

Goodbye father darling. Sorry no time for more am sending this by a bearer. God bless you & take care of your dear self won't you?
Much love from
Diddles

13th [November]
Furnes
Friday

Mother dear –
Write at once to Lieut A Field RNVR, Blackdown Hill, Leamington & ask him to come over to Newnham & see you. He was out here with the machine guns (armoured cars) such a nice boy & was awfully good helping me to find Rollo. It was he dug out his whereabouts for me, & took me down to Ypres twice to try & find him, he knows all the country where Tubby is & so could tell you about the conditions of things. He said he would love to come over to NP & see you if you cared to only was shy of turning up without being sent for in case you would think him a bore. He may be home for a few days only or longer I don't know.
Much love DoDo

Furnes
Nov 17th

Mother darling – Thanks so much for the lovely packet of letters sent by Mrs Knocker – also the photos – aren't they good. Will you please send me one more set of the last ones, & also half a dozen copies of these 1st ones of me? That baby Kodak is A1 & makes amazing good enlargements from the films.

As regards Lucia White please tell her we still have no opening but as soon as I hear of a job that will suit her I will write them. However it may be sometime as awful restrictions have been made this last week as allowing ladies to cross over anywhere near the front. In fact I doubt if they could work it really. Anyhow will they please not mind marking time for the present, of course if they get another offer elsewhere they had better take that. I wrote a letter to Dr Evans asking for India rubber air pillows, tonight a lot have been sent the hospital by Red Cross so they do not want any. Would he send you the £10 for some sheets Alexander of Teck ordered for us & which have to be paid for. I told him I would beg the money off people. It was for 200 sheets & some chloroform – I don't know the exact amount yet, but sheets were appallingly wanted for the hospital & Teck got them for me quickly – so if you keep the money & cancel my letter to Doctor Evans. I will tell you later where to pay it.

I wrote a hurried line to you this morning about Bobbie Cassel. It's frightfully nice of her to give me anything. That leather lining I am longing for as I can use it both as a lining & as a coat to walk about in over my breeks. If there is anything else she or anyone else wants to give I would love some cases containing each a hypodermic syringe & some tubes of morphia & spare needles. Anything from one to 15 or more of these I can find happy homes for at the various little dressing stations near the front. Any parcels to be sent me.

Things much quieter here now. Had a talk with Johnie Baird over bad mark against our ambulances at Ypres & your suggestion of a 'mild answer'. He advised us to leave things all as they were as it would only fuss them to rake things up which they have by now forgotten.

Afraid I shan't get near Rollo any more – he can always come & see me though should he get a day off poor boy.

What is this about Dudley Hanly wounded? Do write me particulars? I'm glad it's only slight – what awful bad luck so early. Poor beggar. He was so happy at going off at last. Thank you for your dear letter about Ommanney. It's just what I feel too – the whole thing upset me more than I care to say. It was haunting some how. I want this to go on to his Mother. Please forward it if you can find her address through the War Office. I've never met her, but know she would like to hear from me. You'll see she gets it won't you darling?

Not much fighting here now thank God. This wet is hell for the poor Tommies in the trenches. It's awful to see the state they are in from it & it takes the heart out of a man to be frozen & soaked & never able to dry. It's sadder even than the wounded somehow to see the state they are in.

[*'No part of the fighting area is more bleak and desolate than the fenlands of the Yser, between Nieuport and Dixmude, or more exposed to the biting winds from the North Sea and the Atlantic'* – *War Illustrated*, December 1914.]

Goodbye darling. How glad I am Mr Da isn't going yet – it's not jam this winter fighting & I would loathe him to be in it.

Much love to you all
DoDo

Nov 19th, Thursday

Mother dear
Just a little line to tell you I am as fit and well as a flea. It's damned wet though these days & no fun for the poor souls in the trenches as they never get a chance to get dry. Not only the rain but the inundations that have been turned loose down here, fill the trenches with water.

Thank you ever so much for the choc & the toffee & all sorts. I loved it.

If anyone near home sends me cigarettes & socks etc for the soldiers I'd love it. I have written Mr Heath to that effect as he kindly wrote & asked me if there was anything the Tommies wanted.

Much love – a real letter anon – I'm so glad Da isn't gone
DoDo

CHAPTER 4

November–December 1914

'Pervyse, one of the most heavily contested points and one of the most
sorely battered towns in the coastal battlefront.'
War Illustrated, 12 December 1914

Sat morning (Nov 21st?) [21 November]

Mother darling – My time for writing is short as I am now camped in a
cellar at Pervyse where we make soup for the soldiers in the trenches there.
It's so cold these days for the poor devils. Ice & snow everywhere & as there
are no 'blessés' these days we thought we might as well do something.
These last photos were of Pervyse & as there is not one house in the village
without a side out. It's not luxury. But there is a very fine cellar intact where
me, Mrs Knocker, Mrs Gleason, a chauffeur & 2 soldiers all sleep in [a] row
on some straw as snug as bugs. We make huge cauldrons of Irish stew stuff
[probably horsemeat] all day. It cooks all night & we take it to the trench
men as soon as it's light. There's very little doing there now only they are
obliged to stay in the trenches all the same.

I've come into Furnes for provisions & am writing this scrawl as hear
someone going to England will take it. Also don't be surprised if I don't
write much these days – no time – but it's quite safe out there you know

Much love dearest

Mrs Knocker and Mairi Chisholm became famous as the only women working
close to the front line at Pervyse. However, it is clear from Dorothie's letters that
they were not alone, at least initially. Mrs Knocker describes the cellar as
measuring about 10 feet by 12 and dimly lit by gratings in the pavement above. 'We
slept in our clothes and cut our short hair so that it would tuck inside our caps ...
Ablutions were infrequent and difficult ... Now and again we would get to Furnes
or Dunkirk for a good soak, but there were times when we had to scrape the lice
off with the blunt edge of a knife and our underclothes stuck to us.'

Thurs [26 November]

Mother darling –
Munro is trying today to get Marjie & Boo taken on at a hospital in Dunkerque. Then later when the dressing station scheme is defined we hope there may be an opening for them. But the authorities here are objecting to so many 'loose' ladies about & we cannot take them until their job is all ready. Especially really as they are 'my' people one must not make exceptions & give vent to criticism among rest of the party – but I am pretty sure he may get them a job at Dunkerque. I do hope so. I am more glad than I can say you have had Tubby back a day or two. Thanks so much for all your letters & parcels – you're a brick – my combies are a joy. I have 'em on now. Tell Mr Heath I have received a gorgeous pair of gloves & thank him very so much – will write later to him – just back to my cave at Pervyse. DoDo

Furnes Nov 27th 1914

Late at nicht [*sic*]

Dearest Mother –
I have just come in from my cave at Pervyse as I am going Rollo hunting early tomorrow. I haven't heard a word so don't know if I'm to find them at Dunkerque or Boulogne or Bailleul or where – or if it's only him or Mellins. All I do know is I mean to have a beano with old Tubby somehow.
   What a vile pen [letter covered in ink blots].
   I can't go on anymore. Thank you & Squeaker so much for the chocs and things, you're a dear to send them me.
   Much love
   DoDo

Rollo's village
Dec 7th about

Mon très cher Herr Papa –
I never answered your last letter for which many tanks [*sic*]. This is our last day at Meteren with Tubby & we have been having huge fun. It does one good to be with one's own belongings again you know & everyone here has been too nice to us. We started off by hiding on all fours under the bed pretending to be the _____! & ended up by going the round of all the

messes & being given vast dinners by all the colonels we had started off by being so frightened of. The result was instead of staying 2 days we have stayed a week. But we felt justified on account of dear old Tubby getting his DSO [Distinguished Service Order]. 'George' [King George V] pinned it on himself the other morning at Hazebrouck & Mellins & I hid in a doorway only a few yards off & watched it all, which was splendid. Wasn't it a bit of luck our just being here for it? Rollo keeps swearing he can't make out why he got it, but it is very obvious why he got it when one hears his fellow officers' opinion of how he has been running things all that sticky 5 weeks. Poor devils, they must have had a ghastly time & what is more done wonders.

We 3 have been snug as bugs here in digs in the village, & all just loafed around & felt happy. It is so restful being just with one's own 'espéce' [species] again. You don't realise till you get away from them, how trying it is being months at a time without people of one's own walk of life, however excellent the others may be individually. It is so odd here seeing all our friends again & it's most cheery. Geoffrey has been a brick & not turned us out a bit which was fortunate & we quite expected it too. Have just seen the battalion march down the high street looking very fit & well & such giants. Rollo has biggest company of the lot & looks like billy among them all.

I go back to my cave at Pervyse tomorrow & will just look up Marjie at Dunkerque on my way home. I expect I shall get kicked on turning up by Munro for taking an extension of leave without orders!

Well goodbye Mr Da dear & for heavens sake stay on the East coast & don't go travelling around Europe. I hope the W.O. will have the same idea too. Much love father darling. Yr Diddles.

Rudolph received the Distinguished Service Order for action near Stroombeck with the 3rd Battalion, Coldstream Guards. His citation in the London Gazette *dated 1 December 1914 reads: 'Conspicuous gallantry in leading platoon during attack on 21st October. He handled it with skill, and held an advanced post for two days under heavy shellfire. Has done other good work in preparing defensive positions.'*

Tuesday [7 December]
'Meteren'

Mother darling –
I am just off back to my cave – having had such a nice rest here & it has been so nice seeing Tubby – we have had great fun dodging Generals & Brigadiers & people & by being tactful & being prepared to 'evacuate' at a minute's notice.

It was so nice having you these days & this week of seeing you all has bucked me up no end.

Yr loving
DoDo

Dec 10th

Mother darling

I hear letters home are to be blocked for a week & heavily censored, so Lord knows when you will get this & I see you mad with indignation at my not writing sooner! I enclose the bill for sheets & chloroform. Would you use the Evans, Clifford & Uncle Lewis £5 for it & supplement the deficit from the other money.

Yesterday we had a big batch of wounded in & one very bad. The doctor said it was no good doing anything & he'd be dead in half an hour. But we got him much better & eventually I got him fit enough to take into the hospital last night & I hear he is ever so much better & coming through which is splendid. He was shot through the lungs. As to the Emergency Club comforts – send them me by all means the hospital would love them.

I had a lovely time with Tubby & the rest was delicious.

Tell Clare to send me any things she has from the village [Monks Kirby] no matter what.

Love DoDo

On 12 December 1914, the Rugby Advertiser *printed a letter from Captain S.J. Carter, Royal Army Medical Corps, to his brother:*

While some fierce fighting was going on I, with other stretcher bearers, was out collecting wounded and at a small dressing station we were assisted by a lady whom you will no doubt know, Lady Dorothie Feilding, the daughter of the Earl of Denbigh. She was not at a base, but at a small cottage with her motor-ambulance, with shells flying around, and she did some excellent work in transporting sick to hospital. She is a lady of whom Britain may well be proud.

Dec 15th

Mother darling

I have just got a very indignant letter from you accusing me of not writing. But the reason is all out going mails have been held up for a week for censoring or something silly so that is why. However I get my home letters as usual which is all that matters really you know! But somehow I think, I see you making a frog mouth at that argument.

I got back here from Meteren alright. That paper yarn about the Pervyse attack by rafts & wading in the water was a pure myth. I expected to find the place a seething mass of dead Germans, but was met here with screeches of derision as the whole affair was undiluted invention on the newspapers' part!! As it turned out I chose quite a good week to be absent in as nothing happened at the cave in my absence but the 1st 3 days on my return we were very busy with odd wounded men & I was able to take on the job while Mrs Knocker had a rest. We have had a goodly few old shrapnel flying round lately – but nothing to fret about, & they did no damage which was luck. Our cave is under water from the rain & our bed floating! So we had to move out & the engineers have rigged us up another residence which has even got glass windows. The only show in place which boasts such luxury & we are very proud of the sensation it causes. Mairi & I were awfully sick with the Teutons yesterday because they nearly smashed them with a bally shrapnel. If they had, I should really have had to walk up the old road & complained to the German C.O. in person about it.

I wish I knew where Rollo was these days – I am afraid we shall drift further away from each other which is sad & rather upsets our plan of an Xmas together. What a joke if Da comes out for a few days 'look–see' – I should love to see his pleasant face. Hug the dear man for me! Much love darling

Yrs Dodo

Dec 19th

Mother darling

Thank you so much for the packet of mixed comforts. They are a joy. Also my lovely boots and flea bag.

Later – just got a line from you & am sending this over to England. The chloroform the £16 sent I will see about – is that bought out of the residue of subscription money or out of Mr Heath's money? He is too kind. If the latter is not spent will you send it to McConnell at 61 Chancery Lane to be put to Munro's fund account. Munro will then dole me out that amount of money for use of the 'Pervyse camp'. We can then just get things as we want them for the blessés & the soldiers if that meets with his approval. That way we can order things in driblets as they are wanted & according to the need & keep that little fund for here only.

For God's sake stop Evy sending out Ramsay McDonald. It would be an awful mistake as would rub up all the authorities over this side. But Munro is writing him about it.

I am very well & very happy. I haven't yet got the 2nd lot hypodermic syringes from Harrods, or the Horlicks milk or Imelda's nice new Mackintosh. They got very delayed. This is a dull letter but am writing in such a hurry – forgive no news. You mustn't blame Marjie too much poor kiddy – she's only human & from their point of view as each mean to wait indefinitely for the other, it would be terribly hard if they couldn't even see each other don't you think? I don't think it can do much harm if they do. Somehow the war changes everything & it's their look out if they don't mind a long wait. Goodbye darling. Thank you so much for all your dear letters & parcels – You do spoil me. But I'm jolly glad you do, so don't stop, will you? I'm sorry your Rollo's pictures aren't better

Yr DoDo

PS

Please out of my Mr Heath's fund could we have another 'flea bag' for Pervyse just like the nice one you sent me. We are one short & one of us dies of cold each night. We would like one the twin to mine. That is really all we want for us, the rest we will spend on things for the soldiers – or do you think we ought to buy a flea bag out of that money? I leave it to your discretion.

DoDo

No trousers alas from James yet! Damn

Dec 22nd

Mother darling –

I am very well – only very dirty. You should just see my neck! These bally Germans have been throwing a lot of things at us lately. As I write I am warming my toes over the fire, & there are a lot of shrapnel fuzzing round – bang – there's another.

It's another – bang! – but it's extraordinary how little damage they do. The trenches are more or less shrapnel proof & very snug. I was so sorry not to see Marjie yesterday I was on my way down & had to stop at Furnes to make the peace as usual. Much love dears send me some Illustrations, Sketches & things when you have done with them at Newnham do – I love them & so do the soldiers.

Bang!

I wish they wouldn't. It's not done.

Much love

DoDo

Dec 22nd

Father dear –
I haven't heard from you for a long while. Do write me the back chat. I hope you will come out. It would be ripping to see you again – of course you may find cars the trouble as impossible to get about without & I do not know to what extent the army would lend you one. I gather Evy did not really approve of my taking one of ours down to Rollo so I daren't do it twice. I should find out about the getting round question before you cross. I don't see why though the Gov't shouldn't take you round. It would interest you enormously I feel sure.

We are still at Pervyse, it's just a month now since we've been up here. We are very fit & very happy but oh so dirty. You should see my neck! As long as there is no heavy fighting going on for ambulance work we can do far more here running this dressing station & the regiments here are very grateful for it.

They still shell a goodish bit & most days we have a few wounded in. As we have a car permanently attached here, we can run them straight back to the Furnes hospital without all that delay.

We had four in yesterday from a s-

This smear a shell fell & made the house shake & me jump!

Well to continue … We had four in yesterday from a shell they got clean in the trenches – a very rare occurrence as they are firing from some way back & nearly all shrapnel. The shells that have come have somehow never fallen on anyone here before. They took a bit off the corner of the cave 2 days ago & made a mass of shrapnel holes in the bonnet of the old Daimler that was standing outside. Luckily the driver was inside the house, but a Belgian who was standing nearby got slightly wounded & we took him into our hospital.

Won't it be an odd Xmas up here. But I am sure far less depressing than Xmas in England this year.

Our only tragedy at Pervyse is our water supply. The only water comes from the cemetery yard where 358 dead Germans are 'interred'. Yesterday the pump stuck & has not worked since & it is feared a Teuton has worked his way up the spout. General disgust but no one is brave enough to look & see.

Meanwhile water is getting very scarce.

Goodbye Mr Da dear. Bless you & much love this Xmas
From
Diddles
Write me a nice letter do!

Father darling
Much love to you this Xmas & do come out & look at the guns & me. I dined with Baird & Teck last night & they are trying to fix it up for you.

Evy has sent us Ramsay McDonald confound him! Everyone is furious & no one wants to be associated with a man whose politics are like his especially at this time – as for his 'conversion' of course he hunts with the hounds now – he'd be a d_____ fool if he didn't. I can't understand why Evy will foist him on us & we are all furious. It will only make disquiet.

Much love Papa dear
Yr Diddles

Ramsay Macdonald, treasurer of the Labour Party and later Prime Minister, was at this time extremely unpopular and had been accused of treason and cowardice. He visited the Munro Corps and the ladies at Pervyse but then disappeared. It transpired he had been arrested by the Belgian Military Police and sent back to Britain. He returned later after receiving an 'all access pass' to the Western Front from Lord Kitchener.

Xmas Day 1914

To my family in general & each individual one in particular
What a life! – Here I am on Xmas Day warming my toes up at the old dressing station – we thought the Teutons would have the decency to leave us in peace, as we expected they would be just as excited over their plum pudding as we over ours. But blessed if the offensive blighters didn't spend the whole morning throwing shrapnel and shells at us, having gone to the trouble to bring a gun up closer too under cover of the fog – a really dirty trick & most unchristmassy I consider. Luckily Providence thought so too & saw to it that there were no 'blessé' with the exception of one man who had a hole made in his head by the spoke of a wheel; a shell burst on a long cart, picked out a spoke & threw it at him.

But that was the only casualty!

[An unidentified nurse based at Furnes says similar and appears astonished at newspaper reports of a Christmas Armistice. *'Furnes had over 200 shells in three quarters of an hour between four and five pm Christmas Day.'*]

It's 3 days now since we have had any casualties, though they amuse themselves by shelling the place a little bit each day. But it is very very seldom they actually hit the trenches as owing to the water they are firing from some way off & cannot observe the result well. The trenches are very good & shrapnel proof & shells don't hurt either unless hit plumb through the roof.

We are going to have a great Xmas dinner up here tonight & have been given a bottle of pluz by the officers here. We have been giving away quantities of clothes lately to a company at a time & they were so grateful we got the most touching Xmas letters from the various regiments, saying how they loved us. One delightful one was addressed by a Tommy very proud of his English – to 'The English Misses at the First Help Station'.

We have got all sorts of wonderful foods for Xmas – various parcels sent to Munro of which he has most generously given us 'care ladies' a generous share.

In The Sketch just received of Dec 16th I see a long and inane account of me kissing my hand to Pipe left at the corner of the road & of me 'arriving at a field covered with wounded'. What fools people are.

I got a killing letter from Hughie, furious at his being on the equator while a 'young upstart like me' is on the spot! It really is rather absurd – considering as he points out he spent 13 years in training for a war.

I got lots of nice Xmas letters from all you dear people, Da, Ma, Mellins, Ager, Squeaker & Taffy & photos from Bettie – it's so nice of you all. Taffy's mittens I would love as I can easily find someone with cold hands to give them to.

Later / Interruption to attend to a soldier with the unromantic complaint of boils – a messy performance. We have been out & collected an armful of bits of shells and shrapnel heads & things from the holes round about made this morning. One, I see went right through a luckily empty trench. It would have given someone a thick lip for Xmas if it had been habited. I never got to church this morning which was rather sad. There was midnight mass on in a barn last night about 3 miles off. I wanted so to go, but couldn't very well as I didn't hear about it until going to bed & could not go all that way alone – if I had known about it I could have got one of the soldiers to be a bodyguard.

Am delighted to hear Da is sat on yet a while on the east coast.

Such a frosty day. Lovely for Xmas, a gorgeous morning but foggy now. We are very merry here – I feel we are friends & are having a much nicer Xmas than you people at home – the front is really the only place where one can be genuinely happy 'on occasions' these days.

Thanks for the Illustrateds. I told you I believe that raft attack on our place was a myth?

We now sleep in a repaired cottage in the village proper & the cave is under water but have our dressing station up here by the station as before. It's damn dark I can't see – Much love all – Luv

Diddles

Monday [28 December]

A nice Xmas to you Mrs Ma – at least as nice as it can be these horrid days. I wanted to see Marjie & send her messages for you but was disappointed. By the way, all my parcels have turned up. Thanks, except just my Gamage trousers they won't send. I am back to Pervyse this morning.

Goodbye Mother darling I will pray so hard for you all this Xmas & that your heartache for the boys won't be too great. I wish to God this war was over – poor little Mother.

Yr Diddles

PS Please thank Mrs Heath for her lovely parcel of clothes just arrived – will write her. The village sent me 2 lovely boxes of sweets – I don't know who to thank – could you find out & say how touched I am – it's so nice of them.

Dec 30th 1914

Father darling –

Thank you so much for your nice letter for Xmas. What a shame of that old devil the Kaiser spoiling your time at home like that. A bit 'ard I call it.

No, the German is still up the pump at Pervyse – very tactless of him – I wish he would go away as he simply ruins the drinking water & we have to drag it from Furnes every day.

I have left the cave for a bit – I find if I am away for long I lose touch with the crowd here & they squabble & mess things up, whereas for some marvellous reason I seem to be the only person none of them want to kick or bite! So when I come I find I can often persuade them to bury hatchets & work in harmony. I have been in here at our headquarters now for 2 days. This afternoon they shelled the station again. Killed 9 soldiers & wounded 15. A horrible affair – I have just come in from taking the poor souls up to our hospital. Some of them frightfully badly wounded. They are making very free with their aeroplane bombs these days – an unpleasant game – as it's so infuriating to be done in by anything as futile as that. If one ends my days by any chance – I warn you beforehand I shall turn up at St Peters with an awful grievance. You know Secker one of our people who was wounded before at Nieuport by one of those bombs? Well he has just returned & was driving peacefully down the Dunkirk road today when they threw one at him again – just missed his car & landed on a house where it killed about 6 or 7 people.

It's a pastime I frankly detest.

Poor old Nieuport is more battered than ever now, I was in there last night – it's a tragedy as a town, poor little place.

I spent last night with Marjie at Dunkirk – it's a dear kid isn't it & she is so grateful to you for being so nice to her and Dudley. You know as they have quite made up their minds to wait for each other I cannot see why they cannot anyhow be privately engaged, tho' not announced. If that was the case they would be quite content to wait.

Of course if pennies end by being sufficient it would be splendid if they could just be married quietly & slip off to Derry. I am convinced they will be perfectly happy those two. Dudley may not be brilliant in any way but I feel quite sure he will make Marjie happy.

Poor Mr Da – what a trial daughters are aren't they – don't you wish we were all born with 3 noses, or spots on our faces or something beastly? It would so simplify matters somehow.

Much love Father cheri yr Diddles

The following appeared in the Rugby Advertiser *of 13 February 1915:*

For her work in removing wounded men in the neighbourhood of Ghent and Dixmude, Admiral Ronarc'h, in command of the French Brigade of Fusiliers Marins, issued a special order of the day on 31 December 1914:

The Vice-Admiral commanding the Brigade of 'Fusiliers Marins' specially mentions in the Brigade order of the day Lady Dorothy Feilding, ambulance lady of the English Red Cross, for having effected the evacuation of very many wounded men of the Brigade – first of all at Ghent, then at Dixmude, and even in that town itself, and for exhibiting to everybody, almost daily, the finest example of devotion and contempt of danger.

By this present order the entire Brigade wishes to tender to Lady Dorothie Feilding the assurance of their deep gratitude and admiration.

It is regarded in the French forces as a great honour to be cited in an order of the day for any special act of bravery, and it may be regarded as somewhat unprecedented for this compliment to be extended to a woman.

It is understood that Admiral Ronarc'h, having noticed Lady Dorothie's work amongst his wounded on several occasions when sharp fighting was going on, took steps to ascertain her identity that he might express his recognition of her services to his men.

CHAPTER 5

January–March 1915

The Countess had visited the front in December and she was eager to do her bit. She agreed for some blessés to go to Newnham to convalesce and Mrs Knocker escorted them on the long journey. The men were all stretcher cases - 'two head wounds, one amputated leg, two men with serious abdominal complications, and one with a horribly fractured thigh' - and Mrs Knocker was concerned that they might not all survive the journey. The Countess was not expecting such serious cases, being 'under the impression that I was bringing convalescent sitting or walking cases who could benefit from the lovely grounds ... and was horrified to see six men each of whom appeared to have at least one foot in the grave'. Judging by Dorothie's letter she was perhaps aware that the men would come as a shock to her mother.

Jan 1st 1915

Mother Darling – Don't have a fit! My blessés are very very charming & I really didn't mean you to have them for a fortnight until 1st I asked the Heaths & Hendersons etc how many they would take in & 2nd until they were further on the road to convalescence.

I sent these men from here to Marjie's hospital to await their time to go to Newnham and until all arrangements were made. Then their doctor bust a bombshell on me, by saying they could not keep them after today as they had had a rush of the more serious wounded.

I couldn't bear losing sight of these men just after I had got permission to have them, so I prayed the neighbours would forgive short notice. I feel they will be glad to have 'blessés' & glad to have some real nursing to do as a result of all the Red X lectures & work they have done.

I don't expect you want any of these at Newnham proper as you haven't time these days but I left that for you. Please forgive me for the short notice but that is the worst of war. The £20 sent by you to McConnell we would spend on getting these men to England & any expenses not incurred by the householders they lodge with – should there be any over we can use it for other things, only as subscribed locally I thought would please them to have a finger in the pie & the looking after the actual blessé.

Thanks for the lovely parcels & letter by Mrs K you do spoil me & don't I love it just.

Much love dears – I hope to come & see you for 3 days in a fortnight if poss.

Goodbye

DoDo

I forgot to tell you Robert Broqueville went back to army proper, not for any grievance but now ambulance work was slacker, he didn't feel he could go on having a 'soft job'. He is now in Artillery. I respect him for his decision. It's 3 weeks now he went & we miss his personality enormously. He was a brick.

It's been very kind of Mrs Knocker taking these men back – can you please put her up at Newnham & be nice to her on the strength of it.

DoDo

Jan 21st 1915 [This date was added later by Dorothie and is clearly incorrect as Marjie and Dudley were married on 18 January. Possibly this letter should be around 11 January as Dunkirk was badly bombed on the 10th.]

Mother darling –

I am sending you this home by Marjie, things were so black here [Dunkirk] they are shelling up half the hospital & they gave her leave to come home. I expect it will simplify things muchly as it takes such ages to communicate by letter & a lot of cross purposes goes on. As it looks imminent do try & fix it up by a licence or something funny as then probably Hughie could be there for it. I mean coming home for a week's leave for the occasion & a week or two on would fit in just beautifully for me, whereas later on might possibly be complicated. Besides I am aching to see old Neb & just think how nice it would be altogether ever so early & ever so quietly at NP. It's too good to be true that the finance question is ok. I think a public engagement is quite unnecessary once Da decides the deed can be done don't you? Once that is decided do let them kick off at once – they've had all the engaging they want already as they've had lots of time to think it over. Time is so short too, this awful war one just has to snatch any minute of happiness one can before it melts & a week or two more or less would mean such an enormous difference to them.

I enclose you the French dispatch [Admiral Ronarc'h's order of the day] by Marjie & a German hat that smells like hell to be kept very carefully for me. I am longing just to come home for a few days & see you all – you know counting from August when I went to the Rugby hospital it's nearly five months since I've had any time at home & I just love to dash back &

hug all you dear people & Hughie too. Poor poor 'Pigs' Trotter – it is too horrible. I can't realise it. What it must mean to Rollo is too awful poor boy. The horror of seeing one's pals drop out day by day like that.

Please God ours will come home safe.

Much love Mother darling you've been an angel to Marjie & the little kid is so radiant at the prospect of things being settled up.

God bless you all

Yr loving Diddles

Dorothie took a brief period of leave to go home for the long-awaited wedding of Marjie and Dudley on 18 January 1915.

Jan 25th 1915
Monday Dover

Just seen Mr Hart who tells me they have been shelling Furnes off & on all the week & in the hospital & they had to move all the wounded. I gather our people are still there so it's not as bad as I thought thank God. They have probably moved all the wounded & are just hanging on as long as possible. That is better it means there was no pain or risk to move people which I feared. I expect we will go up there on landing – will communicate when possible.

God bless you all

Ever so much love Mother dear. You are sweet to me.

Yr loving Diddles

Such haste

Hurrah for Blucher

Furnes, Jan 27th

Mother deah

I was much relieved on arriving to find things not half so black as were painted. The hospital staff was at Malo & our ambulance remained here for the present – we have found a new site for a hospital in a convent about 7 miles from here on the Ypres road. Very little damage has been done to the town it was only that it wasn't safe to have 'blessés' & therefore no use having a hospital in the town – but we hope later to be able to open up this one again & are leaving a few nurses & people as a 'poste de secours' [dressing station] & to see no one else bags the building. There are always odd casualties from the town being brought in – though now all the population has been cleared out. We are going to do a lot of the moving of the hospital stuff to the convent this morning. I am so sick at losing this as a base but hope to return if the Teuton's guns that go for it can be silenced.

I saw Roger Hély d'Oissel, the general last night. To my joy I find he is going to command the part of the French line that we work for, which is splendid, & he will also facilitate our ambulance work which is no small consideration as we often 'come up' against fussy little French officers. Went out down the line yesterday & day before & found everything exactly as I had left it & no advance excepting per the Daily Mail.

I can't tell you much about this as letters get so hung up now if you do which is a nuisance.

In the dunes they are only 8 yards off in places – most unpleasant I should say I can't imagine anything I would dislike more. Not only that but each side sapping like fun to get under the other beggar's trench & blow him up first!

I am so pleased at Hély d'Oissel being in our bit. Evy & I are dining with him tonight.

I must skid off now & pack up the hospital things. One of the little nurses, a Dutch girl, at our hospital was wounded & I am sorry to say died of the shock of her leg being amputated – poor little soul – it's very tragic.

Much love to you all – what fun it was to be home!

Yr loving Diddles

Furnes Jan 28th 1915

Mr Da dear –
The Red X has told us that in March they will have to withdraw all ambulances lent to the French and Belgians as everything they have & more will be required by K's [Kitchener's] new army. We have therefore to collect funds at once to replace those of our cars (about 2–3) which are not our private property. Also accepting any offers of any really good cars that can be converted into ambulances. Our people are writing round to the various City Companies (Fishmongers, Goldsmiths etc) & banks, to ask if they can give us some pennies from their 'charity funds' for this purpose.

Would the Joint Stock or Tinto or anyone like that give us anything do you think? It's a most deserving object & the money would be devoted entirely to the car fund proper as apart from any of the personable expenses.

I am writing to you because I know you won't do anything if you think it's indiscreet, but on the other hand I feel sure some of your city pals will agree!

We have got a very nice new convent for our hospital about 6 miles further due south of this. Further from Dunkerque which is a bore for food transport.

This place is as quiet as anyfink [*sic*] & I don't think they are going to destroy it after all. Very little damage has been done so far. But they won't let us have our blessés here so we have no choice but to move along for the present though leaving a covering force & many stores here.

Goodbye Mr Da – it was good to see you again & I just loved my week at home – really I congratulate myself more each time on my choice of parents.

Yr loving Diddles.

Funds seemed to always be an issue for the Corps. The Daily Mail *war correspondent made the following appeal in* War Illustrated *on 6 March 1915:*

Anyone who is anxious to help the brave Belgian Army in the field cannot do better than support the Munro Ambulance Volunteer Corps now working at Furnes ... No words of praise can be too high for the courage, skill and efficiency shown by all its workers ... We knew very well, when we saw the Munro ambulances speeding out at great rate for some particular point, that hot fighting was going on there. I say deliberately, no finer or more courageous medical or war aid has been done anywhere than here. Dr Munro and his colleagues are seriously hampered by lack of funds ... but money must be had. Fresh cars are needed and needed now.

Furnes, Friday [29 January 1915]

Mother dear – Thank you so much for your nice letters – it was so nice to be home again & see all your dear faces. Real amazing luck to fall upon you all there in a lump – it was grand. We worked very hard yesterday getting in French Algerian troops as a result of their successful attack in the dunes. Evy is taking this scrawl back & will give you the news. I am still in Furnes thank heaven – they haven't shelled it for days so we are as snug as bugs. The hospital is up the road though.

Ever so much love Mother darling.

Yr loving Diddles

Furnes, 2nd Feb 1915

Oh my family –

I've been very remiss about writing, but owing to change in hospitals & places things have been one damn thing after another & the idea that now letters take a fortnight to get to you somehow takes the gilt off letter writing. I intend smuggling this home or bursting in the attempt.

It's 3 days now since we've had a shell in Furnes & things are very snug again. The last 'marmite' went slap through the hospital wall & burst in that inner courtyard between the wards. Absolutely wrecked the washing which was hung up to dry – gave Jane a nasty jump but luckily hurt no one – the nurses had all been evacuated, thank God, as otherwise someone was bound to be hurt as that yard is a hotbed of them in usual conditions. One of their nurses was killed during the bombardment I am sorry to say. Such a nice Dutch girl who joined us about three weeks ago.

Perrins hospital is now about 8 miles down the road to Ypres, of course within range but I am sure they are safe there as it is an isolated chateau & sure not to be potted. It's very nice but of course not so marvellously beautiful as this one.

We have some of our cars attached there & the rest, including me, hang on at Furnes to do from the sea to Dixmude as it's such a much better centre. The Belgians have now taken on a lot of French trenches the far side of Dixmude up to Steenstrade & Binchote. Did I tell you Gen Hély d'Oissel has now the division by Nieuport & in the dunes? He has been promoted again to a still 'buggier' type of general. He's such a dear it's splendid having him close by. Also to our joy he has the whole lot of beloved 'fusiliers Marins' with him at Nieuport – our friends of Melle & Dixmude fights. They are some 6,000 strong & nothing but horse ambulances. Yesterday they asked us to dine & have been charming asking us to go on working for them, & making everything smooth & easy, & so grateful. Such a difference after all the troubles we have had here with these swine of French infantry doctors who consider they do you a favour by allowing you to get obussed [shelled] getting their wounded when they haven't the spunk to go in & do it themselves.

We are attaching two cars to them & will thus work the Nieuport section officially & harmoniously, instead of having to 'body snatch' poor blessés that the French RAMC insisted on leaving there 6 hours before moving them back. Those sailors are ripping to work for & such gentlemen. I can't stick the French infantry at any price.

My old 'dispatches' pal Admiral Ronarc'h is back there too under Hély d'Oissel.

Such a gallant old bird & he too has sent us all sorts of nice messages asking if we will go on working for them again here. They are taking over the Lombardz to St George line & the French infantry the dune bit. It's the very devil that dune & almost impossible to take. It's a natural fortress. After that attack the other day there that cost them 300 men they had to give up the trench they took as it was untenable from mines.

Much love dears

DoDo

Furnes Feb 3rd 1915

Mother dear

'Old Albert' [King of the Belgians] gave me a tin cross [Order of Leopold] today which I am putting up for auction – what offers? My tummy looks grand with a shiny thing plastered in the middle! [The Order of Leopold was awarded for extreme bravery in combat or for meritorious service of immense benefit to the Belgian nation.]

The dear man was very kind & said many nice things. Told me Bridges was trying hard to send us home & was much amused & said he would leave us as we were.

Bless you all – Furnes very quiet now the état major have left.

All rot about our ladies being moved from Pervyse – Evy is talking through his neck.

Yrs ever in the deuce of a hurry
Diddles

Feb 9th 1915

My dear Mother –

Just to show you I am live and well & not obussed yet. I was told yesterday that Rollo led an attack 3 days ago & did very well & was ok – good news isn't it? It appears the attack was successful & they took the trenches.

We sleep outside old Furnes now as our street was none too healthy. They made a habit which we didn't think much of, stoving in the houses all round ours. Thanks so much for your letters. Johnie Baird tells me he is afraid Da's chance of coming out here for a look-see by War Office is nil. The only hope is if he can come as their private guest – a difficult job rather but he will try his best.

Yr loving Diddles

Don't say on any account to people in Paris that Roger Hély d'Oissel is in this district as it would get him into trouble as it is supposed to be a strict secret where his division is. This is very important please as French so particular

PS

Could you send by Gleason or someone a large size primus heater to burn petrol (paraffin no can get). Like the one we have for picnics at home – one that will take a large kettle. We have nothing in our cave of the sort & it's imperative for heating things quick at night & at odd times.

DoDo

Feb 12th 1915

Mother dear

When on earth is Moll going to [get] married? I haven't heard a word of it & I want to know so as to see if I can't get home for 48hrs for it. I am sure I can if I know a bit beforehand.

We are a bit less topsy turvey now & are sleeping outside our dear old town now. Yesterday they stove in the house opposite & smashed all our windows, so as we had left two days before it was rather nicely judged. Poor little place – I hate seeing it going the way of all the others. You know old 'Juices' house where you stayed? The house next that is bust up too & all our old bedroom windows broken too.

We are temporarily by the sea but it's the devil of a way from our hospital only there is absolutely nothing near it so there's not much choice.

I got a very funny letter from Marjie yesterday – she seems full of beans.

I went last night & had a great chat with my old pal, Admiral Ronarc'h. I want awfully to get him a little present, he has been so kind to us & I want a little leather (natural colour or brown) writing block. Something about - or - the size of this sheet of paper with a block & envelopes & things. Above all not large or cumbersome. I have a little one that is simply invaluable. Could you choose one for me please & post it me to field post office Dunkerque & pay for it out of my pennies.

And tell Moll to get a move on & get married before the hunting season is over or I shall never never forgive her.

Much love dears
DoDo

Feb 13th

Mother dear –

Why won't Moll get married? Have the dear things fallen out? Because I am just longing for a hunt & am getting fed up with them.

It's nearly midnight & I am very weary, very bad tempered, very headachy & oh so longing for a little peace right away from everyone & everything for 48hrs – but that's too much to hope for I suppose.

I do so hate this eternal evacuating. It always gives me the blues.

What an amazing shave Tubby had. I never saw 'Eye Witness' do send me a copy if it is anything relating to him in it. He is nearer to me than he was I think. By 'he' I mean the English lines generally & that I hope may mean Tubby nearer to me eventually.

Just seen Roger Hély d'Oissel. He's a brick that man & so good to me & helps us all manner of ways. I haven't been frightened for days yet. I

51

expect I shall soon forget what it's like. I was so disappointed at not being able to startle Evy – somehow we never got him near a shell & I was so longing to bust one up his trouser leg & out through his collar stud – just to liven up 'the front' for him. But he was a sort of mascot – wherever we took him nothing happened.

The Germans go on shucking those damnable lyddite bombs from mortars out of their trenches into ours in the dunes. They do a terrible lot of mischief & there's no means of protecting from them.

Off to bed – so sleepy.

Love to all Diddles

Feb 15th

I wonder where?
Probably in Silesia?

Well all ye little Denbighs & Feildings –
That's grand, I shall try & get off for a few days on the 25th to see Moll kick off. I am longing for a few days mental peace more than I have ever since the beginning of the war I think. I shall probably try & cross on the 24th & then try & stay on a few days afterwards when the wedding cake is sitting hard on everyone's chest. And then – I can have a hunt! – ooer. If it's anything like as wet as it's here it will be about the limit. Everything is a sea of mud. I was out till midnight last night getting blessés at _____! & I got so cold & wet. But we got the blessés too which was the great thing poor things. Yesterday they shelled _____ again badly & I was in there trying to save the washing of mine that got left behind. The Germs [sic] started shelling like fun & I grabbed my washing – tied it up in a red handkerchief & fled with it up the street like a stag for shelter at the hospital. You would have laughed to see me. There always that to be said wherever you are most frit there is nearly always something especially ludicrous that happens that makes one laugh.

That's providence I suppose.

My letters now I send by the English Mission so you get them quick, but I have to promise not to mention names & places or give any information which means damnably dull letters, but on the other hand you get them quick which is the great consolation.

Dear old Roger came & dined with us here Sunday & was in great form. He gets rabid with rage if I pay the Admiral one more visit than I pay him so I have to eke out my calls on the high road with tact!

I also tell him every manner of lie or he tries to stop me going anywhere near an obus [shell] or a blessé which is absurd of him. But he's a dear & has been so kind to me.

Heavens what a day. The wind is whistling round the house & I have got to go & put on a sou-wester & hie to _____ again.

Much love dears. See you soon I hope – I am so longing to be back for 2 or 3 days somehow – more than I have ever wanted ever since the war started.

Yr loving Diddles

Dorothie went home to attend the wedding of her older sister, Mary, to Cecil Dormer at Newnham Paddox on 25 February. Cecil was Assistant Private Secretary to the Foreign Secretary.

Royal Pavilion Hotel, Folkestone
Thursday 11th March

Oh Mama, dear mama –
I wonder shall I own up – but as the paper gives it away I might as well! We missed the damn boat!

In spite of the Admiralty telling me that train would be ok, it was late & no porters & we got to the side just as the old barge moved off. We had to come on here & cross by Calais which is the very devil of a bore & waste of a day.

It was nice seeing you & Mr Da again yesterday when I thought I wouldn't any more & you are both such saints to me & I had such a nice time I don't at all feel like going back.

I don't expect I will be over for ages though now. Let me know Da's plans won't you please & Peter's too.

I see they have got 17-inch guns at Nieuport now to buck us up.

It appears the Mission told Hély d'Oissel that now I was in England I wouldn't be coming back & he wrote me pages in an awful stew. I shall make a point on leaving my card on the Mission the moment I arrive just to show I am back again!

Goodbye & much love to all you dear people.

Yr loving
Diddles

Furnes 17th March

To my father – to my Mother – to my Brothers – to my Sisters –
Salut!
Thank God I've got an armchair & a fire & a few minutes peace – things have been an awful scrum since I got back & I have been spending my time seeing all the Grand Prevosts & Commandants & Ministers & Maires [*sic*]

& Colonels & Generals of Belgium. There have been new & terrible rules drawn up by the allies at Boulogne as regards English subjects working in the lines & for an awful moment (at its maximum yesterday) we thought both we & the hospital would have to drop out of things or officially join the Red X which meant being relegated to Boulogne or some such Godforsaken spot. But the little Belgians have stuck by us manfully as usual, including my beloved 'Papa' Broqueville, so that the clouds have cleared & we are now ok. What we would still like & want all the same for future use in similar occasions is a chit from the English Red X saying we are respectable people & very nice too.

The French round Nieuport have been doing very nicely & taking all sorts of snitches of land & little forts from the German which delights them & Suzanne's Herr Papa [Hély d'Oissel] is very bucked generally. I dined with him last night. He was as nice as ever & most interesting as always. He's a brick that man & is doing wonderfully well from an army point of view.

The Zouaves are very fine troops & there is great rivalry between them & the 'Marins' as to who will do the most original stunt next that is most calculated to worry Germans generally.

Two Zouaves did a very fine thing 3 nights ago in the dunes. By the light of one of the flares they saw the glint of the muzzle of a German machine gun in the trench some 50 yds away. It was a dark night so they wriggled up on their tummies to the German trench & found all the machine gun people fast asleep – so they very gently pulled out the gun & got away with it, not however without waking the Germans & being chased by bullets back to their own trench. But in getting back they noticed two French rifles that had been left on the sand for the last attack about 5 or 6 yds outside the German trench – not at all pleased at having seen them there the Zouaves decided they would go & fetch them too. As soon as the shooting had died down, blessed if they didn't go out & fetch the rifles in, & again got back without being hit though fired at hard.

'Roger' was so pleased he gave them both the 'Medaille Militaire' to buck them up so heaven knows what they will be up to next – I hope they don't get done in.

That's grand Rollo being in for his captaincy ok. They have been having the devil of a time at poor old Nieuport lately. The Germans have brought up one of their four vast 17-inch guns they had at Antwerp. No mistake about it because the General has the base of one of the shells as proof.

There is one hole which is 48 feet across. Perfectly gigantic & the biggest anywhere down the line up to now. They are terribly proud of it & photographed the Col & 40 men in it yesterday without one of them showing over the hole. But they don't put many of those shells in. They cost them too much & besides they say each gun only has a life of some

150 shots before coming useless. The cost to the Germans of each shell fired works out at £450 counting the depreciation to the gun & the cost of the shell. Rather a revelation isn't it?

After all the talk in the English papers as to whether these guns ever existed at all it's rather interesting to have that base of shell. I haven't seen it yet but mean to this afternoon – would you like it mounted as a pendant. I believe it only weighs a hundred weight or so.

Well goodbye dears – I am off to attend to my little Mary.

Much love

Diddles

March 22nd 1915

Maman chere –

I am at the bottom of my bed this morning and quite lazy. Do not worry, only my dear friendly Tonks which occupied me with such zeal that I couldn't stand anymore. It is a nasty 'chill' I think, but that will be finished soon and already I am much better. We are awfully short for cars but your tame millionaire gave us another small 'thou' too for two ambulances to come immediately from London. Jellett, the old man, comes over to London today for chores and I have entrusted this letter [translated from French]. When I am in bed I think in French it's a form of nightmare. Please find out for me if you can in which hospital Tom Brockholes is. I am supposing he can't be badly wounded or I should have heard something about it from you. But if he is in a hospital over at Boulogne do please wire me as I am sure I could manage to get over some how.

Don't forget will you please? I am meanwhile trying to find out from this end but so far without success. What a horrible thing that endless [casualty] list was. Thank God Tubby got left out of that. I am afraid we didn't accomplish all we wanted to either or enough to warrant that ghastly sacrifice of men. The latter was greatly due to our artillery not shooting accurately, only this is private of course, don't say it about unless you have already heard it published.

Our gunners fired a good deal on our own men & 3 times when they were supposed to have cleared the ground & the wire entanglements for an attack shot too short with the result our men rushed right up to the entanglements before they found they weren't swept away & had to retire losing a terrible amount of men in the retreat from the Germans' fire.

It's a ghastly thing anyway.

They say the Germans must have lost nearly as many men though, although we were the attacking party.

Here things are much the same. The French taking a few yards here & there. Just enough to 'kill the German's pride'.

Is there any news of Hughie? Is he at the Dardanelles do you think?

We haven't been shelled once in Furnes since I've been back. It's so damn healthy we don't know ourselves; we had a new home lately without a stick of furniture in it, but now thanks to a week's vigorous looking we have a magnificent furnished flat & a spare bedroom with looking glasses, wash stands complete & now a kitchen range I got in a brewer's horse & cart from Pervyse! Even our plates are swank & have 'Nieuport Hotel' & a crest on them – to the envy of all – yr loving Diddles.

Captain Thomas Fitzherbert Brockholes, 2nd Battalion, Rifle Brigade, was killed in action on 14 March 1915 at Neuve Chapelle. It is apparent from later letters that Tom meant a great deal to Dorothie.

Monday Furnes [29 March]

Father dear

Dr Munro is going back to England & I am asking him to post this scrawl. I had started writing you a real letter only they started shelling us with fat ones simultaneously, luckily not much damage.

Two days ago we had a ghastly morning here. People just blown to smithereens & lots of wounded.

The Corps is going on just the same without Munro & the Belgians & the Mission both say we may go on just the same as ever. That is to say the women.

Thank God for that anyway. I just don't know what I should have done just now if I had had to chuck the active job & go & sit at home & twiddle one's thumbs & think. I honestly don't think I could bear it & ever so grateful that for the present at any rate the English Mission will sanction my working on the ambulances.

Johnie Baird has been a perfect little brick helping us in all sorts of ways & me in particular. He's an awful good little chap.

Oh Father when is this devilish war going on? It's so awful.

Munro is going now. I wish I could write you a real letter. I am smothered in oil having been under the car greasing it all the afternoon.

God bless you – do write me please

Yr loving Diddles

CHAPTER 6

April–May 1915

April 1st, Furnes

Father dear –
Here are some photographs to see. Would you send them later on to Mother
to keep for me please? The one of a shell burst in the square at Furnes is
one I want to keep. Our hospital is about 100 yds from the square as the
crow flies, but longer to walk round as the street waggles. We haven't had
one quite close to the building – that is to say 100 yds for some time now.

Such a gorgeous night last night. Magnificent moon, like day & we went
blessé hunting down near Dixmude. It was very ghostly & ghouly there in
moonlight. I do resent having the Germans right up to the bridge there.
They are just the other side of the river, 25 yds across & it doesn't look like
being able to move them. Most of the civilians left in Furnes are doing a
bunk now with the result that we now have all the eggs & milk & things we
want instead of nicks – so it has its compensations. The English lines are
very close up to us now. I wonder if they will join them actually in with the
Belgians or not? All the Belgians are having khaki uniforms in April and
are awful bucked about it.

It's grand about Italy joining in, at least I suppose it's true, all of the
sentries on the road waved their arms with joy & told it to us as we drove
home about midnight last night. Everyone is too pleased for words.

What a hell it will be if it's only rumour after all.

Goodbye Mr Da dear, this is a damnable war. I wish I had been invented
last generation.

God bless you
Diddles

April 2nd [1915] Furnes

Mother dear –
The English Mission have been bricks to me & I won't have it said they

aren't. They have also given me official permission to stay out here now & say they will no longer oppose it in any way & have written to Red X to say so. Bless them.

I don't think you realise a bit what it would mean to me to not have a job just now. I nearly chucked it last week as I was so afraid I was blocking the work & I told the mission I would leave it to them to decide. Johnie was a perfect brick & has made everything alright & I am so grateful to him & always will be.

Thank you for your letters & news of the boys. We haven't been shelled here for 3 days now. I am just off to Nieuport. I often wonder as I drive into that old place if I'll drive out again but one always seems to.

Our hospital has a lot of blessés lately.

Goodbye, old Jellett is waiting for me & the car bumping its gears out.

Yr loving Diddles

I wish I was a man. It's rotten being a woman isn't it?

April 3rd 1915 Furnes

Mother darling – I have just got your letter written on Maundy Thursday & have been to communion on purpose for you this morning. Poor Mother it must be too too ghastly at home these days & we foolish kids don't seem to be of much use to you. I am so so sorry I hurt you by my letter Mother darling. I wrote it just blindly & at the moment I couldn't understand you writing so casually that was all. Please forgive me & say a little prayer for me – everyone is losing their bravest & their best I suppose we must try & remember that. Poor Col Bridges' boy of the Grenadiers was killed at Neuve Chap[elle]. It was rumoured once before & proved false but I am afraid this time it is official. They were so devoted to him too. It's awfully hard isn't it to try & remember the good side of this war, it's so easy for the women folks to see nothing but the misery of it all & it's hard to be a patriot sometimes. I brought in one little Zouave boy from Nieuport Bains yesterday. He was dying but quite conscious & oh so plucky & talked to me so much about his home in Algiers & his wife who had married just before the war & that he was mad about. He gave me her name & address & asked of me to write her which I am doing today as the poor kid died quite soon after getting to the hospital. These Zouaves are wonderful troops & something so fine about them & their 'moral[e]' & bravery. These are French colonials you know who live in Algiers etc & most of them have a streak of Arab in them which gives them the pluck. We have worked a lot for them now & it's extraordinary how fond one gets of particular troops when you see much of them & they are a good lot.

Jellett & I had a bit of luck yesterday in Nieuport dodging shrapnel they were putting down the road & over the bridge into the town.

Suzanne's father, the 'Gen', is still here I am glad to say & I think likely to be so for some time. He is such a good pal to me & such a fine man. I have always said he was one of the typical best type of Frenchmen existing – one of the few who have both the cultivated side of a Frenchman & the straightness & courage of an English man. Joffre has given him a further promotion this week.

I thought of you so much at mass today Maman cherie & of your sad little Easter at Newnham with everyone gone. Father tells me he sails on the 9th, I hope so it is Alexandria don't you? Goodbye Mother & God bless you for all you have done for me & forgive me won't you? Yr loving Diddles.

Ap 6th about [6 April]
Tuesday for sure
Dear old Furnes

Mother darling – I've just got your letter full of 'goings' – Peter & Da now it's awful. Poor poor you & to think in all this I have been an utter pig & made it harder for you. Do please forgive me Mother dear. I don't know what I wrote & I didn't mean to hurt you like that. I had never seen anything in any paper except the 1st announcement & as that was then 10 days old I felt sure he [Thomas Fitzherbert Brockholes] couldn't be bad or someone from home would have told me and then I got your 2nd letter, before the 1st I don't know why. It came one day when I was at dinner with a crowd & it was ghastly.

Furnes is perfectly peaceful again, it's hard to believe between whiles they ever pot it. Luckily, they don't do it often as the town is practically deserted. I sent Father a photo of a shell bursting in a street near the hospital – ask him to show it you – one of our doctors took it.

And now Dudley passed fit, oh Mother what a nightmare. Moll is a lucky devil she can go on peacefully buying carpets & tripe. [Mary's husband, Cecil Dormer, worked in the Foreign Office based in London.]

I am just off to Nieuport – goodbye Mother cherie.

I said such a big prayer again for you today & will say a still larger one tomorrow. I can get to Com most mornings here, only it's very early. The last mass at 6.30 as the poor padres are too nervous to be in the big buildings any later as that is what Germans have a habit at potting at.

God bless you – I am so sorry about Father and Peter – it's awful for you poor little Mother.

Yr loving but utterly disgusting daughter who ought to be drowned.
DoDo

In 1915, as Commander Royal Artillery, the Earl of Denbigh was posted to Egypt with the 2nd Mounted Division. He would be there for a year. He had previously served with the Royal Artillery in Egypt, fought at Tel-el-Kebir and in India.

Furnes Saturday April 10th?

Mother dear –

I haven't heard definitely Da was sent to Alexandria or not. I expect you have been awfully busy & rather worried seeing him off. It's perfectly beastly seeing people go, much worse than going you know.

Dr Jellett & I now run a new ambulance we have; we undertook to collect for it but as a matter of fact he has done all the collecting really & we have only about £50 to get. However, we have got the car! If you meet any Jews with kind faces & lots of bank notes strangle one for me please.

Our day's work at present is (that is Jelly & my car) at 11.30 am we go to Nieuport Bains for Zouaves or Nieuport Ville for marines & nearly always bad cases then as that is the hour they shell most. We often take the mad cases down to a big French hospital near Dunkerque & it takes so long we don't get back to Furnes till 3 or so – then do a Belgian round by Ramscapelle & Pervyse & in the evening after dinner go out to Kaaskerke, just agin [*sic*] Dixmude because at 9 o' clock the troops are changed & there are very often some blessés. If so by the time we take them to our hospital at Hoogstadt & get to bed it's 12 or 1 o'clock.

Since Munro went it is so nice & peaceful for me. I let Bevan do all the dirty work & ordering & interviewing & seeing to things while I just fire away & hunt blessés which is the job I like & not hanging round the yard being plagued with people & things. We are on the move pretty well all day Jellett & I, and I like steady work so much better.

He's a quaint bird old Jellett, a wild Irish man with the devil of a temper & generally scraps with the others, but he & I get along ok & drive 'Daniel' the car, turn & turn around. It's one of the new Clegg Darracqs & such a nice one – it was a revelation to me to find such a thing as a sweet running Darracq existed after our Daniel at home.

I've got a lovely bunch of daffies in front of me as I write that young Chalmers got yesterday not many hundred yards off the Teutons – such nice big fat ones.

I got a lovely bunch of peach blossom at Ramscapelle 3 days ago. A few minutes before I got there an obus had made an 'orrid hole in the garden but digging in the debris I found some violets & lots of peach blossom, something so nice about finding flowers growing in spite of all the beastliness of shells & war. I enclose you a little bit. [This peach blossom remains in a sealed envelope in Warwickshire County Record Office.]

The soldiers had put a chocolate cream, a great luxury, to set outside the door & the aforesaid 'obus' broke all their windows, covered them with mud but what was far worse put some bricks & a huge sod right into the pudding. Poor dears – they were so disgusted.

Goodbye Mother darling. I went to HC this morning & prayed for you so hard at home – it's far far worse for you I know.

Yr loving Diddles

April 11th

Mother little darling
I am still alive & just scribbling you a line. They shelled us again in Furnes in the morning but this time although they put a lot in did no damage except two slight blessés. The aeroplanes dropped bombs in the afternoon & killed & wounded a lot outside our home. People are such fools. They collect some 300 strong to make a nice mark & then sit & gape in the street & watch the aeroplanes. Then have a grievance when bomb is dropped in the middle of the bunch. Col Bridges was wounded in Nieuport yesterday. Luckily not very bad – one piece through his cheek & jaw small which they got out & a piece in his shoulder – bad luck. Baird got nothing – was dog sick.
Yr Diddles

April 15th Furnes

Mother darling
I gather Peter hasn't gone from England yet though left Watford. Does he have any idea where they are going? I am told they are massing big lots of cavalry in reserve out here now but have given up that habit of putting cavalry men in the trenches since they lost such huge quantities. Which is always a little better otherwise the cavalry came in for both in a very inferior way. I was delighted with Rollo's tommy who wanted to be kept out of danger!

How nice of Arthur James to give us two ambulances. I wired him he was a lamb & sure to go straight to heaven, or words to that effect & wrote confirming it. The reason I wired Clare to publish letter all the same is that we have already the ambulance out here but still want some spare cash for its spares & running expenses & I have let poor old Jellett do all the work so far as regards collecting.

Furnes they shell every blessed day now & aeroplane bombs between whiles which somehow have been the cause of more casualties than the shells; eight people were killed a few yards from this little house of ours. We had two bang in the hospital again, one nearly got two of the cars only luckily a wall took the shock & the cars only got a few dents & lots of dust; another fell in the inner courtyard again. We had a jam tart for lunch that day – great flutter! & the shell bust all the dining room windows & smothered the tart with glass. But we weren't going to be done & pulled out the bits of debris & got our feet into the trough all the same. The Grande Place was riddled yesterday but luckily mostly in the open places & none of the fine old buildings smashed though of course all the glass broken. Poor little Furnes it's too sad.

Yesterday we were lucky & only had about 5 blessés; one old gendarme had taken refuge in his cellar off the Grande Place & was wounded in it in spite of it & I am afraid very badly too. Dr Jellett & I had an awful time getting him out & into the ambulance.

That really is very gruesome, that going round the town looking for poor devils that have been blessé & it's often not very plain sailing either as you never know when the next one is lumping in & whether at you or not. Dr Jellett had one jolly close to him yesterday that way & Cooper had a brick that bruised his back a bit.

I just hate this Furnes shelling. Much worse than anything else.

The only consolation however is that the French artillery is thundering good & very numerous & gives the Germans far worse Hades on their side than on ours. There is no kind of doubt about that. They learn a lot from German prisoners – one – an Alsatian French calmly deserted two days ago at St Georges he was on outpost duty & got fed up so left his rifle behind & lay down near the French sentry & called 'au secours' until they picked him up. Personally I consider it takes a lot of courage to do that as it's a 100 to 1 on your being shot & not prisonered – one of his reasons for deserting was that his wife sent him a packet of lard every week & since 3 weeks the sergeant had kept it – so what with that & his disgust at having been put on outpost he gave it up!

Poincaré [French President] was at Nieuport yesterday visiting Suzanne's Pa [Hély d'Oissel]. The joke was the Germans knew he was there, got a French shell they had taken at Mantage, took the fuse out so it should arrive intact & cut on it with a file a verse to Poincaré asking him to accept the enclosed as an Easter egg! It arrived too, shortly before the President & in time to be shown him.

Suzanne's Pa made me smile telling me how when they [were] looking round the Germans suddenly spotted Poincaré's car & started shrapnelling it. The chauffeur, a worthy Parisian in livery, was entirely overcome & went to ground under the car & refused to come out!

Old P didn't go into Nieuport itself as not safe enough, but was allowed to gaze upon it from 3 miles back & it [was] there they shrapnelled him.

Little father Munro is going out to Ypres soon he tells me. He is rather a pathetic figure somehow. Full of ideals & no backbone to carry them out & then gets very hipped. He's a good little chap & has been a real good pal to me & I am very grateful to him as I should never have got a chance of a real job & chance to try & make good if it hadn't been for him.

To the family in general

April 16th 1915

Furnes is not what it was, they never give us much peace there & go on stirring us up most days with obus & between whiles with those beastly aeroplane bombs which do more damage individually somehow than the shells. They are getting such damn good shots too; one nearly pipped me 3 days ago & I still have a grievance. I was changing & greasing a wheel on the old ambulance outside our house door (not the hospital) in the street when drop[ped] a bomb alongside. Breaks all the bedroom windows (mine included), throws a lot of mud on the bed & fills my throat & eyes with black smoke & beastliness & smothered the car with glass and debris. Luckily, at that moment Admiral Ronarc'h had just passed in his car & stopped to chinwag so I was talking to him a few yards from the car & so got far less glass than we would have otherwise. He cut his hand a bit but we were jolly lucky not to get thoroughly blessé really. There's a nasty draught in my bedroom at nights now – but I am going to hog it & buy a chip of glass & blow the expense!

We've got some lovely big guns now in front of Furnes which we ginger the Germans up with their Furnes – ie their towns back behind the lines. So we get a bit even with them now which is consoling, only they revenge themselves by throwing all the more at poor old Furnes.

We have got a lovely lot of new ambulances now. It is most decent of Arthur James to give me two. He's a brick.

Are all the daffies out at home now? I find a few tired & sad looking ones in the deserted gardens at Nieuport, but they are nice nevertheless only they make me rather homesick & long for a look up the green avenue with the daffies dancing in the sunlight & nice clean grass & blow through you.

Tell me how they are this year please. I'd give a lot to see them & sit on the grass with the family & the tykes & all.

Yr Diddles

April 20th

Mother darling

I have been getting such nice budgets of letters from you lately – thank you so much – you are a marvel the way you send us all, all the news & I am sure you will go straight to heaven.

I am scribbling like fun when I ought to be laying the table for supper. We go out to Dixmude direction every night now which does not give one any quiet in the evenings for letter writing – rather a curse – as it's too late when we come in to [do] anything, it being 11 at the earliest & anything up to 2 am the nights there are blessés.

D

Wednesday

I am sending Moll a young obus to make into an electric lamp & some odds & ends for Squeaker's museum. While I am writing old Jelly is trying to photograph the interior of the room – me included & is driving me silly striding up & down measuring the distance, which drives everything I had to tell you clean out of my head, confound him. We have fixed a very fine obus head to the cap of the radiator of our car & it looks awful swank & excites much admiration. I enclose one for Squeaker to get Slee to put on Sally Sunbeam. He can move the AA sign to the side. It's a German obus head that fell at Ramscapelle. You want to shine it up really nice & shiny & it's 'some swank'.

Love Diddles

On 22 April, the 2nd Battle of Ypres began with the Germans using chlorine gas for the first time on the Western Front. This battle was made up of four smaller separate battles: Gravenstafel, St Julien, Frezenberg and Bellewaarde. It lasted for almost a month, the Allied casualties being around 70,000 dead, wounded or missing.

April 25th, Furnes

Mother darling

I've not written for days but you will have seen by the papers what is happening & will realise we are simply flooded out with work. We get in blessés all night & work for the hospital all day so there is not much time for sleep or letter writing. I am now in pyjamas at 8.30 having breakfast having slept at 4.30 am – our best effort was from 8 am to 10 am as a 'night'.

About a week ago when the Germans got through & over the Yser it was just touch & go & everyone was rather jumpy & very depressed. The Allies lost over 200 men prisoners & 3 guns. Most of this French but now they counter attack every night & are gradually regaining lost ground & consolidating generally. The casualties have been awful; one regiment of Zouaves about 1,500 strong lost 60 men & 15 officers in one night. It has been just like the Yser fight of October again. The hospital at Hochstatt – half way between Ypres & Furnes has, of course, been inundated with every nationality as it is the only hospital up that beat & all the heavy fighting is there; men all over the place & stretchers everywhere & operations going on without interruption day & night. One of our wretched doctors did 63 operations in 24 hours without a pause & was so beat he could hardly stand. All the little nurses & staff are perfect bricks & I can't see how they get round the work. Only the awful cases can be taken in, & then are moved on as soon as it is possible to make room for worse cases. It just despairs one & makes one rage when you see this endless, endless stream of shattered humanity & sees the ghastly work a shell can make of their poor bodies; bullet wounds are so very different & devoid of the same horror. It's the shell wounds that are simply haunting & sometimes one feels ill with the sheer futility of it all, rather than the fact of its being a horrible thing to look at. It's hard to be patriotic when these days of heavy fighting one sees so much of the horror & misery of this filthy war.

It's at night, at dawn especially we get in most of the wounded. The 'postes' are in little farms round Steenstrade that we go to & not far behind the lines. Two nights ago, it was a nightmare, you could hardly think with the noise of our guns, their guns & everybody's rifles & on one or two occasions it is most unpleasant. The 1st night there they brought up Belgian & French reinforcement batteries so fast & had to fire them at once they hadn't time to cut the trees down in front & shot through them. The result was one in every 15 or so burst on the road on the way to the Germans & you stood a jolly good chance of being hit by your own guns 75 yds behind. Once we had the car crammed with men & one burst like that just in front of us & we pulled up with a jerk in time. The same thing happened soon after & a Belgian about 50 yds away was hit – he did that 50 yds to the poste faster than any marathon, nearly knocking me down in the way. When I caught him up at the farm he was hysterical with terror & told me his leg was broken. Having seen the pace he did that 50 yds in I withheld my judgement for a few minutes & of course found nothing the matter with his leg but a little shin wound. He got off with a nasty fright & a draughty hole in his gaiter!

It really is gruesome in these dark little farms, wounded men lying everywhere & the appalling noise going on in every direction. Last night they weren't attacking so hard & it was better.

I must fly to Hoogstadt & help evacuate. Jellett & my car doing A1 & never breaks down 'unberufen' [touch wood], things are much better today & news everywhere very good I'm glad to say. The Canadians are marvels the French tell me.

God bless you all
Yr sleepy Diddles
The daffies received!!

Saturday night [1 May]
1am about

Mother darling
I am scribbling in the half dark in the ambulance having to 'stand by' in case wanted while the armoured train fires, & as this is one of the few available minutes for letter writing I am seizing it.

I wonder if it is out yet about Dunkerque being bombarded. It really is the limit. They have a big naval gun, propped on land at a high angle & are shooting from 37 kilometres off. But the gun has been located & every allied gun on earth wants to have a pop at it. It's in the Dixmude direction, but will be very hard to put out of action as it is cocked at a high angle means they are firing out of a kind of pit & can give the gun tremendous protection & made it almost impossible to hit it. But we will continue to hope for the best.

Tuesday
I am lying on my underneath (damn uncomfortable too) in the sand by the sea, snatching a little peace. I am fed up with the war & very weary, we really have been very rushed lately & so many late nights make one rather tired, more so mentally than physically & I find myself getting very peevish & stuffy.

It must be 3 weeks now since we got to bed before 2 or 3 in the morning & many nights later. Yesterday we were at Steenstrade till 5am as there were a lot of wounded. French infantry mostly & you can only get them in at night, otherwise things have been quieter down there lately. DG [Danke Gott]. One of the most lovely sights I have seen 2 mornings ago dawn at Reninghe over the inundations, & to see the sun streaming up & being caught by the reflections in the waters & the ruined churches & villages sticking up out of it all.

Last night we got to bed at 12 till 3.30 am & then had to climb out because there was a call for a car & then turned in from 6 to 10am again. I got so bored dressing & undressing I shall economise labour tonight & go to sleep with my clothes & false teeth all ready on for an emergency exit. It's so nice in the sun here & the sea & so peaceful except for some Godforsaken soldiers that will shoot at a floating target. I never saw such putrid shots. They most of them seem to be going in the direction of Dover. They are cavalry & I think had better go back to their muttons & leave others to try & shoot a bit straighter.

Hély d'Oissel sent 2,000 of his Zouaves down to reinforce the asphyxiated French at Lizerne & it was they that did that very fine attack & took the village but they lost 800 men out of 2,000, a huge total & all except a tiny handful of officers. They have a wonderful fine 'moral[e]' those Zouaves though of course it depends a lot on individual regiments. Many of the last turned out regiments are more hotel proprietors from Dinard than Algerians.

One Zouave was given the VC & made a corporal lately for doing fine things & he told his colonel he was afraid he wouldn't be much use as a corporal as he could neither read or write. His Col told him not to fret as it was fighting was wanted.

Hély d'Oissel saw this same Tommy in hospital yesterday, he had been shot through both eyes 'stone blind' in the attack at Lizerne & in awful pain but he never complained but said 'My General – you should tell the Colonel that he was right and that it doesn't matter now that I know not how to read nor write' [Translated from the French] I think it's so sad, perhaps all these little things don't interest you, but it's little trifles of pluck & all the millions of individual efforts that count in this war.

The things that do one so much good too & make up for any nights up is the extraordinary gratitude of these men one helps. There are so many of them that think of such pathetic ways to thank you that it gives you a lump in your throat & makes one see red & want to put all these beastly Germans in a pit & chop them up with spades like the boys used to do with jellyfish at Colwyn Bay.

Later – FFF [Female Feilding Fortnightly – a newsletter edited by Clare and circulated amongst the Feilding women] is a thing of joy & I sat on my bed & read it yesterday till I just cried & got to a sort of hysterical giggles. It's the funniest thing of modern times.

We have got a dashed fine garden to our house now. We loot plants from deserted gardens & improve ours. I have photographed it for you because it really rivals the dump now. Do dig me up a few dump flowers in bud & post them me & I will have a baby dump corner.

God bless you Mother dear so much love DoDo

Dorothie wrote the following piece about some of the wounded men she encountered:

Furnes May

It's worth doing a great deal, & giving up much to be allowed to work up near the lines, right at the heart & pulse of things. Even if at times they should be terrible & horrible things. Every little bit one can do to help up here, seems to count so much, because it is immediate help & therefore has far more value, & above all it's the marvellous & touching gratitude (far out of proportion to what one does) that one meets with on all sides, that helps one so to bear one's own sorrow & worries, great or small. But it's quaint little ways the men have of showing their gratitude that often give me a lump in my throat. Sometimes it is the letters they write you afterwards. Sometimes it is just a hot & crumpled bunch of flowers from deserted gardens & very rare to find, tied together with a bootlace or a piece of telephone wire so carefully & tightly that they are almost squeezed out of recognition.

Often it has been the mute thanks in a man's eyes as his life ebbs away, & in his weakness he has not strength or time to say what he means.

Often too, it is their piteous gratitude as they tell you about their wives & womenfolk & you promise to write them all their last messages. A French sergeant, whose 3 grown up sons were all in the fighting line, & who himself had been riddled with bullets while carrying a dangerous message, died at Furnes here holding my hand with all his failing strength & telling me between gasps of pain – 'Tell my wife that I have done my duty ... I am not afraid ... I am not ...' I told her & she was so brave as he wished her to be & wrote me several such charming & beautiful letters without a word of bitterness or revolt in them.

Once it was a Zouave boy, who as I put him on the train, badly wounded, dived in his pockets, & out of an unspeakably grimy pocket book full of treasures gave me a little crumpled horror. It was a little celluloid Christmas card with 'souvenir' written big in pink lettering across it. But he thought it so fine & pressed it proudly into my hand, with a 'It is all that I have.'

A French Fusilier Marin at Dixmude, whose pal we saved & got to hospital in time who otherwise would have had to have waited till nightfall (too late then) thanked us with genuine tears in his eyes & gave me a little miraculous medal to protect me & keep me safe & you see it has.

But once & that last week it was the saddest of all. During that awful hand to hand fighting at Steenstrade when the Zouaves from Nieuport were sent to retake the bridge (lost by the other troops in a gas attack). They lost 80% of their men & covered themselves with glory & took the bridge, one of them had been badly hit in the head leading on the men in the attack. He was blind & part of the lower portion of his face was shot away & terribly bruised – especially his mouth.

We had brought him in from close to the lines there, one rather gruesome night, & I used to see him every day in hospital for a few moments as I came in and out with the wounded. He knew my voice & used to grip my hand & I knew he was grateful & wanted to say so. But he couldn't see, & couldn't speak except a few painful words & God knows what the future holds for him after the war. Well he got better & the awful stream of wounded came on pouring in, so that the time came for him to be moved on to a base hospital & make room for those poor souls needing it still more than he.

I took him to the station myself (19 miles of jolting, jarring ill kept road) & as I left him, on his stretcher there & tried to make him comfortable, I put his purse & little personal treasures in his poor blind hands, not yet accustomed to the awful darkness. He just managed to whisper 'merci ma bonne soeur' & I saw him groping for my hand.

He took it & brought it to his lips – those poor lips, so shattered & bleeding & pressed them to it.

As I went back to the car, with a mist before my eyes & a feeling of revolt & anger against the war with all its horror & futility, there was a little red stain on my glove.

May 8th, same old place

Mother darling, I am so sorry you think I am ungrateful for all you have done for my Cawston Belgians. I am not a bit & do so like knowing what is happening to them & getting your chits about them. It is my fault for not telling you about receiving them when I write back, but often one sits down to scribble & by the time one has written all that has happened since last time it's closing time before one has to write about the things one has been written to from home. It's not that those aren't the things that count for the most because they are but just because you have written them me – I know you know I know!!

Dear me how complicated! My brain is very lethargic today from a quite unusual case ie over sleep. I having done it for 12 solid hours, instead of feeling kittenish I feel like after one's big meal on Good Friday.

They were very rude to us in Ramscapelle on Thursday afternoon. There is a little sheltered nook we always put 'Daniel' the car in, well for some funny reason we didn't that day as we wanted to dig up some pinks for our garden at Furnes, there being no blessés we went to dig up the aforesaid pinks when they started shelling like fun & one bally one landed plumb in the place we always put 'Daniel' the car & we had bits pattering round us as we dug up the pinks. I picked up the fuse & the case of the shell which was so hot I couldn't hold it. Clare shall have it for her museum perhaps. Then it got so unhealthy & they put shrapnel over us. Too high to hurt luckily & we had to dive into the German's dugout for a bit, just as well we did as a fat one fell next poor Daniel, drove a chunk of iron into his tyre & punctured it & sieved the canvas roof & sides a bit. But otherwise didn't hurt the bus which was ok. I should have been most profane if the new car had been broken up. By the way, thank Squeaks for collecting for me. For today's communiqué I see that 'The only incident on the Belgian front was the bombardment of Ramscapelle'. It sounds so simple doesn't it?

Yesterday too they were doing some dirty work on the way to Nieuport Bains & fairly cut up the road, our car was filled up too with poor blessés after it.

Later – The garden here is looking too nifty for words. You can't think how smart it is, I have photographed it for you to see with Dr Jellett's camera, you know I have been ass enough to lose mine. Poor poor Mr Da, I think how hot he must be at Suez, it is a nightmare to think of & here am I grumbling at only having woollen combies at Furnes! He must be nigh dead with heat poor dear. Isn't it nice Peter & Tubby being together at Bethune?

Much love dearie – yr loving Diddles

May 9th

Same old place and address

Father dear – I am just longing to hear a little news about your whereabouts & doing before I quite make up my mind as to whether the Suez Canal is a good place for one's Mr Da or not. Somehow I think not, but I really don't know much about the conditions out there, except that (in the language of Lieut. Commander Feilding) it's 'sticky 'ot'.

We have been very very busy all round here lately & for a few days things were calmer but now they are all beginning again. I am writing in a dugout at present while there is the deuce of a row, attack going on, we ie the French & Belgians were to attack tonight but as far as I can make out the bally Teutons are having a little attack of their own previous & some 4 or 5 hours too early which is a dirty trick they are fond of. But at present every gun in the place is firing, being fired at & the road is quite impassable, they are shelling it so we have to lump it. One of the men from the officers' mess in the cottage along side just came in in triumph with an alarm clock which has had a piece of shell right through its tin body & is ticking away perfectly peacefully & contented all the same. Also a photo of King Albert I saw on the mantelpiece a few minutes ago has been punctured.

Later – lots of relief troops going up the road, I am afraid it is a rotten time for them to go up the road although for the minute they aren't shrapnelling it & I hope none of them get hit poor chaps. I wish I knew what was going on.

There has been a tremendous artillery activity altogether about here just lately. Dr Jellett & I now share in an ambulance named Daniel who was lightly punctured 2 days ago but we weren't in it. However yesterday it really was rather unpleasant & it's amazing how the Almighty looks after our crowd. I was driving down an open bit of canal road (the one I had a nightmare about one night I was sleeping with Mrs Ma) & they amused themselves by having pots at us as we went by & one was Bang in front of the car on the road & for the life of me I don't know why we didn't meet any of the bits. I could hardly see either where the road was to steer straight as there was a good deal of dust & smoke.

[It was not just dust and smoke that Dorothie had to contend with when shells were falling: 'Some of the old canals, particularly around Dixmude, are so choked with the bodies of the fallen that when a shell falls among them it sends up into the sky, not a cascade of water, but a mass of human flesh' – *War Illustrated*, 10 April 1915]

7pm later – such a noisy day. It was a German attack ok but I am glad to say frustrated & no harm done, things are moving all down the line today. I don't know with what result as regards that section.

I have just come in from a trip down with blessés & passed the Admiral (French one's) headquarters on the way & talked to him. He had the most marvellous escape of modern times. They shelled the cottage & a large 6 or 8 inch came right through one room, on through the next, passed under the Admiral's chair he was sitting on & went on through the next wall, having broken both legs off his chair & dumped him on the ground. He was very shaken & semi unconscious half an hour but then got quite alright. I saw the hole & the piece of shell that did it. It was the entire case of the shell, more than a foot in length of it which had not broken up. He really has uncanny luck but I think this takes the bun, you probably won't believe it, I only happen to because I was there just after & saw the bits.

We have a long night before us & lots of blessés – I can't write more.

Yr loving Diddles

May 12th

Mother deah [*sic*] –

We had the dame [*sic*] of a scrap all round Nieuport on the 9th. I don't know if there has been much about it in the papers or not. The Germans did a big attack at 1pm & shelled all the morning & afternoon like old Harry. Especially down all the roads so as to stop any reinforcements coming up, which made it rather sultry on the roads getting blessés to & fro. The troops held splendidly & shot lots & lots of the Huns & taught them the futility of attacking & in the evening the sporting little Marins did a counter attack & bagged a couple of farms & some trenches off them, net result to the allies, German success nil, they had very heavy losses, French casualties about 400–500, very small considering. Our poor cars worked pretty hard as you can imagine for 24 hours ...

The Marins did awfully well this last scrap as always.

The Belgians were to have had an attack yesterday too but at the last minute thought better of it & decided not to start. Not such mugs either, but they are beginning to make rather a habit of it, I am afraid as this is the 3rd time it has happened lately.

They just can't bring themselves to attack primarily because their infantry officers are such rabbits they never dream of leading the men, just send them on ahead & hope for the best. As long as it is 'defensive' they are alright & have improved a lot as troops lately; in fact at Steenstrade in that German attack the other day they did jolly well indeed, much better than was expected.

Dunkirk had 33 fat shells in it again yesterday & I am afraid it will [be] very very hard & practically impossible to knock out the guns that do the damage. They are 2 or 4 guns firing into D not sure which. I haven't been in there since the shelling started, but believe there is a good deal of wreckage. It takes a lot to damage though, for instance I was told today that up to date 700 odd shells have been dropped into Furnes in all & the place is very little damaged indeed. They haven't given us any for some time now. They have had their hands too busy.

The Germans on the 9th put in over 25,000 shells into the 5 miles from the sea to St Georges! We fired back some 11,000 from this side so you can imagine what the row was like. Just deafening. I have never seen so many shells bursting in view at once before, simply on all sides & didn't really do so much harm considering. These are the official artillery figures not mine.

I had a day off today, was feeling rather cheap & back achy & 'wish I was dead' sort of thing, but I am feeling much better as a result. I found myself beginning to get the jumps so gave myself 48 hrs peace.

Bless you all & thanks so much for writing so often.

Yr loving Diddles

Bourbourg
Le 14 Mai [1915]

Mother Deah – you will wonder what this address is all about! It's only that Robert de Broqueville turned up at Furnes this evening & carried me off for the night to this chateau where his Pa is. We are having a very pleasant peaceful time & evening. I am scribbling before turning in.

It's a charming little old chateau with pretty grounds & a weedy avenue full of buttercups & all so peaceful & nice the war seems years away. It's a most pleasant place & I shall come here for a day whenever fed up with life, the war or the Munro Corps.

Thérésé de Jessaint is here for the night too as well as the other Broqueville boy, they are all dears to me. Please thank Squeaks for her letter & you too for being so good & bothering over my wearily lengthy list of deadly garments I wanted you to get for me in London.

They will doubtless arrive shortly & make me gasp & stretch my eyes with their beauty & splendour – especially the pants!

The plants arrived so well & are duly planted out in the garden which is a thing of beauty now, bar rot it really is looking too pretty thanks to all the plants we looted. Even peonies dug up in fat buds don't seem to resent it one bit somehow. The great thing is to be firm with them & insist on their flowering the same as usual. The narcissus when their toes had been cut & put in hot water not only revived, but were opened out by the evening, they smell too good & I loved them just – it was a breath of home. Broqueville has left Dunkirk & taken refuge here since the bombardment. I haven't been into the old town yet since it was shelled, they keep on dropping things into it.

Well I must go to bed; I'm very sleepy.

It's so nice to be in a strange bed & away from the same old faces for a change. I'd give a lot for 3 days at NP on my back in the grass with nothing to do!

Goodnight
Yr loving
Diddles

May 17th, Furnes

Mother deah
I have had such a nice lot of letters from you lately. It is a joy & also some from the 2 boys who seem very happy, it's nice for them being together isn't it?

Things are a little quieter here these days but always something doing. It really was a big show they had at Nieuport on 9th & the Germans got a nasty slap in the face instead of a successful attack.

We have invited the old Admiral in to dinner tonight & the English Navy to meet him. Last time he came here he was nearly obussed & so I hope the Huns won't repeat the stunt, except that now nothing short of having his chair shot away under him worries him.

Will write a real letter anon. This scrawl in haste.

So much love Diddles

Furnes May 18th

Mother deah –

I will tell you the worst at once: I've come to beg! You told me when I was home you would give me something towards my keep as being just as useful as keeping Belgian refugees – well – if you haven't changed your mind I'd be most grateful. For one thing I have also quite run out of cash, will you please post me £5 of own money in French notes if poss, for various expenses, all I have in the world today is 1/6 in German money that belonged to a German before last Sunday's attack.

Dr Jellett & I are at present the only ones in the bally house in Furnes as the other members & Mrs Clitherow have gone home. It makes all the difference in the world having a peaceful spot to go to after the day's work & I should hate to give it up, though it is a little large for the two of us. So I thought I would compromise by paying something on my own to running expenses of same. As I do the housekeeping I'd be glad of any refugee contributions!

Got a very cheery letter from Peter, I am glad he's glad.

Am smothered in oil & am just scrawling this after having had a full morning filling grease caps on the old ambulance. Rather a 'do' as I had hoped for a letter morning. A luxury I haven't had for a long time.

Just off to Nieuport.

Had a lovely ride yesterday in the sands. Pierre de Broqueville, in cavalry, (Robert's brother) is quartered up the road these days & lends me a gee. Had a beauty yesterday. It is lovely to get a real ride & some eccer [exercise] & now the evenings are long I can often have one between tea time when we come in, & before going out again at 9pm.

Later/ 19 Mai –

I have just got your letter saying you have had nothing of mine in the way of letters since the 3rd. I can't understand it as I've been writing very often lately, have been getting my letters censored so they go faster & now they are hung up all the same it is sickening. Just for one moment I got my letters sent in a day & a half thro' the Belgian ministry at Dunkirk but now they have all evacuated thro' the shelling I have to have recourse to the old field post office again which is the very devil.

I also got your message from Da about 'Dorothie's marvellous escape'. I am bursting with interest & want to know all about it please, why or which? The case in court & my unhygienic habits made me smile some. It really is priceless. I always did think there was a lot of excellent cheap notoriety to be got out of the simply dodging of soap & there you are. What more could one want?

The garden is looking too nice, & is now embellished by two most festive young rabbits the Broqueville boys gave me & that rejoice in the names of Robert & Pierre. We are in the dark as to their sex & daren't ask, in case they might turn out to be two ladies & need rechristening which would be tiring so we leave well alone!

I enclose some photos. Will you please just chuck scraps of things like enclosure & photos I send you & Squeaker in a box for me, as some of them I'd like often to keep after you have seen them & then I can sort them out when I come home.

Oh Mother dear I wish to God we were all home again. It's so very very dreary sometimes though one pretends it isn't. It's a year but two months since I left home for the old Rugby hospital, a big slice you know & I've had a slacker's time compared to poor Tubby so heaven knows how sick they must get of it & as for you, it makes my heart ache – poor Mother. I do wish I could do something to make things easier for you. I write as often as I can & will write oftener, thank you so much for all your nice letters. They are so nice you can't think. There's hardly any evening I come in without finding something from home.

Much love –

Yr ever Diddles

I intend trying to get 3 or 4 days down in the country at Broqueville's chateau next week if things are slack. Last time 24hrs was nice but made me greedy & want a few days vegetation & lying round the garden chewing grass.

DoDo

May 23rd

Mother darling – it's a puzzling world & I get fed up with it at times. Here am I out here, wearing trousers & hoping people will look on me like a boy just because I feel & live like one & it seems no one is the least deceived & old Mrs Grundy as active ever! You see since Furnes was shelled the corps has been necessarily split into four small groups: Hospital, Furnes, La Panne & Coxyde for the Fusilier Marins. The Furnes group consisted of the Coopers & Gurney in one little house & Munro, Mrs Clitherow, Jellett & I in the other. Well for the last 2 or 3 weeks, Munro & old Clitherow having left, Dr Jellett & I have necessarily been alone in the little house. There are two other rooms used at odd times by casual members drifting in but at the moment there are no other possible inhabitants. It appears bally Belgians & dirty dogs have been spreading yarns that I had no business to be there alone with Jellett, but there is no alternative. Bevan was asking the Mission advice about the 'lady' question & they were very indignant & said to pay no attention & it didn't matter a scrap. We had just to adapt ourselves to war conditions & everyone realised it & more honour to us because we just 'lumped' things.

I will try & arrange if possible later for Mrs Wynne & I to dig together but at present as she & Bevan do Coxyde & the night trip there, they have to sleep down near on account of late calls & being on the spot. She is in same quandary. So what I am doing is, getting in Hélène, our refugee girl, that used anyhow to be at home all day, to sleep there as well & if possible will get some other members of the Corps shortly to come too. The Coopers & co can't as they are probably going down near Ypres with a small unit of our cars. But anyway I will do my best to get some more members in. Not that we would see any of them as we are out from shortly after breakfast to anything up to 3am! I am just writing you all this in case you might get yarns via Dunkerque or some busybody which would worry you. Whereas there is nothing to be worried about when you know the facts. Jelly is a hot tempered old cuss but a very good sort really & does his work A1 & is one of the most genuinely useful members we have in the corps.

The small house I am living in now is too nice these days with its garden stiff with flowers, & so nice & charming & peaceful it's a joy to roll into after the day's work instead of dirty lodgings or the hospital scrum.

Everything this week is very nice & quiet. I think for the simple reason the Hun has thrown all his ammunition at us last week & is now saving up for an extra fine 'tease' a little later on.

Suzanne's father has been given a very big command, promoted again. Left the Nieuport division yesterday & now has 125,000 men under his orders, it's an enormous promotion & he now has seven divisions under his orders. Luckily he hasn't left the district altogether as the Nieuport one still depends on him & is one of those in his command. It's more that he has been given the other Divs as well. I should have been miserable if he'd left the beat. He's such a dear & has been so wonderfully good to me. His new headquarters are half way between Furnes & Ypres. The refreshing part about him is he never gets a swelled head & is as charming & simple as ever. He was very low at leaving this command as although a leg up, the higher you get on the scale the more office & base work there is & less actual firing line command which is what he loves & interests him. Goodbye Mother dear DoDo

The Countess' concerns regarding Dorothie's health appear to have come to a head towards the end of May and she wired Dorothie offering to pay for her ticket home.

Whit Tuesday [26 May]

Mother darling
I am sending this letter via the sailors & a duplicate as regards its 'girds' by the Furnes post so as to be sure you get one sometime in the near future. Thank you so much for wiring me last night, but honestly I think I would rather come home later on & just vegetate with you in the dump for quite a while. If I come home now this minute I'd only have to come back in a day or two as there are some radical changes going on as to whether the corps will continue working for the Belgians or seek more work elsewhere. I'd rather like to see it through one way & another & until things are decided & would prefer therefore to return in a few weeks time if you don't mind & then to take a good little time off.

I am afraid you are thinking I am in the last stages of exhaustion but for a week things have been beautifully quiet here just in our beat & it has bucked me up no end. Also, next week I mean to take 3 days holiday in the country with the Broquevilles. So you see I shall have had quite a rest cure these days, & will come & have a still completer one at home a little later on.

The 'regiment de Marins', the lot of Ghent days, gave me a dinner party the other day. They christened me 'la Mascotte de la Brigade' & we had an appalling meal of at least 50 diverse foods & drinks – procured God knows where!

Goodbye Mrs Ma dear – God bless you. I am feeling very fit please don't think I am dying, because these last 10 days have been a regular rest cure.

Yr loving
DoDo

Friday for sure & 28th I think [28 May]

Mother dear –
Things are very quiet here still, quieter than there been for a long while. Daniel Darracq sat down last night, a bit of his clutch bust & we are off to

mend it so no time for a real letter. 3 of our cars have gone down to Ypres to be temporarily attached to the English who are short handed & asked for loan of cars, as our people were slack it all fitted in.

The Huns made some sport of us & Daniel yesterday on an open bit of road between Pervyse & Ramscapelle but we won!

Bless you all & much love darling

Yr Diddles

Saturday 28th? [29 May]

Mother darling – I have just [come] in from sending you a wire about Hughie's ship. The Admiral had been given the copy of the German wireless which stated that the 'Defence' had arrived at the Dardanelles & had moved her quarters unhurt because they failed getting the range.

By which I gather they are out there. I didn't quite know whether to wire you or not for fear 1) it may not be true & be another ship & a mistake over the name or 2) that it would alarm you.

But I reasoned if it is a mistake & Neb is not gone Mrs Ma will have heard from him & if he has I feel sure she'd much rather know where he was. Am I right?

I can't help feeling that Hughie & all his people will be so pleased at getting a chance at the Huns after the Goeben episode & as they know the country it's what they'd like best. The fortunes of war are not necessarily any worse out there except of course the horridness of having them so far away.

There was a rumour going too that the Grand Fleet of the Hun had come out at last. But that yarn has been spun so often one waits to see.

If Hughie is at Dardanelles I can probably often get news through Ronarc'h & if ever I do will always wire you anything. But Neb's letter from you I've got since the wire was sent is written from home on the 19th which seems very short time to get out there in somehow & I can't help thinking the German communiqué had the wrong ship down. Here things are very quiet still, but I don't think it will last long.

The English are having huge losses at Ypres. Our ambulance was broken down yesterday & Hély d'Oissel carried me off to dine with him at his new headquarters some 10 miles away. Rather alarming as he's a vast bug these days & all the passages & gangways there swarm with bally Generals & stout Colonels & German prisoners. Six of the latter feed the goldfish in the garden fact!!!!! On his staff is one Major Grant, Coldstream, who knows Tubby of course. He gave me lots of news of the Regiment. He said Jimmy Horlick had a temporary staff job because the shells were putting his nerves on edge & they had to relieve him for a bit. I did not know he had left? Did you?

Cecil Pereira is a bally General & doing A1.

Off Nieuport. Goodbye & God bless you all.

Yr DoDo

PS

Thank you so much for the fiver for the poor refugees – you're a brick.

No, Mrs K & Mairi are doing infirmière job attached to a division & are more on their own now. We never see them hardly. Miss McNaughton gone home to lecture on perils of war (she has never been near!) & Mrs Clitherowe gone home to look after her hubby but thinks she'll come out later. Our Corps changing is over now: it is decided we have 5 cars for Belgians, 3 for Fusilier Marins & 3 are temporarily attached to English at Ypres who implored us to lend them cars – old Lyon in command.

Now that things were settled regarding the Corps, Dorothie felt able to go home on leave.

CHAPTER 7

June–August 1915

Dorothie's work continued despite being on leave. In mid-June she wrote a letter to the Rugby Observer *appealing for funds:*

> *The roads are terrible, and the strain on the ambulances tremendous, with the result that we have been obliged, in view of the heavy work before us, to try and replace nearly all our cars by new ones, I personally am helping in collecting money for one more ambulance still required ... I feel sure your readers will be glad to take so direct and personal an interest in our work, and from time to time I shall be very happy to let them know what this ambulance car accomplishes for the wounded round here.*

On her return to Flanders she took her small terrier, Charles, with her for company.

Royal Pavilion Hotel
Folkestone Friday [18 June]

Mother Darling –
Goodbye – I have seen to the cars & am just off & only time for a scrawl. It has been so nice at home & such a wonderful rest morally as well as physically. I feel I could strangle millions of Huns now all on my lonesome. You have been so sweet to me Mother, thank you with all my heart. I do so want Tubby to get his appt [appointment]. If anything still more for your sake than his. God bless you all Diddles

Le 22nd Juin

Mother darling –
I was so very very glad to get your dear letter just now. Thank you so much & not only for that but for all your love & sympathy to me while I was home. You can't imagine the good it did me. The moral[e] change & rest more than anything & how much better I feel for it. I am dining with the

general who turned up to carry me off & I am scribbling this to go by St Omer post while he interviews the staff. He was delighted with your letter & I have been thanking him from us all for all his help & sympathy.

Last night I got to bed at 4.30 am & they started shelling Furnes at 6. Not much peace & closer to our home which is tiresome of them. One bang frightened poor wee Charles to death & he hid his head & forepaws under the pot stand & imagined himself quite safe! He made me laugh. Dunkirk has been badly potted again today too – 1st time for a month.

Situation is unchanged all along here, no advance to speak of anywhere, I wonder if you had a nice time with Neb bless him. I was so sad at not being able to come too. Goodbye Mother cherie, & thank God for giving me such a dear Ma says I.

Yr so very loving Diddles
PS such a big hug

Furnes 26th [June]

Mother dear. It's so odd to [be] back in the same old place doing the same old things, same old obus, same old faces, same old late nights, same old everything. It's very nice though to be doing something & entirely a degree of hate. I hated going away from home & coming back, but I should hate far more to have nothing to do at home, so have no grievance at all really. Each time one gets the joy of a real good lay at home & is tempted perhaps to chuck things up, one realises it's only because it's temporary that 'bath mats' are so very pleasant & of all the jobs going in war time I think I have the best. Perhaps hard in some ways, but it is most extraordinary interesting being right at the heart & pulse of things & feeling you count & can help a great deal. An indoor hospital life at Balham would be like a general who is 'dégommé' [sic] as the French say shellshocked & sent to run transport at a base at Lands End. Just as useful no doubt, but how dull oh Lord how dull!

I'd rather be obussed any day.

The Germans don't seem to have run out of ammunition while I was away which is a bit 'ard, but seem to have just as much left through a 'mees' as ever.

I never have a dull minute here with Charles. Life at the front is full of excitement with him about. He bit Dr Jelly yesterday while being given a slug! His journal is roughly as follows:

1st day – 3 dog fights Folkestone.
2 – 1 cat Boulogne quay.
3 – 1 fit on D's bed in Furnes at 3am & frightened her to death.
4 – Sufficiently recovered to get run over by a car in Dunkirk, came out

81

smothered in oil & appeared by the exhaust in some mysterious way. Was bathed on return much to his indignation & threatened to have another fit, however compromised & was sick under the table instead.

5th day – went out to the dunes with me & found something perfectly appalling to roll in, a 6 month old Hun at least he must have dug up I feel sure. Nothing less could have been so 'lasting' or entirely satisfactory from his point of view.

But all the same Charles is a dear & the joy of my life, it was a real brainwave to bring him. The swiftness with which he hops on the car the moment an obus appears would do credit to his missus!

Just got such a happy letter from Marjie. Isn't it too splendid Dudley going on so well? Anyway he is safe now & they can't kill him & she can't worry to the same extent. Poor wee kid I am gladder than I can say. [Dudley was a Captain in the 2nd Battalion, Royal Inniskilling Fusiliers. He had been wounded and subsequently captured on 24 May 1915 near Shelltrap Farm, Wieltje during the latter stages of the 2nd Battle of Ypres. In June 1915 he was a prisoner of war at Munster.]

The General carried me off to dinner the other night & was as nice as ever bless him. Major Grant is leaving his staff.

You seem to have had great fun with Neb & I am just aching to get the present he & Clare got me. It might be anything from a stay lace to a Rolls Royce or possibly an emetic or slug for Charles. Tell them to buck up & send it me.

I must go out soon on the night trip & have rather a headache so won't write any more now.

Read Gibbs 'Soul of the War' it is excellently written, a lot about Furnes quite impersonally written & amazingly true as to details. I can't think how he remembers everything.

Goodnight & bless you all

Yrs Diddles

June 29th, Furnes

Mother dear. I got a nice letter from you last night, but saying you had not heard from me, I am so sorry, they must have got hung up again. I got the censored home chat from Hughie & Squeaks which made me smile but I think they ought to have got something more 'frightful' to edit, London mail or Pink un would have given them more work.

Last night a Marin officer, Capt Lafon, dashed in with a long letter from his brother at P[ort] Said who had been out for a ride with an 'English Lord with a daughter in the Brigade in Flanders' & full of chat on the subject generally. How small the little world is. I can also see beloved Colonel the Earl reading my letters aloud to the Afghans on the banks of Suez or whatever type of insect grows there!

I have to be Godmother to a Marin flag tomorrow; that will make Neb's mouth water as it's bound to be a 'thirsty performance'.

I enclose the enlargements you wanted that young Ronarc'h (Admiral's nephew) had done on purpose for you in Paris. Tell me something nice to say to him from you apropos of the trouble taken. Yesterday I was in there talking to him & the old Marin doctor & they started shelling their headquarters again. None quite near the house, but five Marins killed about 200 yds down the road. Poor souls, we went to see if there were any wounded but they had been killed instantaneously & terribly smashed. It's never so bad though when you know people have been killed absolutely outright like that. They are the one's Death is kindest to.

Here Dr Jelly interrupts to say he has a message for you as follows. He desires me to say that I don't eat 15 chops for breakfast & that if I don't do so I shall be coming home with beri-beri in no time – en route for a nice roomy churchyard. He thinks perhaps this may interest you (but I don't think so).

As he dictated I didn't agree & so changed it a bit for your benefit.

God bless you dears

Yr Diddles

June 31 Furnes [1 July]

Mother deah –

I am going down to Ypres this morning to see how our cars down there are getting on. I haven't been in the old place for 3 months & am rather looking forward to a chance of getting down there, of course if I meet Fitzpatrick again I may get heaved out on the way! But I'm full of hope.

It's before breakfast & I'm terribly sleepy, but remorseful because I didn't write you yesterday. Night work is very late now. Since I left Newnham we turned in every night between 1 am & four am with the exception of one evening Hély O carried me off to dine with him. One gets awfully sleepy after a lot of days on end. The troops aren't relieved until 11 pm & sometimes later now it's so late, & then there have been a lot of blessés among the outposts all the Dixmude way, as the Belgians & Huns are at places amazingly near (25yds) (for Belgees!) & it takes a terribly long time to get them in. Last night up there 2 brancardiers [stretcher bearers] started at 10 pm to fetch a wounded man from the outposts & only got him back at ten am next morning. There is some miles of very exposed communication trench, cut zig zag of course with the result no stretcher can be taken in it & the blessé has to be slung in his blanket & carried by the other men on all fours.

Yesterday we had an awful time with a tame Zouave lunatic they very kindly gave 'Mees' at Nieuport to take away. He was just cheerfully barmy, rather like Neb when tight, & was very funny. He had hotly accused his lieutenant of having cut his wife into little bits with his scissors, which just gave his bright pals the clue he might be queer, wonderful how observant these men get you know, so the patient alternately took me for the lieutenant, the wife, the scissors, his best friend, & something most unpleasant & kept trying to climb out at the back when we weren't looking.

I saw Commandant Paillet yesterday, a funny old boy, 2nd in command of the Marins & he found me looting roses in Nieuport. He's rather a wag, & fled down to his office in a cellar & made me out the enclosed 'bon' [chit] with the freedom to loot Nieuport!!!

Well I must run now Mrs Ma. Goodbye & God bless you – yr loving Diddles

PS Charles is such a lamb & is just hot on the tracks of a weevil in the small of his back.

2 Juillet

Mother Cherie – I am dining with Hély O again, like last time am writing you a line while he goes through the orders. He carries me off for a quiet evening about every ten days & I must say I look forward to my 'evenings out' with as much pleasure as you can think. It does one good to get away from everything.

Major Grant is still here but is leaving quite shortly. He tells me Rollo's Div is, he believes, resting & he is intending going down to have a joy ride to look up the Coldstreams about the 8th or so & will try & arrange to take me down with him to see Tubby. I'd just love it & hope to heaven it can be fixed up. But like all good things one longs for it will probably fall through!

Goodnight & God bless you

Yr loving DoDo

July 4th, Furnes

Mother darling –

Such a tea party as we had yesterday! Hughie would have loved it – lots of drinks. I had been asked to be Godmother to the 'auto canons' [armoured cars] Marins flag they had just had made & the dear fat old Col of Zouaves was the Godfather. I found to my horror on arriving at Oost Dunkerque, about 1½ miles behind the lines at Nieuport Bains, all the Zouaves' regimental band drawn up who played God Save the King & Tipperary &

every sort of thing they could think of that had any connection with 'Mees'. Then Col Roland made a speech of some half hr which made me hotter & hotter till I nearly fell thro' the floor in a puddle, & then I christened the 'Fanion' [Pennant] & we drank buckets of champagne & eat hundreds of jam tails till we felt sick as dogs. Then a concert, really quite good, sung by lots of the tommies who are opera singers. They gave me a dashed fine Hun Obus with flowers in it & all sorts of wonderful engravings on it done by the Zouaves & really very nice, a copper plate set into with my name & union jacks & Zouaves monograms & red crosses, & auto canons. In fact every damn thing they could think of.

After tearing ourselves away we went on to the usual round at Nieuport Bains & I said to Jelly I bet we were going to be obussed to learn us to go to orgies; of course as we arrived they were having no end of a time at N Bains. They were firing big ones at a battery in the dunes just opposite the dressing station some 200 yds off & it was really rather ripping watching them burst as they weren't hurting no one, & send huge clouds of sand into the air which took odd shapes almost like huge houses & castles & the sand stays in the air the most extraordinary length of time.

In fact it was very nice little sideshow & I think done on purpose to amuse us. They were so kind & put none near us.

Later/ I am so sorry to hear Peter is in hospital. There is a chance I may be getting down that way with Major Grant in a few days, & will go & see Peter as it is close by. That is unless something sickening happens to upset our plans. Was it a toss, or the result of an obus in a house or something like that? I hope he isn't bad poor kid. Thank you so much for wiring me. They put 17 inch into Nieuport again last night & absolutely buried about 20 men in the cellar in one of the houses. Some are still alive under it all, poor devils, or rather were last night. They have been working to move the debris for 12 hrs & haven't got down to them yet. The whole house crumpled up like a pack of cards. They are awful these 17 inch, like a train coming through the air, I've never heard one close thank God. I'd hate it & run so you wouldn't see me for dust, & I'd be home here & hiding under the bed with Charles in no time.

Good bye Mother dear. I am waiting to hear about Peter, if I get down there soon will wire you of course at once how he is, & if I hear it is anything serious could mange it probably sooner.

Yr loving
DoDo

Henry had been involved in an accident during bomb training. His commanding officer, E.W. Hermon describes it: 'Henry, who was on my left, I am sorry to say got it a good deal worse & his wrist was rather badly bruised but his wristwatch

85

was badly damaged & this saved him from having the tendons of his hand cut I am glad to say. His face too was a bit cut & he went to hospital & two others as well.'

July 6th, Furnes

Mother darling –
Major Grant who has been making enquiries over Peter for me just phones he has rejoined his regiment. But I am afraid this is stale news for you by now & not worth wiring. Had he been bad I could have got down there, as it is Major Grant, the sport, is going to try & take me down there to see him & Tubby next week some time. I only hope I don't miss Tubby dashing home on leave confound him, & Grant can't manage it sooner.
   No time for more now.
   Goodbye & bless you all – yr loving
   DoDo

June 8th [8 July]

Mother dear – I am so terribly pleased because Grant is taking me down to Bethune tomorrow afternoon brother hunting. I am a bit afraid Tubby will be doing his bit of trenching, but it's a case of then or never as Grant has been given a new job & has to leave Hély d' the following day, so anyhow we are going to try & hope to find no difficulty in finding our scabby Lieut of KEH [King Edward's Horse]. I will tell you what the result is.
   About my health Mrs Ma, please don't worry, because, honest injun, if I was seedy I should tell you & Dr Jelly too – as I promised him I would. He is an awfully good old thing & most extraordinarily kind to me in every kind of way. But when we are alone here as we are now he is sometimes terribly 'tiring' being very Irish & rather rough, & very hot tempered, & worst of all very touchy. You know what I mean, like gorrys are sometimes & inclined to make mountains out of the tiniest molehills & take it for granted everyone finds fault with him. Well when he does that (as happens to be doing just now!!!) it makes one awfully tired, because one never never gets a minute to one's self. You see when we were several, it didn't matter, because it didn't notice so much & one just loafed off until he recovered. Whereas now sometimes when I am weary & feel if I saw old Dr Jelly another 5 minutes I should scream, I go off to my room & just slack by myself & Charles with a book until I am fit to speak to again, so I think perhaps often when I go off like that he thinks it's because I'm over tired & I can't very well say it's just because I must have a little bit of the day to myself or it makes me nervy. So you mustn't think I am seedy – until I say so – I am writing this to explain & it's private of course.

But old Jelly is so very kind & such a real good sort in every other way that it easily makes up for his irritableness as everyone has their faults, & as he is older & very respectable, as Nana would say, he is about the only member of the corps I could dig with like this. And I don't for a minute imagine I'm not a bit of a trial myself at times.

So there we are, it's all part of the discomforts – mental especially – that one has to take as the days work. Goodbye Mother dear – yr loving DoDo

Dr Jellett had been commissioned by the Countess to keep an eye on Dorothie's health and his letters to her illustrate their shared concerns, especially regarding Dorothie's appetite.

Furnes July 7th 1915

Dear Lady Denbigh,
I think Lady Dorothie is in very good health, and stands the life here on the whole very well. I am however sometimes annoyed with her for not eating better because when she does not eat properly at one meal, she is rather inclined to want still less at the next, and so on. A lecture from you in this respect would do her no harm, and also on taking as much sleep as she can get ...

We were in Ypres the other day and I found a very excellent tonic for her in a deserted chemists shop which I had her trying to get here I think it will do her a lot of good. I am going to make her go back for a week or two in August.
Henry Jellett

9th [July]

Mother cherie –
I saw Peter today for a couple of hours & found him scabby but still smiling & a good kid. His wristwatch – or the remains of it – will be a great asset to Squeaks museum.

Rollo alas was in the trenches & I was told although easy to go to it would get various people into trouble if I tried – so I had to give up seeing him.

Will try later on I hope with better success.
Goodnight
I love you very much – Do you love me?
DoDo

July 11th, Furnes

Father Dear – I was feeling very gloomy just now & wishing I was dead, when I got such a nice long letter from you & full of interesting enclosures. Thank you so very much. I am getting you particulars I can about the pom pom cars & will tell you the answer in my next letter. The full particulars you gave me in your last letter I sent Tubby to read & return me, but of course he never did the latter, so as I stupidly had not duplicated the bit about the anti-aircraft guns I am undone. But there are some English anti-aircraft people with big armoured cars with 2 or 3 pounders on board up near here & I expect they can give me information.

I now have Charles out here with me & he is the joy of my life though sometimes keep things damn lively. Anyway never a dull minute.

I am glad you liked the General's letter to Mother, she showed it to me & I was much touched. You can't think what a perfect dear that man has been to me out here. He is no end of a bug now & commands one of Foch's 3 armies which means 150,000 men under him. Luckily his GHQ are only some 10 miles from here & so I still often see him & he carries me off there now & then for suppers & a night off.

I enclose a photo enlargement of me & the dear old Admiral taken by his nephew & given me on purpose to send one to you & one to Ma. He looks an awful old ruffian but his heart's in the right place as are those of all his men – an A1 lot.

Life here is much the same & the old line never changes. There is only Dr Jellett with me & the faithful Hèléne, our minion, in the Furnes house now. He is rather cantankerous & tiring at times but a good old thing. He's got an awful Irish temper though & is very 'rough' which is rather 'enervant' [irritating] at times. We do a lot of night work these days, now it's not dark till 10 or later, it's seldom we turn in before 1am at earliest.

I went to see Peter 2 days ago which was nice & found him happy & scabby. Also relieved to find he had a nice 'safe' job at present always something to thank the Almighty for.

When home the other day I thought Mother was looking rather worn out, she will do too much & sits writing endless letters till 3 or 4 in the morning. I am so sorry really to hear Squeaker is going to do a Red X job, it made a big difference to Mother having her there & stopped her being too lonely. If Squeaks goes to London it will be ghastly for Mother all alone at NP.

Oh Father dear, I wish this ghastly business was over. Even when it is over, God knows what will be left to us, it's almost simpler for those that get blown up, I think it's easier than for those that are left with just a heartache.

It's so late & I must go to bed I suppose.

I do wish I could come & see you for a little bit & get away from all this beastliness & sorrow.

It's the endlessness & futility of it that is so despairing.
Good night dear & God bless you & keep you safe.
Yr loving Diddles
Such a big hug

Le 11th Juillet

The Furnes post seems going to pot. Now takes 5 days to you alas. Rollo's diary was censored between me & you not before. Ypres absolutely desolate. No civilians or soldiers just ruined & it hardly even gets shelled now except the roads for transport

Mother darling – got more nice letters from you yesterday. Yes! I think that's an excellent idea to come home barmy & cut you all up in bits with scissors like the Zouave – just think what a lovely article for the Rugby Advertiser.

Charles after being smothered in sulphur & motor oil for a week is hardly itchy & barely knows himself.

The garden is looking very nice, but will soon be done I am afraid as they are mostly summer flowers. In fact, when we looted for it I forbade old Jelly to dig up chrysanthemums because I hoped to be in Ostend when they flowered. However he is right & me wrong. Always a tiresome state of affairs!

He is mad with me today because I got up for mass. I have only been able to go twice since I've been back so made an effort this Sunday, & he says I ought to be shot as we went to bed at 2am. However one won't hurt me. Goodbye & so much love DoDo

July 12th (about)

Mother dear –
I was sad to hear Squeaker was going to Park Lane as it will leave you so very lonely at NP. Your family are, I am afraid, the limit – there isn't one out of 10 left where they ought to be.

Poor poor Mrs Ma. But honestly won't it be horribly dreary for you with little Squeaks gone? She is such a dear kid & she & you get on so well.

A big German offensive is expected all along between Ypres and the sea end of Aug or Sept, in fact during the autumn – of course the poor old allies advance that was to take place in April is rather a frost! But they say the Germans having now sat so effectively on the Russians are bringing back huge quantities of troops & guns for this Western offensive. Till then I think there won't be much doing. Just the same steady fighting & endless

casualties without either side getting any further,
   Oh la Oh la
   Such a dear letter from Da he sounds very happy.
   Yr loving DoDo

July 13th (about)

Wed for sure [14 July]

Mother Dear – Just got an indignant letter from you saying you haven't heard from me since the Pennant baptism with the auto canons. I can't understand it because I have written often I think. Anyhow I was under the impression I had.

Charles is sitting beside me on the itch as usual & I have just caught him a swot, & he as usual gazes at me reproachfully & says 'I wish I was with the dear Countess she loves the itch'. In fact, he misses you frightfully & I am sure you do him too, no more dead rabbits left in the library now, how lonely you must be.

I have written to ask Marjie to come stay with me for a week, it would be quite safe because this house is on the edge of the town & I would take such care not to dent her & now things are slack I would see quite a lot of her. I wonder if she'll come. I could arrange her temporary passes though not permanent ones of course. It would be so nice having her for a little bit & I don't think would bore her.

This house is too smart now & is getting very like Frankton. Has nifty curtains (from Ma), priceless furniture (Nieuport), wonderful gold-rimmed dinner service (Ypres) & lovely brass, copper & china antiques (Flanders generally) hanging all round the walls. And beautiful garden at the back with terrier in same by name Charles, one hen by name Mabel, one rabbit by name Pierre.

In fact it's really almost too nice & comfortable now. I don't think I'd ever have the courage to go back to real war & real dirt & never taking off one's trousers.

Do ask Graham to put the lid on it by making me a cake & posting it me. A nice one, stiff with currants & weevils; we never lunch in but have a sandwich in the car & it's a luxury to have a cake in the house to cut chunks off to take with one & I am both too lazy & too busy to make one myself. I do like Ma. I do like Graham.

Just off to our nightly round near Dixmude. There is a little white house at the X roads, up to now a sort of mascot & untouched, which has been used as a dressing station since Oct & which we have been to I should be sorry to say how many times. I had a great affection for it as its 'luck' has often stood us in good stead, especially the 'Yser' days. To my sorrow two nights ago I rolled up as usual & found it a wreck having been badly shelled that forenoon & again yesterday. The dressing station is now a neighbouring dugout & I weep salt tears over the ruins of our poor little house there whenever I see it. Luckily no one was hit in it as the 1st two shells fell short & gave them warning. There have been blessés up there every night for a very long while.

The Hun is doing no attacking to speak of these days but is damnably flush of ammunition & 'arroses' [sprays] all roads & dear old Nieuport with nasty heavy obus. They have set their hearts on smashing those locks at Nieuport, but as fast as touched the engineers build them up & all those fat 17 inch are wasted. A lot of houses have been stove in though lately in Nieuport by them this week & many poor devils wounded & killed in the ruins. When a 17 inch comes down it's like old Mrs Busby (she of the legs) sitting down, & things just must give.

Goodnight & God bless you all

Yr loving DoDo

Sunday
(July 11 or 18)

Mother dear –

Such a day & a night yesterday. Howling gale and rain – I was soaked twice & swallowed a few ton of sand & mud in the dunes & on the roads in the course of the day. You can't think what those roads through the dunes are like in a storm. The sand simply beating down & the air full of it & it hurts your face so driving against it one can hardly steer. Then the night was black as ink, & of course it was skiddy & poor blessés in the car Dixmude way & the road invisible. But whenever there is a dirty night & I think how nice to be at NP with a gin, in a red flannel jacket, I console myself by saying, 'Thank God I'm not a sailor' & hitching up my pants & spitting over the side of the car & the mere thought of wretched devils patrolling in torpedo destroyers makes the night out here a picnic. If I was a sailor I should desert every time there was a storm.

The General was given permission to see Zette & Mme HO at Boulogne for 3 hrs, first time he saw them since mobilisation & he was barmy with joy at seeing Zette again, however the French are now at last giving their officers a week's leave. They deserve it poor devils.

Bless you all DoDo

July 19th

Mother deah –
I am fed up with the Furnes post & will try the English medium via Dunkirk again. Today is Monday, I think 19th, tell me when this gets & tell me on replying that it is the Dunkirk post.

Nothing new here, always blessés at night this place we go to Dixmude way. It's ages since there has been no one there now, whereas before every night in four or so there used to be no wounded.

Haven't heard news of Tubby for centuries.

Thank you so much for all your nice letters.

Goodbye & much love
DoDo

It's so hard to get to communion now as I practically never get in till well after midnight, 1 or 2 am & Dr Jelly insists on my having grub when I get in as he says from a health point of view it's too long to go without food. Otherwise I could get communion in the mornings at 9.30 often although mass is so early, 6.30 am, that I seldom can get to it. Whereas the priests will give you communion if you ask for it. But I s'pose the Almighty takes that into consideration.

DoDo

Tuesday 20th about

Mother dear – I wrote you a letter this morning with on the top of the paper written 'Tuesday for certain about the 20th' & saying I was sending it by the English post & when it arrived let me know. It's arrival would now be doubly interesting because I dropped it out of my pocket in the course of the day. God knows where & it remains to be seen if it's fallen in a puddle, under an obus or in the hands of some good Samaritan who will eventually post it. It was on this blue paper & envelope. [This letter was received at Newnham on 31 July having been found and posted by two Belgian soldiers.]

Today, our usual & almost uncanny luck held good again. It was at Pervyse & the old house with the cellar that you saw up near the station, well the cellar is all stove in now & full of water, with no roof & a child's cradle & a red cotton umbrella floating mournfully in the dirty water. It all looked so disconsolate I wanted to photograph it for you as it now is & you must thank that photograph when you get it for saving our lives. We had just stopped inside the doorway to do the photo when a clutch of four shells fell at intervals of 10 yds apart up the road we had just been standing on. Half a minute sooner & we simply couldn't have helped being hit. A sentry who was standing there was killed, poor soul. Dr Jelly was there & did what he could for him at once, but the artery in his neck was cut & he died in a few minutes. If only he had had the tiniest chance of life, we might have made the whole difference being there, as our car was a 100 yds off & we could have taken him right away. As it was it was all very gruesome. It's hard to get accustomed out here to the extraordinary swiftness of death. It takes someone like that a few yards from you & then perhaps in a few minutes you are right away, in a new atmosphere & perfect safety & in different surroundings with people laughing & talking & it seems a century since one stood alongside death.

But somehow out here the thought of it doesn't frighten me an atom as it would have in the old days. It just seems natural & one never thinks about it. But it makes it very hard to realise the existence of a future life, or rather the need for one. After all, people are alive one moment & cease to be the next & why should there be any kind of future? When one sees Death in ones & two in every day life, there seems some sort of necessity for something further, but now that Death deals in hundreds & thousands one thinks of people as being the same of any of God's other creatures, & why we should have anything more than any of the other animals is hard to understand & honestly I don't understand.

You'll think I'm barmy but I'm not – I am just writing what I think at the moment

Yr DoDo

21 Juillet

Mother dear –

I am dining with the dear General again & always make a point of writing you while he signs his papers after dinner, in the hopes that letters posted you this way reach sooner.

Had a quiet day today. Didn't go out till the afternoon, came in for a noisy half hr at Nieuport, but the Hun wasted much ammunition & touched devil a soul. However Charles was teased proper, I thought he was lost or stolen, hunted the houses round & then found him after all under a rug in the car. As usual as soon as he's in the dark he considers himself out of range. But it [is] especially an allied gun going off any where in his proximity that annoys & frightens him. One funny episode of the day was a Major's orderly who had gone out to get his CO fresh eggs & had put them in his trouser pocket for safety. Arrives an obus some 15 yds off, a little one, but enough to give the orderly a bad fright & he ducks madly which of course broke all the eggs! A sitting position is not conducive to the safeguarding of a clutch of eggs in the trouser pouch! It was very funny to see the orderly's face of disgust when he diskivered [*sic*] the tragedy & to see the egg mess. It made me 'smile some'.

I have another wheeze for getting to see Tubby. Have discovered an old pal of the early days of the war, an Artillery Major who is at Bethune and is coming to sup with me tomorrow at Furnes. I feel in my bones that if ask him nicely he will aid and abet me getting down for another day to those parts. This time when Tubby is out of his ditch.

> Goodnight
> Je t'aime
> DoDo

Furnes 24th [July]

Mother Dear – I've just come in from a great review down at the sea where the various medals have been spooned out, 2 generals among them including Hély d'Oissel.

The old Admiral had to do the decorating & you should just have seen him, lovely new suit on, smothered with buttons & medals & not a speck of dust! Looked like a bally field Marshal & no end of a nut instead of all covered in mud & top boots & hands in his pockets as usual.

I am just delighted at news of Dudley. Major Lumsden of Bethune who is going to try & get me to see Rollo, wrote me last night 'your brother is no longer in the 3rd Coldstream but on the 2nd Div staff.' I think it's a mistake on his part as I'd have heard from you, so aren't really taking it to heart unless it's confirmed. I wish I could really think it was true, but I can't I'm sure you'd have told me else.

Goodbye dears. It's pouring rain & has been beastly this week also I've got such a stomach ache.

> Gott Strafe 'Tonks'!
> Yr loving
> Diddles

July 24th

Father dear –
I have at last found news for you about your anti-aircraft guns. The ones you mention have done very well indeed & been a great success. Their only fault was the range the ammunition had. Their present shell fuse only lasted 2,000yds so were very apt to burst prematurely, but now a new lot with 8,000yd fuses have been served out to them. Funnily enough there are some close up near me here of that Osbaston detachment & some at Ypres. These

have actually brought down one machine in our lines, have teased many others & been most effective in stopping effective aircraft spying on the part of the Hun. But they have been heavily shelled here & one of their officers, a boy called Knight, was killed I was sorry to say & several of the men wounded last week.

The crews are A1 men & the various invention of Osbaston's a great success. I hope this will interest you & am sorry to be so long answering your questions about it.

I got such a long interesting letter of yours to Ma yesterday, all about Alexandria & the various bloodcurdling yarns about German naval officers – all corroborated by the naval officers here who say they're quite true. Col the Earl in fact, is becoming no end of a wag.

I'd give a lot to hear Alouette, there [are] some Algerian troops just rolled up here & with the rippingest regimental band. All sorts of snake charmers instruments & tomtoms & weird things. It's rather like marching to a fat old lady being pinched at regular intervals till she squeaks who also is being walked just fast enough to make her wheeze.

If they attack with the band they ought to do great things & terrify the enemy to a suitable state of pulp before leaving their trench.

Much love mon cher monsieur Da

Such a big hug – Diddles

July 25th

Hurrah hurrah
I saw Tubby & Peter yesterday – had a whole day down at Bethune thanks to the kindness of Major Lumsden – both as fit as fleas I am mad with joy at Tubby getting that staff job.
Yr loving DoDo

Major Frederick Lumsden commanded No1 Howitzer Battery of the Royal Marine Artillery which comprised of twelve 15" howitzers. He would go on to great things. He was awarded the DSO and two bars and the Victoria Cross for his bravery between 1 January and 11 May 1917. He went on to win a further bar to his DSO. He was tragically killed in action on 3 June 1918 and is buried at Berles New Military Cemetery, France.

July 26th night

Mother Dear –
Got 3 letters from you tonight bursting with back chat.
I want to tell you about my day with the boys. Major Lumsden, the kind man, sent his car all the way up here for me & sent me back at night. Also

went to endless trouble collecting the 2 boys for lunch & the afternoon & hacking them down to their lines.

Rollo smothered in swanking staff bands & full of bounce & looking too well for words. Honestly really & thoroughly well & in great spirits. Peter too with hardly a scab left & full of smiles. We pottered about all the afternoon & Lumsden took us all to see the big Coventry 15 inch Howitzers he is in charge of. The shells are half as much again as the German 17 inch ones they throw at us here & that bucked me up no end to think how we too must be frightening them in return.

I am sleepy & must turn out for Dixmude trip in a few minutes. They shelled Furnes tonight during supper. About 15 fattish ones which never exploded & some small fry which didn't.

Alarmed our tweenie but otherwise did nowt as I know of thank Gawd [*sic*]

Yr loving DoDo

Sometimes Dorothie was so tired she could barely string a sentence together:

27th July

Morning Ma –
    I luv you –
    'aven't time to write –
    How sad the swallows have gone –
    Yr lovin DoDo
    Aunt Mabel sent me 200 cigs. I luv her.
    PS dear Countess I luv you – Do you luv me? – Charlie

July 28th

Same old place

Mother darling –
Haven't I been good lately? I've written such lots of letters. Our latest Furnes bombardments are a great frost as the obus don't go off, so don't be alarmed.

Total casualty last time was a severe fright to our tweenie, one who rejoices in the name of 'Zenobia', she evacuated up the road, at a 120 per hour in pin curls with a stocking round her face in the approved manner when suffering from a face ache or inflammation of the grinder.

The Admiral's 2 young sparks, young Ronarc'h & Duforge, tried to pull my leg last night but it failed & I am a hen to the good (named Alice) which is always something.

The front door has a window over it, or rather had because one of the bombs broke the glass naturally, & the result is there is just a draft as I haven't been able to afford glass except for my bedroom.

Well they turned up at 3am with a sack & a cat & a hen in it. They squared the sentry at the X roads outside & climbed up & dropped the hen in, & then the cat who had a long string & a tin box with shrapnel bullets in it to rattle & a caricature of me. They had carefully ascertained that Charles hated cats & of course expected him to be sleeping in the kitchen & to give chase & raise hell generally.

However Charles being in my bedroom it fell flat because the cat escaped in the garden, leaving his tin box behind & Hélène put the new hen in the pen with 'Mabel' the hen & Pierre the rabbit. I heard a row but didn't bother, it seemed quite usual somehow to hear a hen on the landing & didn't interest me enough to get me out of bed. It teased old Jelly a bit as he got up in the dark & nearly fell down stairs & couldn't find the matches or the hen. I am going to invite these two to supper & have hen for supper to amuse them!

Yr loving
Diddles

Friday for sure July 29th I think
(30th really) [30 July]

Mother dear –
I got your long dear letter last night for which many thanks it was a help too because one's poor mind & judgement is rather inclined to get lost in the dark & inclined to chuck it up at times.

What I mean is, that although the war brings one closer to prayers, doesn't diminish one's faith as a Catholic in the smallest degree, it makes one rocky over the root principle of any after life at all, or rather seeing the suddenness & completeness of death so often & so very close to one, somehow does away with the whole theory of a future of any kind. Why should there be one? There isn't any need for one for us any more than for any other animal. But I do believe the need of religion in a race because it brings out all the noblest & the best morally & incidentally stands for betterment & continuance of the whole race generally doesn't it? Therefore I think that even if there is no future existence at all, one has no right to squander one's life or things slide, or humanity as a whole would go to pot. See what I mean? It's seeing Death in such numbers & such simplicity that makes me think this. Because somehow the fact of Death in the abstract has no 'fear' now like it used when one thought about it in the old days. But although still wanting to do the square thing on earth it doesn't seem to matter to the smallest degree what happens 'after' – or if there is an after or not. It just doesn't matter anymore somehow. I think people just live & do their best & then die & there's an end of it – it seems so easy to believe in God but no need for heaven!

Dear me how complicated it's all getting – I'd better leave it! Because after all I'm one in many millions & I don't really count or matter what I finks.

Have had a quiet day today, haven't been shot at once & haven't seen an obus nearer than 500 yds or found more than one 'malade' [*patient*] to conduct to his hospice. And I am having a quiet evening with the General – so all is as it should be.

Would you like me to come home for a bit end of August? Dr Jelly will be going back to his kids then, as he hasn't been over since Nov last, & if you like I'd try & arrange to come at the same time – as we share the car it is simpler to go on leave at the same time really.

Arthur James 2 cars. He gave me a Renault which ought to be out soon now, but there's been a lot of delay on the part of the makers. Then a Vauxhall which came out 3 weeks ago, this latter car was a perfect wreck just painted over to look nice, a body put on & sold to Arthur James as an ambulance; no more use as a car than a sick headache & I hated his being done. So I wrote him & he has been very kind about it. The result is he is giving us the ambulance body and fittings to put on a chassis we have already, & the man who sold him the chassis is taking it back without any expense to Arthur James except just the ambulance body. It was rather awful to have to write & tell AJ the car was a stumour [*sic*] but I didn't want him to be 'done' – much love DoDo

2 Aug

Mother darling – such a good cake & tins of toffee turned up yesterday. Thank you very very much. You are sure to go straight to heaven & Graham too. But perhaps the Lord will spare you both long enough to 'do it again'. I most sincerely hope so.

Furnes is still here & nice & peaceful. Nieuport had an extra doing yesterday afternoon. Rather sad, I was done out of a hen for dinner, on the way into Nieuport we saw a decapitated hen lying on the road, whether by obus or motor I know not (but out of spirit I know) and just done too, & asking to be picked up for the larder, only Jelly & I both were suffering from cold feet as they were shelling the road & the last 3 had been rather close, so we put our nose in the air & pretended we didn't want it. However on the return journey we eagerly scanned every inch of the road, it being then so nice & quiet but a wily & braver looter had been there 1st & we went home hen-less after all – a bit 'ard – but will larn [*sic*] us to funk. By the way 'Alice', the Admiral's hen that came in thro' the staylight at 3am & that I meant to eat, must have heard me say so & she is now laying eggs fit to bust, & I haven't the heart to strangle the old girl anyway until she gives over. Charles is well & sends his love to everyone & has just received such a nice p. card from Piper – which has pleased him.

Yr loving Diddles

Saturday [7 August]

Bourbourg

Mother dear – I am in the garden at Bourbourg (Broqueville's) doing absolutely nothing & very nice too. Charles is shivering pathetically & shaking the whole bench because I won't have him on my lap. I am down here for a couple of days – it's so quiet & pleasant & quite a jolly garden. I am glad to be here just these days too because a couple of days ago I ricked my back, just how I don't know, & it was hurting a lot. It's much better now though, the Dr looked at it as it is going off by itself, just a ricked muscle that's all, but it's a joy not to go bumping about in the damned ambulance in & out of potholes all day.

About what the Germans said re blowing up a gun on the Furnes canal. It was all bunkum. They were shelling the bend where the gunboats often fire from, & hit a barge, an old sunk affair, & blew it up. We saw the hits from where we happened at that moment to be standing watching a few fields away. The aviator spotting for the Germans no doubt saw the bits too & went back triumphantly thinking the gun was blown up. Anyway they made a statement to that effect in their communiqué the next day & they probably believed it themselves, tho' in reality the gun was nowhere near at the time.

The sailors (English) have been firing a lot lately & done very well.

I shall be home I think the last week in August and first one Sept. Will that suit & please you? I should like to be at Newnham of course just like last time. Do see if you can get Marjie to be there for me then too please & of course you might whisper to Mrs Ma too should you see her, that I'd be mighty glad to have her about the place too.

Much love dears

DoDo

Sunday
(Aug 8th 1915)

Mother dear

Just going back to Furnes having had two nice quiet days here. My back is much better & I intend to slack too for the next few days until it quite stops as it's not good enough else.

I've just stolen armfuls of flowers to take back with me, in fact was so ashamed of the quantity & the gardener's wrath that I wrapped them up in a rug & pretended it was 'only a corpse'.

So long & much love

DoDo

Aug 12th

Mother dear – I've been rather lazy this week about writing I'm afraid.

I am still slacking. Part run down I think & then I ricked my back & that put the lid on. Dr Jelly can't find anything the matter except an intermittent pulse, which is wearing off as my back is getting better & he says there is no need to worry. So if anything should happen or my neck or loin fall off I shan't fail to let you know. Otherwise take it for granted I am quite ok again by the time you get this letter. I'm not doing any night work at all for the present.

I brought back two baby white bunnies from Bourbourg – christened George & Mary – only my Mary isn't at all true to nature, as she is most coy & nifty, wears one ear up & one ear down, & has a black patch over one eye. The ensemble is fast to a degree & the other Mary wouldn't at all approve.

Charles is hunting 'Alfred' in the coal house. He is black & I am fed up with him. Alfred is a tiny wild bunny the Fusiliers Marins gave me in Nieuport one day – when 3 inch long. He is now grown up & as wild as the devil. Digs himself out at night & hides in the coal hole, which gives Charles something to do all day, besides giving Hélène something to do washing Charles afterwards.

There was great flutter 2 nights ago. The Belgians telephoned there was gas approaching in front of their lines at Steenstrade again – Consternation! Vision of Huns arriving at Furnes at 3am. Reinforcements sent up & artillery opens fire vigorously for at least half an hour to disperse the gas fumes which continue to rise undaunted until with the dawn & daylight our bulgy Belge diskivers it is but a fog rising!!!

Goodbye dear

So long

The rain is blotting my letter – a sure sign the Almighty thinks I've written enough.

Yr loving Diddles

PS I quite forgot to tell you the Admiral presented me with the French 'Croix de Guerre' two days ago, it is the order just been issued for all who have been mentioned in dispatches. [This is related to Ronarc'h's special order of the day dated 31 December 1914 regarding Dorothie's bravery.] The Admiral presented it me with pleasant words, what time he kept his head & firmly embraced me on both cheeks. It being the custom in France to hug the Tommy you decorate! It's rather a nice bronze medal. I'll show it you when I come home which will be about 25th Aug. I enclose a bit of the ribbon. [The letter still has the ribbon attached.]

Aug 14th Furnes

Father dear – It was nice getting another letter from you – bless you. Do it again please. I am glad you liked the photo too of me & the Admiral. You know the old dear presented me with a damn fine tin cross the other day. The French 'Croix de Guerre', a sort of Military Cross minor to the Medal Militaire. The Admiral said some very nice & touching things to me when he gave it me, & said it was the one gave him most pleasure to give of them all because it was genuinely deserved. Nice of him wasn't it? I enclose you a bit of the ribbon so that you can see what it's like. The cross is a nice little bronze one with crossed swords & not gaudy like the Belgian order.

Furnes is much the same: odd moth-eaten bombardments that some how never seem to hit anyone, perhaps it is partly because the Furnes population is greatly thinned now.

I am going home on 25 Aug for a fortnight, Boche permitting. I don't know why but I've been rather a rag lately, back aches & things & get tired over nothing. It's a pest & I am slacking & taking things easy in the hopes it will soon go. It's such a bore feeling cheap out here as it interferes with everything. But don't be anxious as it's pots better already.

Charles is well, & so brave now, he barks at shells. He is very funny. They whistle as they arrive, makes him perfectly furious & he dances about barking madly. But if they burst anywhere near, his courage at once oozes, he dives to ground under the car. His memory is good too because he was rather frit by one, at a certain street corner in Nieuport some 3 weeks ago & now whenever we pass the place he hurries by with his tail between his legs. It's really rather curious.

Isn't it splendid Rollo having that staff appointment? He does deserve it so, & poor wee Mellins was wearing herself to a rag with anxiety.

I don't think your mixed bathing parties with bits of fluff from the chorus is all seemly in a Colonel & Earl, to say nothing of a Pa of 10.

Ever so much love dear & such a big hug – yr loving Diddles

Aug 16th

Mother dear –
Things are still quiet here & I mean to come home on the 25th but people are still unanimous in thinking the Hun is going to push his little all up for Dunkirk by the end of Sept.

They made two moth-eaten little attacks in the dunes 2 days ago which were duly squashed.

I am still doing no night work & being lazy & my backache is nearly done which is refreshing.

My mind is a blank & I can think of nothing witty, amusing or untrue to tell you so will close.

Y loving D

Aug 19th

At the General's

Mother dear –
A line to thank you for the various letters & to ask forgiveness for writing you such dull letters lately I've been lazy. They shelled Furnes nicely yesterday, a real good hate but nowhere near my house & no one hit either. Charles so indignant & barked his fat head off. He is so brave now he always barks at obus. He is down for Croix de Guerre too & wants you to tell Piper so.

The General sends you his love. At least I say so but here he chips in & says it's not proper & you will be offended!

I fink not
Love from DoDo

Aug 20th, Furnes

Mother dear –
I am crossing either the 23rd or 24th, I am not quite sure which, via Boulogne. I will wire you as soon as I know for sure.

Dr Jelly is crossing by the same boat & since writing to you, he has decided he would rather I went on way through London to be vetted by physician. He will take me to someone he knows early next morning after arriving in London. Then I propose catching the 12.15 down to Rugby – gets in at 2 something – Dr Jelly will come down with me as he would like to see you & tell you what the doctor says. He has to go on to Ireland that night, so I suggested he come out to Newnham with me, & we would send him in to catch the Irish train in the evening.

This would be better than your coming to London to see him as 1) I want to save you a racket. 2) Dr Jelly says he doesn't mind a scrap whether he fills in the time between trains at Rugby or in London & 3) as we may only know the exact day of crossing at the last minute, you would probably miss any wires we sent, so I think, it's best to leave it decisively at that.

Don't worry – I'm not dead, or likely to be for the next century, only Dr Jelly just wanted me to see the bloke in London on my way down as being simpler than leaving it till later. So you mustn't think please, it's because there's anything the matter, because there ain't. It's just I'm that amiable (ahem) you know I always do as requested. I expect you will see my lovely phiz almost as soon as you get this.

Isn't it nice to think I shall be at Newnham in no time?

Ever so much love

DoDo

PS Gott strafe Tonks!

In her letter on 12 July Dorothie mentions an imminent German offensive expected in August or September and it appears to begin just as she goes home on leave. The Rugby Advertiser *reported on 21 August that 'The Germans are showing considerable activity [on the Yser front], and are evidently preparing for a new effort. The French, British and Belgian artillery is now hotly shelling the German trenches, and the Allies are well prepared to crush any attempt to break through.' Throughout her letters Dorothie is surprisingly accurate in much of her information. Her contacts with the officer corps undoubtedly provided most of this, probably confidential, detail.*

CHAPTER 8

October 1915–January 1916

Dorothie's health was obviously suffering and she was away from the front for two months. From the following letters it is clear that she had made several abortive attempts to return and that her family were concerned at her decision to go back again, so much so that Henry was on his way home, probably to try and reason with her.

Friday (Oct 22nd 1915) Written from John Street Mayfair London

Mother dear –
You were a darling to drive me down yourself, see me off – thank you so very very much. As to my 2 months of idling & being waited on – words fail me – to tell you how nobly you bore with me & spoilt me.

It has given me a new lease of life especially morally & that is mostly due to you & home sympathy. I really am feeling ever so much more fit mentally & after all it's one's brainpower & willpower that carry you, or let down your body as it did mine.

But home has overhauled it & it can go on forever now. I shall be glad of work again.

I will write more tomorrow – God bless you many many times for being such a dear to yr funny old Diddles.

Saturday (Oct 23rd 1915) London

Mother Darling –
I was out when your wire came & so only got it late. I think I had better go along over as I had got all my papers visa'd for crossing tomorrow & I have had so many false starts, & had already wired the hour a car was to fetch me at Calais. It's not that I don't want to see Peter because I do & am so very sorry to miss him, it's real hard lines & he might have chosen it more tactfully. So I am departing by the early breakfast train tomorrow & am dining here tonight with Evy quietly. I have done all the diverse gadgets I meant to – goodbye darling & thank you many many times for being my

Mama!

I saw Geoffrey Elwes yesterday, who said Bill was going on much better & he was sure would get right eventually. That's good isn't it?

Ever so much love to you all & such a big hug from DoDo

PS

I have just received your letter about Bill. Poor poor kid – I am terribly sorry as Geoffrey's news was so emphatically better, but must have been older after all. I do hope he will get well, but if it means his being crippled for life – that is worst of all.

Thank you for your dear letter, I hope you understand about my not coming back again. I honestly feel it would be better for me to get on & do something just now when I happen to be wanted to arrange things. Goodbye Mother dear & God bless you

Diddles

Bill was Mellins' brother, Captain Francis Edward Basil Harding, 21st Battery, Royal Field Artillery. The state of his health was a constant concern over the following weeks.

Oct 26th Furnes

Mother darling –

I am back again quite safely & it is all so odd!

I took Moonie by the hand to the boat, & then they tried to arrest us on landing as I had omitted to get one 'paper', invented since I last crossed, to give me power to disembark! & there was no time to get it at Folkestone & catch the boat so I got onboard in spite of the officials, who to get even wired to Calais that I was a suspicious character & not allowed to land!

To our joy & amusement a dowdy officer & two hairy sentries with bayonets came & arrested us in the cabin & said we weren't to land!! But it all petered out by their receiving an answer from the Belgian GHQ 10 minutes later in answer to their enquiries saying not to be a fool & to let me off.

I went & saw the others yesterday, who Jelly hadn't told I was coming to surprise them & they were struck all of a heap when I strolled in.

Charles is frisky & a bit scabby & delighted to see me.

Hélène & Zenobia nearly off their rockers with excitement – bless them.

I saw the General too yesterday who sent you his love & said to thank you again for a charming letter you had written him. It appears the Mission had quite made up their minds I had gone for good now so I must go & cock a snook at them just to show there is no ill feeling.

Torrents of abuse on all sides for being le dernier des dernières of slackers & for being away so long.

How is Peter?

Hély d'Oissel was very sorry to hear I had missed him & promised to let me be taken down to Bethune to see them both when he gets back to make up. So that will be nice.

Having got under way I decided to come over all things considered.

False starts are like having a tooth out 7 times instead of once. I have found such a loffey [*sic*] lot of cigarettes waiting for me here. I shall be sick as a dog in a few days – from unaccustomed (spelling?) luxuries.

I hope Bettie & Taffy are spelling better. It was disgraceful & distressed me much to see the faults they made – it's an awful thing not to be able to spell & they really must try & improve.

Goodbye Mother dear & Oh thank you more & more in all your dearness to me – I can't say all I feel. But your love & sympathy have helped me so much. I feel I just must have active work to do, or I couldn't keep up; on the other hand I feel we have so deserted you, & left you all the hard & dreary work, with everyone gone. I wish I was more help.

Yr so loving Diddles

Furnes 27th [October]

Mother darling –

Such mud! & such rain! as have taken trouble to greet me here.

I looked out of my bedroom window fatheadedly this morning to a vista of fields & mud: gendarmes & mud, rain & mud, lorries splashing mud, pot holes on the road full of mud, & 'Daniel' a mass of mud.

Most exhilarating when one remembers it is now a daily affair for 4 or 5 months. I had got so accustomed to nice dry roads, I had omitted the fact that mud is a Flanders speciality.

Went to N Bains again & saw all our diverse funny friends, doctors & Tommies at the different dressing stations, all very pleased to see Charles & his Missus again & Charles delighted to renew acquaintance with one particular cat he spars with at 3 and 5 every afternoon & that he hadn't been able to visit for 2 months! The cat looks forward to it too.

Two gorgeous rainbows in the dunes, & it was rather a fine H Majesty's theatre scenery effect: the dunes with the sun shining on them, the mist lifting, a huge double rainbow in the middle &, at just the right moment, a nice shell burst, a fine black splotch just against the rainbow – most futuristic!

A neighbour of ours, a Belge near 'no14', was blown up last week messing with an unexploded shell in his back garden close by – poor chap.

It is absolutely impossible to impress a Belge with the futility of this particular sport, it is ingrained in him, 'Mees' however is very firm & always refuses to play it, & I think on the whole she is right.

The Munro Corps is doing very nicely & all divers rifts seem done.

The work seems [to be] going very well & old Jelly is certainly running it far more thoroughly & competently than Bevan did, of course now it's easier there are less people, but things badly wanted sorting out & as long as Bevan was boss we couldn't interfere. I am going to see the hospital today. The house here now boasts what Hélène calls an 'oh hell clock', beats Marjie's into fits, rather clever of Jelly. It was in bits – part woodwork broken & works all any'ow. He collected same & has got the thing working after much labour & I gather 'oh hells' – hence Hélène's christening of it! But the result is magnificent.

So long darling
Diddles

Oct 28th [1915]

Mother dear –
We had a great meeting of the corps yesterday & everything most amicable. Things are being done on more businesslike & economical lines & I think the result will be a vast improvement. At least I hope so.

Reste à vois! [Remains to be seen]

Charles I have just flipped. He has a mania now which is to sit in the coal box, it has two good points from his point of view: 1 it is near the stove & fuggy, 2 it makes nice patterns on my clothes afterwards.

Yesterday they shelled Furnes again but no damage.

In the afternoon elsewhere an obus burst 4 to 5 yds behind the car on the road as I pulled up. But beyond making a few holes in the back of Daniel did nothing – rather luck as it was on the pavé, the bits often travel – such is life – who cares.

I saw the dear old Admiral yesterday. The Marins have had very heavy losses these last 6 weeks. Fritz is very offensive with ammunition – I wish he could run out sometimes.

Yr loving Diddles

Oct 29th 'no 14'

Mother dear –
Just going down to beastly old Dunkirk to do all manner of gadgets. Thank heaven the rain has stopped for the 1st minute since I got back.

107

I got two such nice letters from you last night. Thank you very much for them & for all you say.

I am so glad to hear Bill is a little better, but am afraid it is still very bad. You won't forget to send me a line as soon as you hear anything, will you please. I am glad Aunt Emma [Bill's mother] got over after all.

My garden here is very sad & desolate, only a few mingy nasturtiums to represent all its past glories – it is depressing.

Besides Jelly is in a bad temper this morning & that is depressing too!

Or perhaps it is that I am in a bad temper.

P'raps that's it?

I shouldn't wonder!

Hélène is so well & so bucked to see me again. She thought I wasn't coming back until the spring for, as she remarked, 'There is mud – Mslle hates so much mud – why should Mslle come back to the mud?'

On the whole she is about right.

The war news is bad & it's despairing here to see the absolutely no change in my absence except very heavy losses & nothing to show for it.

Goodbye all

Yr loving

Diddles

31st Oct

Beloved Mrs Ma –

It is damn cold – 'ow are you?

There is a wind here that blows right through you today. In at your boots & out by the lug. Have just had an e-normous lunch with the British Mission. All very affable & very pleasant & old Teck full of beans.

Very good lunch too & I am as full as an egg.

Hély O was there & says he is arranging for me to go & see the boys at Bethune – isn't that nice of him? I will give them a little time yet as I don't know when Peter gets back.

I must go out with Daniel now. This is a scrappy letter I fear.

Goodbye & so much love to you all

Yr loving

Diddles

1st Nov 15

Mother dear –

Oh dear more rain & more mud! I am just feeling as flat & backboneless as a kipper having been squashed so flat at mass just now; it was in a tiny chapel bursting with bulgy Belges of both sexes & all smelling like bad margarine. No room to stand let alone sit or kneel & if anyone can raise a prayer under these conditions they aren't human.

So I gave it up half way & have come in to write to you instead. Anyway I feel less profane so doing & I expect you agree?

Anyway the margarine smell is slowly dying away which is always something & I can say a Deo Gratias for that with proper fervour, if I can't for anything else.

The English sailors have had a bad time this week. Fritz had set his heart on knocking out their batteries, but fortunately failed – tho' entirely by luck. The management being excellent.

The floor for miles round was like a sieve.

They are all very well & all the same lot, no changes except of course the poor boy that was hit while I was home.

I am dining with H d'O tonight so will take this up for him to post, as it gets over so much quicker.

Evening at the general's –

Goodnight & thank you for your letter. I am so very glad to hear dear old Bill is better. Please God he will get quite well now. A lot of firing at N this afternoon & a good many losses I fear.

Much love darling DoDo

The 'English sailors' Dorothie refers to are the men of the Royal Naval Siege Guns who manned long-range naval guns in the sand dunes near Nieuport. Their mission was to provide long-range artillery support for British bombardments from the sea and to assist the Allied armies. Several of these naval officers became good friends with Dorothie, who they called 'Lady D'. Halahan was their Commanding Officer and Brewill, known as 'Burbidge', was in charge of a gun which Dorothie called 'Mother' in an attempt to outwit the censors. Two other officers, 'Ginger' and 'Deb', were also involved with the battery and became friends of Dorothie. As the RNSG had no medical facilities, arrangements were made for the Munro Corps to provide a doctor and ambulance as required. As with everything to do with the guns at the beginning it all appears a bit ad hoc.

Newnham Lutterworth No I'm not!
I'm at no 14 & it's the 2nd Nov or 3rd

Mother dear –
More rain – oh dear & I have just been doing accounts – 'ate it just.

At mass this morning my prayers were interfered with once more, this time it was an old lady kneeling next to me, who kept flopping down with a wump [*sic*]– saying one 'Ave' about & then diving out of the church for about 30 seconds, & then coming back again. I think it must be that awful habit invented by some infernal pope, whereby the faithful are obliged to pay 58 visits to the church, & get over the system by coming in & out one after another. I know it's a game the convent children always play in Holy Week, anyway this old lady had it bad, by the 42nd time she had come in & out I started getting palpitations from the nervous strain.

Yesterday there was heavy firing at N — about 3.30pm. Fritz shelled the Marin trenches with fury for half an hour & Minenwerfer & trench mortar 'torpilles' too & a lot of rifle fire. But they didn't attack – so I don't know why they did it. The poor Marins lost a good many men about 30 or 40 & four officers killed & wounded.

Fritz has been doing this every 2 or 3 days, all October they say. Never attacks, but shells a small bit of trench each time very heavily, just as if they were preparing an attack.

That was an interesting letter from Da about Greece.

I fear USA & Greece are non-starters that nothing will shake.

Jelly is typewriting like mad & wobbling the table, blow him – so I will stop – as it drives all intelligent thoughts out of my head.

I am so glad Bill is better

Much love dear

DoDo

Nov 4th

Mother dear –

I have just eaten 5 lbs of Marrons glacés & can't describe to you the feeling of satisfaction, reflection & nausea that have taken possession of me as a result.

I'd sell my soul for Marrons glacés any day & as Jelly & Charles don't like them I eat the lot which is so satisfactory. The Gen sent them to me yesterday bless him, also he asks me to 'lay at your feet his homage & respect'.

He was delighted with your letters & very touched, when you have time write him again because he has the fixed idea now that you don't believe him when he says I ought to be good & that I have told you to pay no attention to anything he tells you!

As this is far the case, & words can't describe the trouble he takes to anything for us, I should be grateful if you would remove the illusion when next you write.

Just up to see Mairi & Mrs K- at P-. It appears their dugout was sunk in a bit by an obus yesterday. I hope they aren't having too bad a time up there.

I am so glad Bill is better but beyond Bettie's scrawl about it, it is all I have heard.

Must fly now – have spent the morning on our heads getting half cwt of mud out of Daniel's guards.

Yr loving Diddles

Nov 5th 15

Mother dear –
A quiet day today, went up to the hospital to see the blessés, lunched with Mairi & Mrs K up there too. It appears poor dears they nearly had a fit yesterday. The English girl was wounded & the Belgian lady killed & a Belge dashed up to Mrs K & Mairi to tell them I had been killed so they tore down in a car poor dears in an awful state.

I am glad to say the 2 English girls are going on well. They were only touched & escaped by a miracle.

Yesterday a lot of shelling too at N but quieter today. There were no blessés & we met Duforge (Hughie's friend ADC!) blowing up a mine – a German one come in on the coast by itself; it appears it is a new variety, they haven't seen before so it was treated with great reverence.

Blown up with gun cotton but disappointing because tho' half filled with about a barrel full of gun cotton squares (like bricks as Hughie had a sample of) it had got overdamp from long exposure in the water. Result just the case blew up & scattered the gun cotton all over the shore but it didn't go off with a magnificent burst as we expected but only a half hearted affair.

Still it was interesting to see one. Charles developed a love for chewing & chasing the gun cotton squares & by the time we left was full of it.

That was all very well as long as it was damp but on coming in he would sit next the stove & I expected him to blow up any minute.

It is now 10.15pm & he hasn't gone off yet so I trust he will pull through after all – if he lasts over night.

My beloved Admiral R is promoted which I fear means he will be moved. I sincerely trust not but we shan't know for 2 or 3 days, if it means he or his brigade moved I shall be very sad indeed. We have worked for them so long & they have done so splendidly one gets very attached to them.

Of course it's a leg up for the Admiral but I am not unselfish enough to wish him moved.

One of the English (Halahan's) guns had a very bad time today but no one hit I am glad to say.

I have borrowed Gurney's gramophone & Jelly has gone on the night round so it's nice & quiet & I have been enjoying myself with a young concert of records that Gervase Elwes & Hubert Eisdell sent me of their songs such good ones too – it's charming to hear something nice.

I must go to bed now – goodnight – DoDo

5th Nov 15 night

Mother dear –

Just got two very nice letters from you – very many thanks for your prayers from me on All Souls, darling. I slipped out to an early HC at the convent chapel here.

Today & yesterday, tragedies at Furnes: yesterday they shelled the town & a soldier was killed not far from 14. Today a lot of aeroplane bombs in our district again & hit slightly two English ladies (Red X) newly arrived who have been feeding the poor Belgian refugee kiddies at a 'lean to' school some 500 yds from here. They aren't bad I believe, it happened while I was at N today. But a Belgian lady working with them at the same work was killed I am sorry to say.

Thank you for sending me my 'blessé' book. I am sure I showed it you Mrs Ma as it was for that reason I bought it home last time & the others saw it.

It is a book in which the Gen enters the 'mentioned in despatches' of all the men in the N district in the regiments for which we work. It is a nice idea & I like my book very much indeed as I know so many of them – Zouaves & Marins. There are a lot of new entries to go in since Aug that is why I sent for it.

I hoped you looked at it before sending it, if I was idiot enough not to show it you at home – I am so sorry if that was the case.

There is a rather nice picture of Daniel in the dunes at the beginning by the General.

I went to R——-pelle today, the 1st time since my return – ye Gods what a mess! You know it was knocked to blazes while I was at home. There wasn't much then to wave your arms about – but now it is pathetic.

There is scarcely a bit of wall left to take cover behind now & all the old 'postes' & the diverse sheltered nooks Daniel used to be berthed in, are flat!

It was very fortunate none of the bombs today fell on the children's school. As it was, Hélène tells me the poor mites were scared to death & screamed & thought the end of the world had come. It was terribly near to the school & would have been ghastly had it been hit.

I have been giving lots of the kiddies scarves & things round 14. They are so bucked poor little souls. The next door to us is a family of Mama &

her married daughter living together in a wee cottage; population is nine kids under 14!! So you see you must be thankful for only 2 stugs at NP! The husband was killed at Furnes & they are terribly poor so I do what I can for them. Tell Bettie if there are any old children's warm clothes at home, jerseys etc they would be so grateful for them.

I wrote Nana about my blessé book to save you trouble but it apparently failed in its object!

Much love dears

Goodnight DoDo

Nov 8th 1915

Mother dear –

I am afraid these last 2 days I have been rather busy & had a lot of corps things to write so you won't have heard from me – 'scuse me. Tonight I dine with the Gen so this will get you quicker to make up. I have an 'evening out' on Mon there excepting if there is any work on.

Young Field blew in yesterday & sends you salaams. He is a Capt in artillery now as all those 3 pounder cars have been made army & not RNVR which seems far more sensible, they were in action a good deal he says that last advance & did quite well only lost a few men.

Furnes has been quiet since I last wrote I am glad to say.

Things just the same only Fritz has been shelling the French rather badly all week.

We haven't yet heard if Ronarc'h leaves or not I very much fear he will & it is very sad indeed. I wish to goodness they hadn't promoted him – we have worked for them since the very beginning & it would be very tragic now to lose sight of them.

Charles yesterday amused us at N Bains – he has become the most awful thief & is always on the steal. This time he had collared a Zouave's 'biftek' [beefsteak] ration & was slinking along a wall with it. The biftek was just in the process of being swallowed & half down the throttle, when a French 75 battery suddenly opened fire close by & made the most frightful echo & noise against the side of the house. Charles thought it was all because he had been found out, had a guilty conscience & jumped into the air with fright, threw up (ahem!) his biftek & bolted for the car! Much laughter from the Zouaves!

I will write you more this evening from the General's.

8pm/alas – it is only too true. The Admiral is being given a sea command & the whole brigade broken up & sent back to the navy as they can no longer spare the personnel.

113

I can't tell you how truly grieved & sad I am. It is impossible to work so long for such a magnificent set of men as they have been without becoming deeply attached to them. I do not mean to individuals although as you know they have always been such good friends to me I shall miss them dreadfully but also the Brigade in the 'abstract'. They are such a splendid lot & I love them all. They have such a 'moral[e]' & are such a gallant crowd. I feel like them as Rollo does of his Coldstreams. It is like a bit of one's self & I feel just as sad at seeing them go as he was to [have] his guards brigade leave him or still worse be disbanded.

Goodnight dear – Much love DoDo

No14

Nov 9th

Mother dear –

They shelled Furnes again today but did not do much damage except one poor old lady was killed in her house.

I am going to see the Mission tonight. Johnie Baird is just over from England & may have some news – all this about K [Kitchener] is very confusing.

You know the two English Red X girls that got wounded here the other day? One of them is back again already & has just been in to see me, she is a Miss McNeil, the MP's daughter, a very nice girl. Do you remember she came home on the boat with us from Gib[raltar] that time we stayed with the Archie Hunters? We saw a good deal of her then & she was travelling alone & put in our charge? It is funny her being now some 300 yds away isn't it?

Such a wet day today. Fritz inactive & besides shooting at Furnes which he can't miss with his eyes shut he hasn't been at all offensive.

I was too energetic for words today & spent from 9.30 am to 4 pm, with lunch interval for 'OXO', under Daniel on my tummy, scraping the mud off with a coal chisel. Jelly upside down the while in the engine girds the result is magnificent & Daniel clean inside & out & he doesn't know himself.

Tis sad to think he will be as bad in 2 or 3 days.

Much love dears

Diddles

No 14
10th Nov 15

Mother dear –

Dined at the Mission yesterday & Johnnie full of chat – he says K is for Egypt only & not Balkan forces.

I can't think of any news for you, I posted a letter last night & I must write this early in the morning so as to post it by the sailors in the afternoon & nothing of interest has happened in the meanwhile. They shelled Furnes feebly yesterday & killed one poor woman in her home.

Civilians are scarcer & scarce now.

Rather a nice yarn about my Marins I forgot to tell you – one funny old commander, mad keen & very excitable, & a bosom pal of the Admiral's, went out in an aeroplane (strictly against rules) to drop bombs on Ostend last week.

He enjoyed himself hugely & had a real good 'hate' when to his despair on the way home when they had nothing more to drop, he saw a large squad of Huns! The aviator flew low, & the commander dragged off his top boots & threw them with all his vim at the Boche at which he felt better (but had somewhat cold feet by the time he got back to Dunkirk!). Like a Marin!

Goodbye Mother dear – Je t'aime tu sais? [I love you you know?]

Diddles

15 Nov 15

No14

In bed/Gott strafe Tonks

By the way please pay no attention to Jelly & my old appetite, he has it on the brain! I never do eat much out here. Don't need it somehow – it's only at NP one wants to eat for 10! Out here I need half the food & sleep I do at home always.

Mother dear

I got so many letters from you all of a heap yesterday, I fear I will have to [go] some days without. All diverse dates from the 9th to the 12th about choose to arrive on the same day.

I am in bed with a stomach ache, Charles, a Jim [hot water bottle] & lots of books, not bad on the whole as it means an idle & a peaceful day. I was to do my usual Mon supper at chez the Gen but have had him come here. He tells me he has had a charming letter from you & was very pleased. What with you telling Jelly I'm to have Bengers which I hate & the Gen I'm not to have Marrons glacés which I love, death is losing its sting!

This morning, Grand événement [great event], Mrs Knocker & Mairi came in & sat on my bed bursting with excitement & Mrs K proceeded to apologise for all the diverse unpleasant remarks she ever made to me & to swear she never meant them, wouldn't do so again. Much surprised I marvelled exceedingly & then the reason: she is engaged to a Belgian 'Lieut Baron Harold de T'Serclaes de Rattendael' & it is now announced & she is in devil of a flutter. It appears he is young & an Apollo & of a most noble 'family & quite ready to become a Protestant to please me my dear – isn't it sweet of him? But I think it might make unpleasantness out here if he did – so I shall become a Catholic instead & I want you to tell me how to do it etc etc!!!!'

Can't you see me, missionising Mrs K!

I at once assured her she had far better leave everybody's concerned religion as it was for the moment & think it over a little more! Anyhow she intends to get married some time before the spring & will probably live at La Panne & Mairi & Helen Gleason (who will return from America shortly) run the Poste at Pervyse together.

They have got one of the first houses as you go into the village arranged & fortified with cement & sand bags & dugouts & are quite safe & comfortable – a Ritz compared to what it used to be, although of course not so offensively Ritz as 'no14' is these days.

I had tea with Esther McNeil yesterday. Please tell her father I will always do anything I can to help her in any way. She lives only 300yds away, & I shall be only too glad to help her always. She is such a nice girl. The woman she lives with, Mrs Innes Taylor's nerves have gone to pot since that bomb. She is very jumpy & weepy as a result & I don't expect will get over it. But McNeil is absolutely normal from that point of view & none the worse. The little cut she had is now healed too, the 3rd a Canadian, Miss Saunders, is in hospital at La Panne for another fortnight yet, but will equally be none the worse eventually.

They run a clothing & food distribution for refugees & also feed the school children free. They are doing it very well & everybody is devoted to them.

A few of my Marins will, I think, be left but only about one-sixth & the Admiral of course going to a big command – tis most tragic.

Thank you so much Mother for your two dear letters – I loved them.

I am so terribly sorry about Bill – poor poor kid – so much love dear from DoDo

Nov 18th 15
Furnes

Mother dear –
Did I ever tell you the Admiral, before leaving, mentioned in despatches Dr Jelly, Mr Gilling & old Lyon & has proposed them for the X de Guerre same as I have? We haven't heard yet if it has been accorded or not as they

The Feilding children c.1903 (from right to left): Rudolph, Hugh, Mary, Dorothie, Agnes, Marjorie, ...nry, Clare, Elizabeth and Victoria.

...Da – Rudolph Robert Basil Aloysius ...gustine Feilding, 9th Earl of Denbigh.

3. From left to right: Rudolph, Viscount Feilding (Rollo), Cecilia Countess of Denbigh (Ma), Imelda, Viscountess Feilding (Mellins), Dorothie and Clare (Squeaker) at Newnham Paddox.

4. Far right: Doctor Hector Munro. According to Dorothie 'He's a well meaning & enthusiastic little man, but as to being in charge of anything or anyone, let alone himself, it's a jest.'

5. The original female contingent of the Munro Corps (from left to right): Mairi Chisholm, Elsie Knocker (Dr Jellett – 'Jelly'), Helen Hayes Gleason and Dorothie. May Sinclair was part of the original corps, but did not last long.

6. Dorothie shortly after her arrival in Flanders. 'It's topping being up near things and so jolly interesting', 8 October 1914.

7. The reality of spending some time near the front line in Flanders. 'It must be 3 weeks now since we got to bed before 2 or 3 in the morning and many nights later', April 1915. Note the Coldstream Guards badge on her tie. The Feildings had a long and illustrious association with the Coldstream.

8. Belgian armoured car 'auto-canons'.

9. Dorothie with Elsie Knocker (left) and Mairi Chisholm (right), November 1914.

10. Fusiliers Marins at Melle, October 1914.

11. A lighter moment for the camera – Dorothie taking refreshment as Robert de Broqueville, who was in military command of the Corps, looks on. Dorothie notes on the reverse that this 'picnic' was hurriedly broken up by Teutons.

12. A typical Belgian dressing station, 'poste de secours', location unknown, c.1915.

13. Dorothie at the second house in Pervyse.

14. Admiral Ronarc'h (second from the left), 'a dear old boy', with Dorothie and his staff.

15. Dorothie at the wheel, with Mellins. The immediate family visited the front on a number of occasions.

16. Dorothie's note on reverse: 'Shell bursting in Furnes Grande Place. No sign of me as you see!' March 1915.

17. 'D in "Daniel" in Furnes just after a shelling of the Grande Place. Everybody out looking for "bits"!' Undated.

. 'Perfectly gigantic' shell hole at Nieuport, 15 yards across, made by a German 17-inch shell. March 1915.

19. Dorothie with Ronarc'h's staff at the review to celebrate a successful Zouave attack at Lizerne. The Regiment lost 800 men out of 2,000.

20. At the same review (right to left): 'Hély d'Oissel with back turned, a French aviator got VC, French Colonel got order, Marin officer being decorated with Legion of Honour by Admiral Ronarc'h, young Ronarc'h tying ribbon.'

21. Dorothie and Dr Jellett, 'Outside our new home', No. 14, Furnes.

22. Dorothie's garden at Furnes, many of the plants purloined from abandoned gardens in the town. She describes the 'garden stiff with flowers, & so nice & charming & peaceful it's a joy to roll into after the day's work instead of dirty lodgings or the hospital scrum', 23 May 1915.

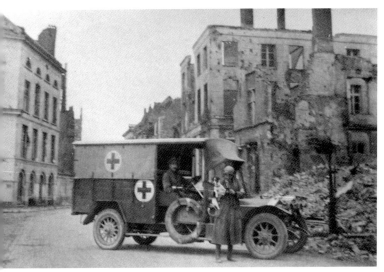

23. Dorothie with Charles (the dog) in Ypres, June 1915. Driver identified as 'Secker'.

24. Dorothie posing with an *obus*, a practice she frowned upon in her letters: 'a Belge near ''No. 14'' was blown up last week messing with an unexploded shell in his back garden close by – poor chap. It is absolutely impossible to impress a Belge with the futility of this particular sport ... ''Mees'' however is very firm & always refuses to play it.'

25. Marin trenches, Nieuport. Note copious use of sandbags.

26. Reverse of photo reads: 'Ambulance at Furnes. Driver was hit.' Proof positive that Dorothie and the Corps ran real risks.

. 'Me up an observatory watching some firing. This was taken by a wag up there!' 1915.

. Dr Jellett and Dorothie dressed for the harsh anders winter. The ambulances were on the hole open to the elements; one can only agine the discomfort.

29. Centre: Hughie – Lieutenant Commander Hugh Cecil Robert Feilding, HMS *Defence*.

30. General Roger Hély d'Oissel. When Doroth[e]
met him he was commander of the 7th Cavalry
Division in the French Eighth Army. Known as
'The Gen'.

31. General Hély d'Oissel with Dorothie outside
his bunker, where he used to carry her off for
dinner.

32. 'The Bloke' – Commander Henry Crosby
Halahan. A close friend and confidant of
Dorothie. He worked with the Royal Naval
Siege Guns in Flanders.

3. From left to right: Burbidge, Chalmers, Deb, Dorothie, Jelly and the Bloke.

4. Burbidge's 'Mother' – a 9.2 inch railway gun of the Royal Navy Siege Guns. Fifth from the right Lieutenant Arthur William Lancelot Brewill, known as 'Burbidge'. Dr Jellett can be seen to Burbidge's left. Sitting on the gun directly above Jellett's head is Charles, Dorothie's dog.

35. Third row, from right to left, Jellett, Burbidge and Halahan, presumably with some of the Royal Naval Siege Gun crews, undated. Note the number of mascots.

36. Ginger and Deb in the Dunes, 1916. 'Real nice healthy, happy, English boys & such good sorts', 24 November 1916.

37. Rollo (left), 3rd Battalion Coldstream Guards and Peter (right), who initially was in King Edward's Horse and later joined the 2nd Battalion Coldstream Guards.

38. Dorothie entertaining Prince Alexander of Teck in the garden at Furnes. Unidentified companion, possibly Winkie Speight.

39. Dorothie modelling her gas apparatus. She wrote in April 1917: 'It's a dirty business gas and rather frightening.'

40. Dorothie's wedding to Captain Charles Moore at Newnham Paddox was front page news despite their wish for a quiet ceremony. Note the convalescent soldiers bottom left; the house was a hospital from 1915 to October 1917.

GERMAN PLOTTERS FOILED BY A GIRL: See P.2

DAILY SKETCH.
THE PREMIER PICTURE PAPER.

No. 2,597.   LONDON, FRIDAY, JULY 6, 1917.   ONE PENNY.

LADY DOROTHIE FEILDING'S WEDDING: WOUNDED SOLDIERS GREET THEIR HEROINE.

give them very reluctantly to ambulance people, except for special reasons. This because at the beginning it was much abused & diverse Red X 'embusqués' [shirkers] pulled strings & awarded themselves medals at the base!

The Marins have invited us to a farewell party tonight, I foresee an awful orgy of at least 25 courses, 58 divers drinks & many speeches, oo-er. These things take years off one's life.

We had a young one at No 14 a few nights ago for the chief Marin doctors & it was very successful & very merry because I didn't give them more to eat than was good for them! or let them be pompous!

Been doing a lot of work this morning with buckets of damn cold water washing the body of Daniel while Jelly as usual put his head & ears in the gear box.

No time for more now.

Goodbye dear & thank you so much for writing me so many & such nice letters.

About 1,300 Marins are being left to represent the flag. The idea being it would be a bit 'ard if at the moment 'de la victoire' (ahem) they were no longer represented having done so much of the dirty work.

The remaining 5,000 go to ships. Duforge (Hughie's pal) is remaining with the few left behind here he tells me.

Much love
DoDo

Friday – for sure
Nov 19th? [19 Nov]

'No14'

Mother dear –

Well the Marin doctors invited us to supper last night as I told you yesterday & I am glad to say it was not quite such an orgy as was expected & I got off with only 4 different coloured drinks & a liqueur that was so strong – God knows what – it nearly gave me a heart attack.

Then speeches at the end aimed at you & you feel you'd like to fall thro' the floor – you know the kind! But they said many kind things about what we had done for them & how sad they were to leave. And they meant it too which was nice of them. Then they drank my health 'la brave, la dévouée et la charmante' [the brave, dedicated and charming] & I had to try & tell them what fine chaps they were too etc only I didn't do it half so well.

This morning a little review in the dunes at which H d'Oissel said goodbye to the Brigade de Marins, a march past of Zouaves & Marins etc with their flag & it made me very sad indeed to realise it was the last time they would

117

'defile' anywhere anymore. I just love my Marins & get sadder & sadder as it is time for them to leave. In a fortnight there will only be the one battalion & a few odd people left to represent the brigade flag. It will be nice to have just a few 'Poms Poms Rouges' about the place still.

Our cars are being attached to the infantry brigade which is replacing the Marins.

It's extraordinary how the Boche knows everything going on, several days ago he shouted over to the Marins in their trench 'I say when are you being going away? We thought you had gone?'

This before the men themselves even knew they were being taken away!

Good bye Mother dear

Yr loving

Diddles

21st Nov 15

'no14'

Dear Mother –

I enclose you a letter from dear old Ronarc'h which you might put by with my letters for me please. I hope he may possibly get down here for a day to say goodbye as when called up he left at 10 min notice & no one knew he was off – me neither, which was very sad. He was wired for suddenly.

I fear Our Lady would turn in her grave (or hasn't she one? I really forget?) at my being likened to her respected self.

Oh dear it's so cold today, everything freezing like mad.

Yesterday they strafed N—t like anyfink all day & put I don't know how many obus into it. Total casualty (as everyone went to dugouts) was one of the doctor's medicine chests! The obus had gone right through the chest & you should have seen his instruments when Fritz had done with them, one pair artery forceps he gave me with a bow as a moment of a 'Kultur' invention of a special instrument for 'cutting in tricky corners'!

So long dears.

Yr loving Diddles

Nov 23 15
Furnes

Mother dear –

I fear I haven't written you properly for some days but some how every minute I have been at 14 someone has bounced in about something & I couldn't get going on letters.

Our Marins are being gradually replaced & some are gone already. It is too sad I just can't bear saying goodbye to them all. They have all been wonderfully nice to us & they are my own particular regiment; even if the Admiral hadn't been promoted they would have been disbanded as they can't spare naval officers for infantry work any more; you can make a good infantry officer in a few months but the same amount of years to make an efficient naval officer.

The Admiral tore back for the afternoon here 2 days ago to say goodbye. He came without any warning & called at no14 but I was at N—t, luckily I got a message saying he was at his HQ & would I go at once so I legged it with Daniel & got there just in time to see him for 5 minutes before he left again. He was so sad at going & we were all very sorry too. He was such a nice mixture of capability (from military point of view), courage & absolute simplicity minus all swank, that made all his officers & men worship him, as a result he got everything from his men, where many might have got nothing.

The old boy said many kind things to me before he went off & then said to me run away quick – as he was so sorry to see me go – so I fled.

Today I have just passed all the Zouaves on the road coming to relieve the Marins, & I felt I wanted to shoot the lot.

Our cars are going to continue working for the brigade that succeeded them, & also for the remaining battalion of the Marins.

I have just been lunching with Mairi C at Pervyse. The only complaint I had to make was that she had adopted nine refugee cats of all colours & shapes & they keep peering over the back of the chair, into your lap when you aren't expecting & they gave me jim jams.

There is one vast one with a satanical smile just like Alice in Wonderland's Cheshire cat.

Mrs K is being married soon & Mairi's father is coming out to run the poste with her.

Much love DoDo

At the General's 28 Nov

Mother dear –

I have just had a delightful day down at Bethune with Rollo & Peter. Walter Baird at the last minute had urgent business & couldn't take me, & I was very sad indeed, when that saint Halahan offered to take me down so off we went he & I, had lunch & spent the afternoon with the boys. He dropped me at H d'Oissel's on the way back where I dine & then back to 14. Both the bricks were looking very well indeed & I was delighted to see them again. It was 3 or 4 months since I saw them.

Much love – great haste
DoDo

Le 30 Nov

Mother dear –
I have come down for a night to Broquevilles. They sent up a car to fetch me & I am having 2 days & a night off – a most depraved holiday!

I have just been out for a ride with Pierre de Broqueville, the 1st one I have had since Aug. It was most pleasant & we went a very nice ride up St Omer way, only about 6 miles from it & lots of English, big hills, a jolly view & special nice sunset this evening. I shall go for another ride tomorrow before going back.

Fritz has been less offensive just lately.

Goodbye & goodnight & thank you for all your nice letters.

I think Egypt is an excellent plan.

Keep it up! Da would love it so, & if anyone deserves a jaunt & a rest, it's you!

Yr loving
Diddles

3rd Dec

Mother dear –
2 or 3 of the Marins came to supper & say goodbye last night including old Commandant Paillet (who commands in the Admiral's absence) he is a great wag & a dear old boy.

I am just dashing off to get passes at the GHQ & have spent the morning getting mud off Daniel's underneath.

As I write I hear Jelly damning Hélène & 'oh hells' come drifting down on the breeze. I don't know what it's all at anyway as Hélène is out shopping, I don't s'pose twill fect [sic] her much!

I have now upset a mug of milk all over the table. I'll get strafed now I s'pose!

I'm off before I'm diskivered.

DoDo

Dec 4th

Mother darling –

I am so terribly sorry about poor Bill & especially for little Mellins, these last weeks must have been awful for her; for Bill, he is spared the horror & the terror of being crippled. One simply cannot wish that for anyone one cares for. It is the worst of all & a living death.

Bill's always so tremendously alive & young & happy. I cannot very well realise it all. I went out to mass & HC for him & Mellins today.

I enclose a long letter from Da & a silly one from the 'Novel Mag', to the latter I send a curt & somewhat rude epistle as follows 'Dear sir – most certainly not – DF'

Much love darling –
Yr DoDo

'Bill', Francis Edward Basil Harding, died 1 December 1915 at the age of twenty-eight and is buried at St Sever Cemetery, Rouen.

6th Dec

Mother dear –

This being Monday & I going up to the General's. I am writing a letter beforehand to give him to post.

It is simply awful about poor old Bill – I can't get it out of my head – it haunts one so.

I am so glad Marjie is up & better as she will be able to keep poor Mellins company I hope quite soon.

There is the most awful gale here today. I have been going the round of the cellars at Furnes trying to buy a kitchen clock.

Here all the shops, or a great many, go on selling their goods in the cellar. Even the jeweller of town told me today he still had all his things here. Although his house, with the exception of the basement was properly smashed up by a shell a few weeks ago.

As all the inhabitants have left I can't quite see who his clients for tiaras are! But he assured me he still did quite a good trade.

The last of the Marins left yesterday but there will always be a few about as they have decided to leave about 1,200 men here to represent their flag but I preferred the 6,000 of them!

Ronarc'h has been sat at the Admiralty for the present to unravel predecessor's muddles & he hates it like poison. He says he prefers a land command to a Paris office stool! Poor old boy. Apparently the new French minister (Navy) is A1 but the last one just left, left things in the most hopeless state of chaos & inefficiency.

The corps things out here doing quite well I am glad to say.
Well good night maman
Much love
DoDo

10th Dec

Mother dear – it seems a long time since I wrote. I don't quite know why. Have been interviewing all sorts of lousy officials all the week. On account of our taking over new work for the troops succeeding the Marins. It isn't at all the same now. Then we were attached solely to their brigade of 6,000 & did entirely & solely for them & it was like a large family. Now our cars are attached to the army corps & just do a small part of the general work. The cars do as much but it's not so individual or so pleasant. These officials too are all such fusspots, so different to the Marins & always making silly complicated difficulties.

In fact we regret our Marins more each day from every point of view & are all 'on the grievance' in consequence.

2 days ago we were going up to Lettenberg (the Belgian poste nr Dixmude we go to at night) by day; it's rather an exposed road in daylight & there is a 'safe' road coming up from behind, & a less safe one coming up horizontally. The latter is the better road so we took it after a short discussion. No sooner having arrived at the poste than they started strafing the 'safe' road like mad with 8 inch, & we had the satisfaction of watching a very pretty little hate for 20 min into some empty houses that didn't hurt anyone. Red roofs make a grand red smoke as they go up.

Moral, never try to be prudent.

Also I have discovered a new pattern 'abri' or dugout up there by a ruined cottage. I heard an obus coming & thought it was for me, & so did a dive into the only remaining portion of the building double quick time which turned out to be a Euclid! Such a picturesque place to be found blessé in, & would make such a nice column in the Daily Mail.

As a matter of fact too the obus went miles on & it was all for nothing.

Such a wet day yesterday & today too. I had a jaw with Mairi at Pervyse 2 days ago, she was very fit, her father is coming out to join her there & run the poste with her. Mrs K is getting married in Jan & I haven't heard yet if she has decided to become a vegetarian, a Parsee, a dancing dervish or a Catholic. I shouldn't be surprised if she got a little mixed in the choosing & turned out a bit of a mongrel. Then again if he is a papist & says she a dervish, what would the 'kittens' be??

In fact a very deep theological discussion that would make a nice subject for correspondence in the Tablet that could be directed by Snick.

Please put it en train for me.
  Goodbye & much love
  DoDo

Dec 12th 15

Mother dear –

Gen Bridges has just dashed in to say farewell. He leaves the 'Mish' to go as Major General to a Div in the 1st Army, good enough isn't it considering he started the war as a Lieut Col? Johny Baird is going on his staff but the Prince will stay on to maintain the dignity & grandeur of the Mish.

Bridges & I haven't had a scrap for months & months, over the 'Femme au front' question. That is all we ever fell out over. I always agreed with him entirely, but quite firmly declined to be moved! & all his diverse tactics to move me were foiled!

Personally he has always been very nice to me & he is a jolly good soldier & bound to do well.

It's a great bore. I have diverse new photos to send you, but il n'q a pas moyen [there is no way]. Lately all photos are torn up that are sent by either Belgian, French or English posts so it's 'ardly good enough.

I am feeling rather sick as I have eaten too much cake for tea.

The stugs sent me a most luscious pork pie in tin. I strongly advise it as a 'medical comfort' to be sent to a Red X nurse at the front.

  Goodnight & love from
  DoDo

George Tom Molesworth Bridges, head of the British Mission in Belgium had obviously disapproved of ladies at the front. He had served in Somaliland at the turn of the century and was awarded the DSO in 1904. At the outbreak of the war in 1914 he was a Lieutenant Colonel in the 4th Hussars and greatly distinguished himself during the retreat from Mons that autumn. Many stories have grown up around his exploits.

Dec 18th

Mother dear – I must write you for Xmas, though I can't believe it is upon us again – or so near either. But I want to wish you with all my heart that it won't be too sad or too anxious a one for you; you have been such a wonderful person to all your curious sons and daughters. You can't think how grateful we are for all your love & help through life. The Almighty really was splendid the way he chose our parents, without so much as one

123

of us on the spot to arrange it either! Poor Mother – the war has brought you many anxious hours I fear but please God it will be over some day, & it is a little better now the 2 boys have safe billets & you needn't be so terrified for them.

I do so hope your visit to Mr Da comes off. He will be so mad with joy & it will be so good for you too.

It is late & I am going to bed with 'Jim' the hot water bottle & that arch Hun Tonks (won't this surprise the censor?? How disappointing if he never opens this one!)

So goodnight Mother dear, & God bless you more times than I can say for all your love & sympathy. Indeed I'm grateful & you know it don't you?

Yr so loving

Diddles

You mustn't worry about me you know, I haven't been obussed, not close for weeks & weeks & weeks & weeks.

Really & truly shelp [*sic*] me, as Neb says.

21 Dec

Mother darling –

I wonder if you have settled anything about Egypt yet? I am waiting breathlessly to see.

You said in one letter, that with the dead one is much nearer to them, than before, & that one looks forward to meeting them again. But Mother, try as I will, I just can't make myself believe really & truly in my heart & hearts that we shall any of us ever see them again. I think there is just an endless blank that begins after death & that all things finish there.

I try & try to believe that there's a future, but I can't any more. I suppose it's seeing so many lives go out in their youth & strength, like the wind blowing out a light: people were, & they are not & that is all.

While alive one must do one's best to help everyone, & that is best done by doing right but why we should expect or need anything after I really can't see?

It seems to me quite right like that & I am quite content.

Yr loving DoDo

21 Dec
At the General's

Mother dear I am so frightfully sorry that the Egypt trip looks like fizzling out. I did so want you to have a real good holiday & see dear Mr Da, & Squeaker too, it would have done her so much good & she was looking forward to it just frightfully. I think more than perhaps you realised.

But after all you may go yet I s'pose, though I feel somehow you aren't really trying any more & will let things slide which is very wrong of you & I shall scold you for it proper so pull up your socks Mrs Ma, & go to Egypt like a good girl – don't forget mind – I mean it – this is such an ideal time for you to go from every point of view. Quiet over here on the W front for the winter, the boys a nice safe billet & things can't possibly happen in Egypt yet a while, though if you put it off any longer – you will be really had then & serve you right if you do!

I am really very angry with you – I mean it – I mean it.

Fritz has woken up these last 2 days, today he threw 900 obus round poor old N but no one seemed to mind in the least & yesterday he had quite a little hate & chewed up the roads a lot, one place getting over the debris today the poor old ambulance 'Daniel' had to do the prettiest bit of alpine climbing he's met yet in Flanders. Got stuck too on Mont Blanc & had to get gunners to push us off.

One battery of French 75 had got real hell near by, every gun shelter knocked to Jericho, & a mess of twisted girders, sand bags, debris round & on each gun yet not one damaged to matter & no one hit. It is one of the best escapes I've seen for a long time & how the guns weren't put out of action permanently defeats me.

The gunners were very bucked today, told us proudly they had dragged the guns out from the décombres [rubble] safely at night & had put them up in a new position nearby & were just going to have a pip at Fritz to say 'yaa boo' & show they were none the worse! They were perfectly delighted with themselves!

Yesterday at 5am the Germans started a gas attack on all the Gen's troops to the right of the Belgians & the English lines down to opposite Ypres. But everyone was expecting it & they opened a diabolical artillery fire, so that the Germans were never able even to leave their trenches.

Also the new pattern gas masks were very successful & the men stood it perfectly this time, which is very satisfactory, as being the 1st time there has been no trace of panic or disorganisation as a sequel to those ghastly gases.

I am dining with the General tonight & he sends his love.

Goodnight dears

DoDo

125

26th Dec

Mother darling. Many thanks indeed for telegraphing to me for Xmas & about Ronarc'h. I am glad he has a button.

I sent you a wire too on Xmas eve – I wonder if you got it?

Here I had quite a nice Xmas, lunch at 12.30 in a hurry, a round to N— with the car, where Fritz amused himself with obus, but total casualty one dent in a soldier's tin hat! At any rate the only one in our vicinity. Then a dinner with the English sailors which was very nice. The 'Mish' had asked me but I had already promised the sailors a long time ago. We had an absurd evening with a great battle with toy howitzers & dried peas as ammunition. Charles was a great nuisance at the most critical moments of the battle, as he was feeling awfully frisky & would dash in, devour the ammunition & try to slay the howitzers!

They have got a new man, RNVR Lieut Lord Maidstone (married Drexel Yank girl) there now, very quiet & seems nice.

We even had pale pink candle shades tho' it's true the candles were stuck on to pieces of obus & the shades cut out of pink blotting paper by Ginger! – still it was very fine.

Xmas eve I went to my Marins' midnight mass which was very beautiful and impressive. Just a little ready made altar, & a big crucifix all smashed by shelling, & nothing but the Marins, who sang hymns in Breton, & all of them came. I was very glad I was able to go. The Gen arranged for me to.

Teck is supping here on Wed at 14. Hélène in an awful flutter & says 'What on earth is she to give a real prince to eat? – c'est affreux!!' [It's frightful!]

Thank Bettie for her nice Xmas letter. I fear it was a very sad one for all at home.

Here both sides were very very quiet all day not like last year when each side was out to spoil the other's plum pudding.

Barring a bit of shelling at N in the afternoon it was quite quiet everywhere & last night not a sound anywhere which was refreshing.

Goodbye Mother dear.

Love from DoDo

27 Dec at the General's

Mother dear – Our mails have been terribly hung up lately owing to hanky panky on Fritz's part in the channel, the result being we only get mail once every 3 or 4 days as there are fewer boats for the present. This of course equally applies to the delay in my letters to you. By the way I was surprised to find that letter via the Gen took 6 days. Just notice how long this takes, as I think that one must have been a freak.

I got such a dear letter from you tonight, my Xmas letter. Poor Mother dear – I am so sorry your family have been 'stuffing', they want smacking! You say Peter was stuffy last time, do you mean morally or a cold in his head?

I loved your letter & thank you for it so much. Also a nice one from Squeaks, Bettie & Taff which I will answer anon. I am very disappointed at Egypt being off, you shouldn't have put it off & off but gone earlier. It was very wrong of you you know.

Goodnight Mrs Ma & so much love – DoDo

At the Broquevilles'

Dec 29th

Mother deah –
I have a beautiful & lovely plot I have hatched, to make up for your not having gone to see Da.
It is that you & Squeaker come & see me!! Pa Broqueville & I have arranged it all & it is as follows:
1) You come & stay here (not far from Dunkirk) with Broqueville for a week. He is a week here & a week at Havre alternately so you have only to choose any of the times he would be here. He says he would be delighted to put you up any time after Jan 14th you select. He suggested this scheme himself, you bring Squeaker too of course, that is most important, & I promise you I won't take her to the lines or get either of you blown up.
2) Passes I will arrange for you – you wire me 'delighted – could manage any day after –' I then arrange with Broqueville the earliest date that fits in with him. I send you a letter from him authorising you to come which will secure you passports etc quite easily in London.
3) You go to Boulogne or Calais from whence his car (me in it) brings you here. I will arrange to come & stay here then too of course & will give myself a few days holiday.
4) Then we will collect you a temporary pass & you & Squeaks will come & stay a night at Furnes at 14, be introduced to Hélène & Charles, the General & all the rest.
5) Then you return here, get into a car when you like & return to Boulogne & voila!
Total expense 3rd class ticket to Boulogne 25/- & I will stand Squeaks hers. So Ma dear, send me a wire please if you intend coming soon as it will take me a week to get the necessary passes over to you, & you a couple of days in London to get passports etc, visa'd.
Won't that be nice now? So mind you do it. I should love to do you the

honours of No 14 & so would Hélène & I would love to give little Squeaks a little jaunt to make up for Egypt falling thro'.

Now don't put it off like Da, or you will find NP a hospital & you tied down later on.

Furnes hasn't had a bomb or shell on it for 6 weeks & no 14 being outside the town proper is as safe as Tooting now or I wouldn't invite you. Also it's a palace now & very comfy & a beautiful spare bedroom & Squeaks must get into mine to get up a proper fug together.

So do please, please come. I shan't be back in England for months & months yet after my long autumn leave & it would do you good too.

Luv DoDo

Dec 30th

Mother darling

I gather you must have got our invitation last night & the General & I decided last night to strafe you no end if you invent silly reasons for not coming out. Had a great supper party here last night, Alexander of Teck, Hély d'Oissel, Halahan & Jelly & I & Charles.

Had a very fine supper as the Gen brought us asparagus & someone sent us foie gras for Xmas.

Helena very 'émue' [emotional] at Teck coming & nearly chucked a fit whenever she met him, & was horrified because he insisted on doing butter & carrying out the dirty plates!

It was quite a joke & he enjoyed himself, he's a dear old boy & not at all pompous.

He is now Brigadier Gen & head of the Mission instead of Bridges so is very bucked with himself.

Must go to N-t now, two days ago the commander's car ahead of ours was rather badly hit & the radiator torn. Luckily the man was in a dugout & the commander on foot near by at a battery & so no one hit but a poor old mule.

We had to wait for a half of an hour before we could get by – love DoDo

Jan 4th

Mother dear –

That's just too nice about your being able to come out. Hélène is madly excited at meeting Squeaker whom she hasn't seen yet. She remembers you quite well from Dr Joos' house. What fun we will have, I will smuggle you up here for a few days & knock off work, as you won't be allowed in the lines now it's much stricter but I can take you up to the English hospital & show you the beauties of Furnes & get the General etc to come & see you here.

No 14 is too smart for words these days. I trust you will be duly impressed, it is nearly as luxurious as Frankton & very different from pigging in old days.

In fact if you or Squeaker feel it isn't warlike or exciting enough & disappoints you, I will sprinkle a few barbed wire entanglements around the bedroom, remove the mattress & the soap, break a window or two, in fact anything to please you.

I see Rollo is mentioned in despatches again, isn't that splendid?

But I hope he won't be in a position to earn any more for a long time yet – if ever. It's a hobby full of drawbacks

Yr loving DoDo

CHAPTER 9

January–May 1916

The Countess and Clare spent over a week at the front visiting Dorothie and attending the wedding of Mrs Knocker to the Baron de T'Serclaes. Shortly after they left, the Germans launched an attack in the sector around Nieuport, as reported in the Rugby Advertiser *of 29 January 1916:*

> *The attack near Nieuport ... was preceded by a bombardment in which no fewer than 20,000 shells were employed, ended in the pulse of the Germans, who were unable to advance except at one point, where some groups managed to penetrate the French advanced trenches. A grenade struggle, however, cleared out the enemy, who suffered 'appreciable losses'.*

Jan 23rd

Mother Darling
It was such fun & so nice having you over here. You can't think how I loved it, & it was fun showing you Hélène & no14 & all the flora & fauna of the district. We have an awful lot of gadgets & car repairs to do now to make up for being so lazy!

It was awful making such a scrum for you at Boulogne by that damn boat going before her time, it was a real dirty trick to play on a Countess & our editor.

Did Squeaks get her precious obus home alright? Mind you let me know, she is set up in copper goods for her life anyway.

It's a dear brat that & I'm so glad she enjoyed herself.

Goodbye darling
Yr loving
DoDo

Jan 25th

Mother dear –
Things have been humming a bit here since you left. The Boche took it into his head to attack both the General's sectors yesterday. He was repulsed, but

got 30,000 obus off his chest, & cost us a good many casualties. They shelled poor N very badly indeed, one tower very broken & the other knocked clear down by 12inch. There were about 150 casualties up this end, but the Boche did not get far & had to give it up.

By bad luck we had arranged to take that day off for repairing Daniel & replacing diverse worn spare parts. When both his forewheels & radiator & steering column were down the firing started! & it took us all the afternoon till dark & after before we could get him together again so he wasn't much help alas. Today was quieter, & we have just got in from a long trip with blessé from N to that faraway French base hospital I showed you from the road. Yesterday was halfhearted as attacking went, very few actually left their trenches but the bombardment was very heavy. I have got the most awful pain in my underneath yesterday & today. I don't know what it is or why but I hate it so I'm going to bed early with Jim – so excuse a short letter.

You chose your time to come quite beautifully.

Much love

DoDo

26th Jan 16 at the General's

Mother Dear –

We had a little hate back on our beat today to make up for Fritz's one of 2 days ago. Total casualties were more than I told you yesterday at N district, about 180 in all, but lucky not to have more. Wasn't it hard lines Daniel being laid up just the one day we happened to want him most? But things are rather excited these days generally. Burbidge fired today & got one shot within 10 yds of 'Mother', but otherwise less close than usual. Usually whenever he fires they have a bad time.

The pain in my underneath has gone I'm glad to say, it wasn't at all popular & I think realised it!

Have just got yours & Squeaker's letters from London, poor you to have so awful a journey. I do hope you weren't too done up. I am so glad you enjoyed yourselves. I only hope you liked coming as much as I liked having you, it was very depressing for 2 or 3 days after you had gone tho'. I am delighted no one yaffled Squeaker's coffee pots & obus. It would have been the end of all things. Much love – DoDo

Jan 28th

Mother Darling –

Only time for a short scrawl as am off to N. Spent a scurried morning in Dunkirk doing chores or rather I sent the old MD off to do chores & went got my hair washed. A real luxury. I said to the fat lady who shampooed me 'My hair is very dirty isn't it?' She answered cheerfully – 'Yes, mademoiselle and smells like fish'. Tell Squeaker that accounts for that curious smell of bloaters she complained about in our bed at 14.

No14 is still very lovely

But today we've been given a black swan to eat. Hélène very émue & says it won't fit in the oven & what form of a bête [beast] is it anyway?

If we die of indigestion you will know why.

Charles I feel will like it.

After these few stormy days things very quiet again DG. I see the English papers say it was another bid for Calais – what rot!

Much love DoDo

30 Jan

Mother Darling. Just see how nicely my pen is writing? Aren't you sorry you gave it to me?

Great strafing today. You know the 'cloakroom' at 14? The little alcove off the baronial hall that Hélène refuges in when Fritz bombs? Well the T Surgeon diskivered Charles had made a 'cache' for bones in his spare overcoat … sensation … Charles very depressed at the loss of his loot too.

What do you think we had for supper tonight? A black swan from Australia. Or rather he's been going on for 3 days now & he has reached the soup stage & we are getting decidedly weary of him. Cooking swan too has a most curiously penetrating smell & everything one touches from British warms to pyjamas has a pungent swan odour attached – I confess I'm rather tired of it.

Saw the Commander today who tells me he may have to go to Bethune to see about some business & guns & he has sworn to hide me in the tool chest as before & I can play around with Tubby while he does jobs, which sounds most pleasant & I only hope it will come off.

There is only a fragment of Shoppee's tower left after that last shelling at _____ & the 2nd one you saw from that mound is absolutely down, only a mound of bricks & I am sorry to say a French officer observer was killed in it.

Shoppee, luckily for him, was not on duty that day as his batteries weren't firing.

We had a concert for the blessés at Hoogstadt yesterday, given by different soldiers; it was quite good & of course the success of the evening as far as the blessés were concerned, was a vulgar man who sang about quite unmentionable subjects in quite unmentionable terms, in a piercing & very distinct voice!

We took McNeil & the Saunders girl up with us.

Goodnight Mrs Ma & God bless you. Did I tell you 'Burbidge' has been lent to the Belgians for a week or two & as it happens a Belgian is as a red rag to a bull to him so he was much chaffed & has gone off muttering imprecations & with a large roll of barbed wire to make an entanglement around himself and his gun to keep Belgians out o' reach!!

Yr loving Diddles

Sat [12 Feb]

Mother dear –

About the girl coming here. Esther McNeil tells me the Saunders girl who was hit has decided she is too nervous to return so that knocks the idea on the head of Esther coming here as she can't leave Mrs Taylor alone. But Mrs T has consented to any pal of mine working with them so I want someone to come out. Marjie has been seeing Molly Shreiber but she has drawbacks: German name, rather old 35 or so (or more) & Esther would prefer a girl her own age to work with & me too. Also I fear she is rather 'superior' & inclined to look down her nose. I s'pose she would do if we can't find anyone else. There is this Speight girl Jelly writes you enclosed about. She sounds nice & is quite willing to come if you approve. I wrote Marjie to tell her to come & see her & write me how the girl struck her.

Marjie wrote her a rude letter turning her down & me an angry one saying she was damned if she would get a 3rd rate friend of Jellett's!

She really is a little fool. I told her to see the girl without committing herself to anything. It is absurd to turn the girl down without even seeing her. Age 25. So will you please do something & if possible see the Speight girl yourself instead of Marjie & tell me what you think of her before fixing anything up definitely with Molly Shreiber.

I will leave the decision to you as to whether the girl is nice or not. Marjie is so unbalanced at times!

I too don't want her if she isn't nice, but you can tell that in a minute. They are a good family & not dentist's daughters as Marjie seems to think!!

So please be a dear & get into touch with Marjie about the Speight girl & if possible see her yourself as well as Marjie. I should be very grateful if you would do it as soon as possible as things drag so & letters take such ages.

Yr loving
DoDo

There is a gap in the letters here from February to May 1916. Dorothie appears to have gone home on leave for some of this time but there are obviously some letters missing.

133

When the letters start again, they still seem to be on the same subject: arranging for a girl to go over to live and work with Dorothie and to help Esther McNeill at her canteen. Also, Dorothie is excited at the prospect of a visit from her brother, Hugh.

May 2nd

Mother dear – Will you write a little letter to old Jelly – don't say I asked you!! About someone coming to live here. I have explained to him & he was very nice about it, but I think a little inclined to think it is a reflection that you & Da aren't satisfied with him – see what I mean? Whereas he has always been most kind & taken great care of me so I think it would please the old man if you just thanked him much for past favours & future to come!

I forgot to write you this yesterday. Had a very busy day today, Belges had a bad time at Dixmude, we went down there & lent a hand, you will see about it I expect & Fritz was also on the strafe at N in the afternoon.

I was stuck for half of an hour on the road which he shelled a bit of it ahead to blazes, made nasty holes too, as if the road wasn't bad enough already, eventually he was kind enough to let us by. [*'Germans attempt assaults east of Ypres, north of Albert, and on Belgian front, but are stopped by artillery fire.' War Illustrated*]

Our cars carried 150 blessés last month, just been doing returns, not bad for 6 people. We had an inspection yesterday by a new boss who complimented the unit on their efficient work & said he had no improvements to suggest as they weren't possible. They have done very well all the winter our little lot & are very bucked.

Much love
DoDo

May 3rd 16

Cherie Madame.
Seems as if I'd written you raver [*sic*] scrappy letters lately. Reason was I had lost my bee–loved pen. It has now turned up having secreted itself in a pair of 'pants. Youngthermens – wool throughout Harrods bargains floor 3/11½'. Luckily pants and pen intact so I can write again to the sainted Commandant with an easy mind.

Hughie will only get 2 or 3 days here. I am very disappointed, I hoped for longer. I shall just be getting fond of him & lose him. Same as with one's nits.

Day afore yesterday an awful heavy bombardment down Dixmude way from 4am till 6am. Shook even no14 & I got up & expected Fritz into breakfast such a noise it was. We went down there after to see what was going on & took some blessés. Fritz had shelled very badly indeed & took a trench. The bulgy Belge however pulled up his pants & to everyone's surprise counterattacked & took it back & made some Hun men & an officer prisoners. There were, of course, rather heavy casualties as a result of all the shelling but I had feared something rather serious.

Am writing in the garden, it is lovely & warm & sunny since I got back & flowers all out but the dust the devil on the roads. You see there's always a vehicle of some sort in front of you all the time so you can imagine how much one swallows by the evening.

Have got lovely vases of lilac at 14. I bribe a red haired urchin next door with toffee to get it & no questions asked! I know perfectly well they climb over someone's wall & steal it!

But I can't be expected to guess that can I now?

Was making up monthly returns for our cars. The five for the French carried

[Censor has removed paragraph]

Things are very spasmodic here now. Alternate days of acute hate as 2 days ago & absolute calm & peace as yesterday. It's always extremes now.

Fritz hasn't thrown anything close at me yet. He's going off. Last time I got back from leave he d___ well near did me in very first time out at N do you remember? Maybe you wouldn't but I do!

Charles is very well & much better. The Bloke got him some patent stuff for his ears & they aren't bald anymore.

I am so glad of the good news of Dudley's exchange looking so hopeful. Little Marjie wrote me a radiant letter.

I had an acute attack of pip in the 1st week back here, the penalty of too long & too nice a leave & pleasant parents.

You see if you had [a] beard like the Berkeleys or Pa beat us, we shouldn't mind going away half so much.

Thus is the irony of fate – but God save me from a beard.

Yr loving DoDo

May 6th 1916

Bon jour mon Colonel –
It's time you wrote me a letter & it's time I wrote you one so let's pull up our pants & I'll start.

Just been given a new ambulance. A 'Buick' with a A1 body comprising every sort of folding, collapsible, non-upsettable, labour saving, lightweight & squash your thumbs device as would delight Mr Bertie. It blew in today being the gift of the 'Wire rope makers company' God bless them. I am expecting Hughie to turn up quite soon now. It's only for 2 or 3 days he deigns to see me though which disappointeth me.

A good deal of strafing going on at N these days. That last mile of road has had a very thin time lately & is much dented.

'Burbidge' was down in the English lines the other day & was looking at a twin to 'Mother' run by gunners & the crew consisted of 56 men, when they asked him how many he had they nearly had a fit when he said '13 and 14 if I take the cook!' which is a fact. The cook being a gunlayer or something!

I haven't heard if you have definitely got that E Coast job or not. Please tell me what you are up to.

I am delighted exchange of British prisoners is going through so well. Got such a radiant letter from Marjie about it.

Much love to you all – Diddles

May 8th 16

Mother dear – I am expecting Hughie here on Sat, which will be a joke, Burbidge is away on leave & returns the same day with him I believe.

The last two days here have been very quiet & nice. Don't spec [*sic*] it will last long.

My brain is flabby the nicht & I can think of nothing to write you.

Dear old Ronarc'h has arrived at Dunkirk & I had lunch there with him yesterday, a perfect joke & I laughed till I was quite ill! One is accustomed to seeing him leading very much the simple life, whereas there he has a young Versailles, a chateau belonging to the French Admiralty, all to himself. There are some 15 anterooms & salons in pale green & gold etc & canopies that look as if they would crumple if you sat on them. It is so utterly unlike his old surroundings of dugouts & wrecked houses that everyone has a fou rire [giggle] whenever they see it & he walks about with his hands in his pockets gazing at it in a lost kind of way.

He has a lovely huge garden with lots of flowers which has been placed at my disposal! I looted a large bunch of lilies of the valley and lilac to begin with. His nephew young Ronarc'h back with him again as ADC [Aide de Camp], a nice lad & used to be here.

I am very sorry to hear Peter is going into the Coldstream. It means all that anxiety again but I admire the boy for it & quite understand his point of view. He's a good lad to do it. But we were so glad to have them both out of it. Thus is life.

I
Can't
Really
Think
Of
Any
More
To say
DoDo

May 11th 1916

Mother dear – I have just remembered something I had meant to tell you. Do you remember when I was home the Gen wrote me about the Zepp bomb at D which went right through the bed without bursting but killed one of the occupants? It was not two girls as I understood but an old couple. The woman, 70 odd, was killed at once in her sleep. The Gen, talking to the old man next day, asked him if it hadn't been an awful shock. He said 'No monsieur, you see by the time I had struck four matches and got a light (3 went out) I had quite got over it. Also my wife was very old & quite usé [worn out] & is far happier where she is!!!'

Tell this to Marjie it will cheer her up. She imagined all sorts of terrible emotions the second girl had been going through ever since.

That is the length of time I should require people to mourn for me. The time it takes to strike four matches! So nice & sensible.

Neb comes on Sat. Spends the 1st day with the Bloke, as he is nominally due them for passes etc & they will lend him to me Sunday evening! As I have been asked to sup with him there the Sat evening I shan't miss much of him.

The Bloke has been a perfect saint taking a lot of trouble about getting a pass to take him to see Rollo, sending him down in his car etc.

He wouldn't have been able to manage any of it except for the Bloke's niceness over it, so I trust he will appreciate it.

Charles is crouched up agin my leg doing the shivering stunt. He wobbles my writing block!

Went round of the Belge lines today to see if they wanted cars or help any where but it's very quiet & well run & all seemed happy with their lot. They threw a lot of things into N this afternoon but the only casualty we fetched after it was one old reservist with lumbago. I don't know whether Fritz considers that was worth the expenditure of obus. Especially as the patient had it before the bombardment.

But I suppose he knows best.

Well goodbye Mother dear – a great big hug & much love – haven't heard from you for 2 days. I wonder are you dead?

Yr loving Diddles

16th May

Mother dear – a million thanks for my snice books. They are all just the ones for out here that one can read again & I was very glad to get them. Many thanks.

Great fun with Neb, we have been over everything & under everything & to see everybody. The only thing he hasn't seen is the war! Fritz treated him with the same 'orrible respect he showed Father & has been behaving like a stuck pig & refusing to fire anything at anybody to Hughie's disappointment & our disgust! As now he will never think we ever get hustled!

Burbidge came back from leave last night & supped here with the Bloke. The sailors have been perfect saints to Hughie doing him proud & getting him out here. Yesterday was just like a bank holiday picnic & the Bloke took Neb & I exploring & we had a most amusing day.

Just heard from poor little Marjie, Dudley is in hospital I am so sorry poor kid.

17th May

Mother dear –
Had great fun with Hughie here. He will tell you about it. It was like a glorified bank holiday.

I can't think why the damn censor cut out things in my letter to you about the Belgian fighting at Dixmude the other day, it was at least 3 days after it appeared in the newspaper communiqué, that I wrote [Cut out by censor] & the joke was I wrote you no more than was published in the French 'Matin' which only goes to prove the rule that all censors are better dead or else as an alternative, in a home for inebriates in the Sahara where they couldn't be officious.

It really is too silly.

[Cut out by censor]

Yr loving Diddles

May 20th

Mother darling –
Great aeroplane raid in these parts last night, none in my little town but in
the one where Gladys & Marjie were [Dunkirk] – some 40 to 60 blessés –
bad business. We brought down one machine, the machines kept coming &
going over us all the evening & much firing & search lights all over the sky.
I went to bed about 11 but Hélène got up at 1am when they came again &
retired to a dugout a few doors away with Charles under her arm & stayed
till 3am! As she omitted to wake either Dr Jelly or me I can only conclude
she puts her values as above! Which amused me muchly.

Quite an artillery hate up here in the lines yesterday. The French
chivvied Fritz some & he retaliated without distressing anybody which is all
as it should be.

I got a very fine view – such a clear day – you could see for miles.
Much love from DoDo

22nd Mai 16
No14

Mother darling –
So hot & dusty again strafe it. After dinner last night the Bloke brought in
two comic Canadian sappers, a Col & a Major, who are working for them.
They were perfectly killing the expressions they used & kept us in a
convulsed state but didn't seem to mind a bit how much we laughed at
them! I wonder if we would mind their roaring at us the same way. The other
day the Bloke was in bed with flu & the Major turned up to see him & asked
if he was 'on soft tack'. Hearing yes, he called 'Jack – where's that there
hen', Jack then disappeared into the car & produced a long legged, very
alive but emaciated bird with apologies for its thinness, saying 'it's so
darned hard to choose a bird with its feathers on though this looked the best
of the bunch.'

It then came out he had merely stopped the car on the road on seeing
some hens & 'persuaded one to step in his car'! The owner was not
consulted nor is likely to be as the Major swore the Bloke needed it most.

They are awful thieves the whole gang but marvellous workers &
delightfully refreshing to talk to!

The Colonel I hear confided to the sailors afterwards that I was 'a
darned fine girl that, who would follow a man as the track is cut out, & help
him all the way.'

Charles is perfectly filthy. He paddled in black slime in the forenoon &
rolled in car grease in the evening. He is now looking at me with a pleading

watery eye of innocence & suggesting he wants to sit on my lap – but I'm not taking any.

A lot of firing yesterday up here. Thought at a moment it was going to be bad, but it quietened down.

Another air raid yesterday at the place where Marjie & Boo were. They broke all the windows in Admiral Ronarc'h's new smart chateau, a bomb burst in the garden while he was at lunch & 1) broke the windows 2) broke his best tree in the garden & 3) killed the sailors' mascots consisting of a magpie & a cat!

Poor old Admiral, I think if one put him in an island in the Pacific bombs would diskiver him somehow. He is a sort of magnet for Fritz!

We brought down three German machines though. The English accounted for 2 & the allies one. So on the whole I consider we are up on the air raid.

There isn't much glass left in shop windows there now I hear.

Much love DoDo

May 21st 1916 ... The German aeroplanes have carried out two bombardments since yesterday in the region of Dunkirk. About twenty bombs dropped in the evening of May 20th killed four persons and wounded fifteen others. About noon to-day another enemy squadron dropped about 100 bombs on the suburbs of Dunkirk. Two soldiers and a child were killed, and twenty persons were wounded. Allied aeroplanes went in pursuit of the enemy machines, and succeeded in bringing down two just as they were re-entering their lines.' Flight, 25 May 1916.

25 May [1916]

Mother mine – it's days since I really wrote you.

Went look-see down the far end of Belge line beyond hospital yesterday, where haven't been for a long time. They have been rather active down there. Found a funny little Capt who delighted because he could talk English & showed us round & stood us drinks. He came up to me triumphant & said he had found something for Mees that he knew would please her. He then told me with bated breath it was 'A PIECE OF REAL SHELL'!!! I had to be frightfully interested & surprised & pretend I had never never never seen one before. It was solemnly wrapped up for me to take home & Hélène is the proud possessor of it.

The garden is looking very snice. That little light pansy that looks like a large violet, you sent me a scrappy bit of last year, has grown enormous & flowers like mad. It looks so pretty. I have written the Bloke's bitter message to the Col. By the way I wish they would make the dear man a brigadier. It's a dirty shame. Down with K. Hoch der Kaiser.

I wonder if the censor will cut out that blatantly disloyal passage. If not he ought to be shot.

Goodbye dears – I wish Dudley could be got to Switzerland quicker.
Poor little Marjie.

Yr loving
Diddles

May 25 16
No14

Mother dear,

I wonder why that imbecile base censor froths at the mouth so over my
letters & opens them all? He must be very hard up for a job, poor dear, or
else look upon me as a suspicious party. If the latter why doesn't he write
& tell me so & we could have it out.

I am convinced his spite against me is entirely due because of that letter
I sent you months ago about Egypt. The censor thought it was information
I was sending home if you remember, whereas it was a duplicate of a letter
sent me from England & already twice censored, in England & Egypt long
before it reached me. Then as I returned it to you, behold the brainy base
censor goes to think I am a nasty little spy sending mysterious messages!!
If I knew the old fool's name, I'd invite him to come & have a gin & bitters
& point out to him the futileness of his ways.

But I don't suppose he could get as far as this as all censors are suffering
from senile decay and pot bellies or they wouldn't be censoring would they?

Much love
Yr curious dartor [*sic*]
Diddles

May 25 [1916]

Father dear –

The Bloke wanted me to tell you that the rickety place you & he watched
the shoot from has been 'napood'. It was hit with incendiary shells & all
burnt up. One officer slightly wounded, only great luck no more. You were
so sure it couldn't last, he wanted me to tell you.

I am glad you have an interesting job that you like. But why does it come
to an end at the end of June? I don't follow?

There has been a lot of firing on this beat lately. That last bit of road into
the town you went to with me has had it very badly the last 3 days. One poor
devil buried 7 metres deep under the debris of a cottage, of course killed.
Some other men blesséd there too while we were in the town & we took
them along.

We have scored though in air raids as on this beat only we brought down 5 in 3 days. They are very pleased in consequence.

No time for a real letter

God bless you

D

May 29th no 14

Mother darling. The General is coming to dine here tonight so I will ask him to post this for you. I've just got your letter with the good news of Dudley's name being on the exchange of prisoners in Germany. That is perfectly splendid, as even if it does drag now that eventual anxiety is relieved. I was so afraid they might have changed their minds.

No, your letters to me are never opened by any chance – it's only home going letters they have a down on.

Certain amount of strafing these days especially on the road into our local metropolis.

Just writing in the garden & an aeroplane over. The town tocsin rang saying everyone to his cellar & all the anti-aircraft shot like mad with such vim it began to rain bits of shrapnel down on our heads in the garden here at 14 & drove us indoors. Then when it was all over the plane came down & landed in a field close by & turned out be an Ally after all! I wonder what the pilot had to say about [it].

Funny yarn about one of those comic Canadians working for the Bloke. The other night an excited little Belge officer danced up & told him he was a spy & where was his orders, & he, the Belge, had been told nothing about the Canadians coming. The Canadian in charge absolutely ignored him for some time & then drawled 'Well, that's funny you were never told. I know they told King Albert & President Wilson & Charlie Chaplin & how the hell they missed you beats me.'

I don't believe the Belge's limited English was equal to the jest!

Admiral Ronarc'h came to see me yesterday & was very chirpy. He still has no panes in his house, so says beginning to feel more like home!

Yr loving DoDo

Dorothie went home in early June after receiving the news that her brother Hughie had been killed during the Battle of Jutland. The devastation his death caused to the family is obvious. Her mother wrote:

June 3rd

Darling –

God has taken back my beloved Hughie & a big big gap is made in the family. He was so much to us all. But how much we have to thank for in having had him. Down to that very last leave of his when most of us saw him & he got the trip he so much wanted to make. Wanted most, next to his 'chance', & that too God has given him.

There is little to grieve for, when one thinks of all he was. Most one cries out thank God for the years we have had of him, with never a regret or anything but joy in them.

But all the same Diddles he has gone & we are here without him – the first sorrow we can trace to him! So we mustn't sorrow for he would not have liked us to ...

Oh I am so glad he saw you & Rollo. He wrote me when he went back last autumn 'I was so glad to have Diddles there. It is difficult to compare the seven delightful sisters you have given me but of them all I think she is the one who is the most to me, & whom I most love & admire.' God bless & comfort you darling as I could wish to do myself.

Yr loving
Mother.

The Battle of Jutland was the only major Fleet action between the British and German Navies of the war. It took place in the North Sea not far from the coast of Denmark.

Dorothie's brother, Lieutenant Commander Hugh R.C. Feilding, was an officer on the armoured cruiser HMS Defence, *which was the flagship of the 1st Cruiser Squadron commanded by Rear Admiral Sir Robert Arbuthnot; the other ships of the Squadron were* Black Prince, Duke of Edinburgh *and* Warrior. *This class of armoured cruiser was considered obsolete by 1916 and were to suffer heavily in the ensuing action.*

The battle had been going for some time before the Defence *became involved. Arbuthnot led his squadron straight at the crippled German cruiser, SMS* Wiesbaden, *disabled a little earlier and lying roughly between the two fleets. In the process of his attack he nearly collided with Admiral Beattie in HMS* Lion *and her consorts of the battlecruiser fleet coming the other way.*

As Defence *engaged the* Wiesbaden, *out of the mist and smoke the modern German battlecruisers led by SMS* Lützow *appeared. The range was, in naval terms, practically point blank at around 6,000 yards.* Defence *bore the brunt of Lützow's gunnery. A witness stated: 'She went up in a huge sheet of flame 1000 feet high, and not a vestige remained 5 minutes after, but falling bits of iron which fell all around us. No-one could have known, they died instantaneously.'*

It was 1820 on 31 May 1916. 'Hughie' and 902 other officers and men went down with their ship.

CHAPTER 10

July–August 1916

Dorothie was home for almost a month as the Feildings struggled to cope with the loss of Hugh.

8th [July] in train

Mother dearest –
Just a little line to thank you for coming up to London to see me off & getting up at that godforsaken hour too. It was very nice of you & I loved seeing you; it was nice too seeing Hughie's pals, Hall & dear old Freddy, his friends are like a tiny bit of him somehow. It hurts in a way, but one is so glad to see them all the same.

You mustn't worry about me darling I will be as good as gold & not do silly things. Also I will come home oftener for little bits like this last time. You like that best don't you? Goodbye dear & thank you & Da for all your love & affection & niceness to yr funny but devoted
Diddles

Dorothie returned to Furnes but only briefly; shortly afterwards she was back in Blighty collecting Winkie Speight who was joining her in Belgium.
A few days previously there had been heavy bombardment around Dixmude and Steenstrade.

Mother darling –
A wobbly line at Folkestone in train – nothing to say but I am thinking of you a lot & wishing I was with you.

Winkie's entire family came to see her off. The Gen is a nice old boy & two very pretty sisters. All very excited at Winkie going off, only just got her passport through in time to start today rather lucky.

Gorgeous sunny day & a nice crossing in view. Won't get to Furnes till late hours of the nicht but I will send you a wire tomorrow from there to say we arrived safely.

All my love darling I can't say much but I fink such a lot!
Yr loving Diddles

20th [July]

Mother mine –
I sent you a wire last night to say we had arrived safely & am scribbling a
line before going out. I have taken Winkie up to Esther's place & left her
hard at it. Esther is very glad to have her as Mrs Taylor is likely to be in
hospital for many weeks with a sort of nervous breakdown & E is single
handed. I gather she is secretly delighted at bossing the show & I shouldn't
be at all surprised if she managed it far better than Mrs T. Winkie much
amused at no14 & shared the 'tin one' with me. I am ordering one for her
all herself – quel luxe!

It is so nice having her here. I used to get just too horribly lonely here
alone with old Jelly, all we have in common I don't suppose takes a cubic
inch of space.

It was a thing one just had to put up with & I didn't realise how hard it
was to do it until now there is someone of my own age & kind. She will be
a nice 'comfortable' companion Winkie & she seems delighted to be here
too. I don't even mind an atom now it is quietening down again & things are
much as when I left.

'Big Charles' [a second Royal Naval siege ggun] was on the bark
yesterday & made such a row. He got some things thrown at him but they
didn't hit him.

Burbidge & Mother have been lent to the English for a bit but are due
back today I think or quite soon anyway. None the worse. Didn't have half
such a sultry time as they do up here whenever they do anything.

Hélène frightfully pleased to see me, but grown so fat she can hardly fit
through the dining room door.

The garden is looking very nice & quite a lot of sweetpeas out. Here is
a sample with all my love darling.

Diddles

21st July 1916

Mother dear –
I have just been looking at a wonderful work of art old Jelly made in my
absence. He turned an old ambulance into a modern semi-wagonette – semi
lorry, every stitch of which he made himself. The result is a collection of
devices that would rejoice the heart of Heath Robinson. Considering it was
all made out of nothing in the back yard, it's dashed fine!

I said to Jelly yesterday Matron knew him & her husband said he was a
great friend of J's. To which Jelly replied 'Oh, a poisonous little bounder
with a stout wife. He always pretended to be a bosom pal & I couldn't get
rid of him & he brought all his beastly relations to doctor for him for
nothing!'

I smiled at the two accounts & expect you will too.

How are all the blessés? I am sure everything is going on just as well without me & that Tessa's panics were groundless. I can't tell you how glad I am Mrs Annan is there. I saw at once she was just the person for the job & she is such a dear comfortable little soul to have in the house.

Our people have had a good lot of work while I was away …

Winkie at least, like Mairi Chisholm, [is] one of the people who will never be 'hurt' or 'gorry' if one doesn't always want to be tin tacked to them but that equally you can frivol & chatter with when you want to.

Jelly is well but rather on edge, he wants a change or some leave away I think.

Oh my darling, I wish I [could] bring back a little of the happiness into your heart that left with our Hughie.

God bless you & care for you & love you as does your worthless
Diddles

22 July

Mr Da dear –

Here is Flanders once more & I am thinking muchly of you all. It was so nice seeing you so often down at home lately. You must come out & stay with me again here will you? I will order a nice little hate for you as you were so sad at striking a quiet spell last time.

I saw the General yesterday, he is not moving for the present anyway as far as he knows of which I am very glad.

Burbidge just come back from a little excursion half way down English lines with Mother. Very pleased because he says they let him work in peace & he didn't get it back in the appalling way he does up here.

Big Charles has been going too but not at the place you think. He makes a great noise & I trust teases them in no small measure.

The sailors are all very well as are also our people. Lots of improvements in gardens & dwellings, looks as if everyone was settling down for the rest of their natural lives to this existence.

Good accounts of the push from further down [Somme]. HO says the French very pleased indeed with the result because it is very steady & methodical & they have made as many prisoners already as they have lost casualties, which is rather wonderful isn't it?

Winkie Speight is a great dear & just the person out here.

She sends you her love, if you remember the scullion & asks you how the 'good old Irish gentleman' that she was very taken with is getting on.

I am very sleepy & will to bed. I am so glad you agreed with me about coming home on leave as I know Mother was glad to have me & I could help a bit during the cookless regime.

Goodbye Colonel dear, you are such a nice man. I won't enlarge on the theme or you would grow out of your hats.

Yr loving Diddles

23 July 16

Mother darling –

Have just come back from the 'Mission' seaside resort. Took Winkie down in the evening to show her the voisinage [neighbourhood] & went for a long walk down the beach. A glorious evening & pretty Flemish lights, the only redeeming feature in a god forsaken country.

Also went to the hospital to see Mrs Taylor, Winkie's boss, she has been awfully ill & I think it will be at least 2 months before she is fit to do any work at all. So it's rather lucky Winkie is here to help Esther.

Also saw the Deb's men in hospital there that were blesséd the other day. One such a nice boy who had his foot carried away by a shell before it burst; he says he felt nothing but a heavy blow as if a sandbag had fallen on it & then saw his foot on the ground.

We took them sweeties & gadgets & they were awfully pleased, also HO had just given them a Croix de Guerre. The footless boy in the greatest spirits & not in the least depressed – they really are marvels some of these blessés.

Just got your letter saying Squeaker au fond of the ovens. I suppose she is cooked by now. I wonder if she was as nasty to eat as the chocolate cake she made. I should think the taste would be very similar.

Winkie has eaten 32 crystallised apricots & will soon, quite soon be sick. Jelly on the other side is correcting proofs about female livers, full of the most revolting pictures of stout ladies mit corns on their appendixes so doubtless too shall be sick shortly.

Can't think of anything of the least interest to say, hence this palpitating information.

[Following written by Winkie]

My dear Commandant I hope you are in the pink as it leaves me.

This a topping place & I feel as if I was living in a blooming cinema show all day. My neck has fairly got the crick from looking at aeroplanes.

Best love from your one time scullion now a flea bitten canteen worker, Winkie.

The damn mosquitoes haven't left an inch of my face au natural.

[Dorothie continues]

How I can go on? Yes she is a priceless sight. There is a mosquito plague on here, & she looks just like a 'baby Maud' come over with a rash.

I took her down to see Teck today & she resisted as she says she was sure he would think she was always flea bitten!

To her great relief he was out. I too am devoured & the mild itches I used to indulge in at meals at NP that distressed matron so just aren't in the show at all.

Ever so much love my darling Petite Maman – God bless you Diddles

24th July

Mother darling –

Would you please give Da a message Peter Chalmers of the Lion sent me. He says he is very sorry indeed he couldn't manage to see Da but his leave was cut down & he only dashed through London instead of spending some days there as he expected.

I am nearly frozen having been sitting in the garden in the dark.

Charles smells like nothing on earth, having dug up a bit of the crown prince at N today & rolled in it. Dirty dog in every sense of the word. I have suggested to Winkie she might wash him, remains to be seen if she does, but I doubt it.

Mairi came into brekker today – looking a great duck. She's a dear child, took years off Jelly's life by telling him that Baronne 3rd class or Mrs Knocker is coming to take a house in our town near no14! Sensation – as I foresee her living on our doorstep with a train of lousy Belgians avec.

I'm told Somme way active again & that we are doing very well which is good. Things not much changed here.

Goodbye darling – such a great big hug from yr very loving Diddles

26 [July]

Mother darling

I have just been talking about you with the General who dined here. Winkie has fallen in love with him. I shall soon have to write to her mama about it.

Charles is going mad. We have a huge stone ball in the garden twice as big as him & he spends all day biting it & will soon have appendicitis as he has eaten great lumps out of it.

A man from the Somme just been in, says it's very slow work & costing us very heavy casualties. I suppose it's to be expected.

I am amused at Bettie as a VAD. I can't see an unruly blessé paying much attention to her austere commands but I am sure she is supremely happy & working like a navvy.

Burbidge, Ginger & Deb came to supper last night to be introduced to Winkie & we had a grand cat hunt after the patron's cat in the dark after.

Goodnight darling – there is much cross talking going on & I can't write.

Yr loving Diddles

28th July 1916

Mother dearest – I have just got such a nice long letter from you of the 25th for which I fanks [sic] you. There was very heavy firing up at our local metropolis today but more noise than damage I am glad to say & not a great many blessés. It had been very quiet indeed for 3 days & this suddenly started for no reason, it was a very sultry day & smells hung long, the place up there smelt like a classroom at school after a chemistry experiment!

There was a very pretty little review in the sands today & the General invited Winkie & me to go & see it. She hadn't seen one before & was duly thrilled. I showed her my beloved Marins & all the local celebrities. It was a lovely sunny morning & really a very pretty sight. I am glad she saw one.

A general giving of decorations at the end & much hugging to be done by the General, of hairy old Colonels & people. I was damn glad I hadn't got to do it. There are drawbacks to every walk in life it seems.

This morning went down the further away part of the Belge lines, all beautifully quiet & fields of poppies & cornflowers waving in the sunlight. The war didn't seem very close; on quiet days the nearer you get to Fritz the further away it all seems.

Winkie is becoming a great Flam scholar, she takes daily lessons with the little nuns & sits making uncouth noises, a cross between a hiccup & a snort & then informs us it is Flam for 'Pass the butter, Miss'. Hélène anyhow is duly impressed even if we are not!

I had a Marin suffering from 'itch – attack of – acute' in the car today & as I had to take him 7 miles & it is most catching I think of him each time a mosquito bites me & wonder if I've got it.

Goodnight Mother mine. I must to bed, all my love & I am thinking a lot of you. I think I will hug you by proxy – choosing jam as the proxy.

Yr loving
Diddles

29 July, no14

Mother dearest – a nice warm day today & a little more like summer. We have been sitting in the garden quite late & now Winkie sitting opposite me reciting Flemish verbs out of a grammar & it is nearly more than I can bear.

She & Esther McNeil get on splendidly & the latter is delighted with our selection of a working partner for her.

The Bloke came in this evening & I took him for a walk as I wanted to ask him about the fleet action [Jutland] & hadn't wanted to with everyone around so hadn't had a chance before. He had heard from different sailors, all saying how unfair the despatch had been to Robert's squadron & he had also seen several people who had been in the action. They all said what we had had written to us about it & endorsed what Callaghan said so forcibly to Da about it.

So there is no doubt at all the good their sacrifice did to the other ships & that all helps doesn't it? Because one knows how proud & glad every man of them would have been to know what the Fleet thinks of them.

Goodbye darling little Mother & God bless you

Yr loving Diddles

30 July 1916

Mother dearest –

Jelly has been in the sulks all day because Winkie hardboiled his egg for breakfast. He really is an awful fool & very unbearable to associate with when he has these 'gorry' fits & they are becoming more frequent every day alas. I doubt not but that one of us will go mad shortly!

The beloved old Admiral Ronarc'h came in to see me this morning, as nice as ever. He really is a dear old boy & Winkie has fallen in love with him too! It is becoming quite a habit with her I am afraid. Today I took Winkie up to see the Belgian field hospital & we took all the blessés sweeties so they were delighted to see us, as we left them hiding half melted bullseyes under their pillows we are bound to be popular with the nurses.

Have you any news of Tubby's movements? I wish he could get up here for a day before he moves further away.

Goodbye my darling little Mother & God bless you.

Yr loving Diddles

During the summer of 1916, the emphasis of the war, for the British and French armies at least, moved southwards, however this does not mean that Dorothie and the Corps were having a quiet time of it, as pointed out in War Illustrated:

'*Although but little has been heard lately of this important sector of the Western battle-front which embraces the Belgian sand-dunes and canals, our splendid ally has month by month continued to hold the line against the enemy. Although bombarded incessantly by the enemy's big guns, these French heroes have never yielded an inch of ground.*'

1st Aug 1916

Mother dearest –
I have just eaten a vast egg & some chocolate creams for brekker & some how the two don't mix & I am feeling ghastly sick. I feel nothing but a bomb would bring me back to my normal state. My tummy feels under my armpits & I wouldn't be surprised if Winkie had to operate – God help me!

I must go & do the cars' guts now p'raps that will help me to forget my own so no time for a real letter. Heard last night that a hoard of hairy Zepps were on their way to England.

I wonder if they will do any damage, I expect not, but they might do worse than go & bomb Ireland a bit – do it a lot of good – or p'raps they have come with a long landing net to try & rescue Roger Casement from the Tower window. It would make a nice Heath Robinson drawing.

All my love dearest
Diddles

2 August

Mother dearest –
Do you love me? Enough to give me anything I mean? Because while I was away the few remaining face towels fell to bits in my absence & were annexed by Jelly & Hélène as dishcloths & motor rags. They were originally some old worn out ones I had been sent. So when you are doing linen & come upon a few old holey ones too far gone to mend don't give them to poor sister but send to me to use up as they are & thus both she & I will delighted be.

Not a word yet as to what the Zepps did in England.

So piping hot these last days that last night we couldn't bear it any more & took our supper down to the beach for a picnic. The most lovely sunset & lights & hot sand & Winkie & I paddled & got just soaked up to our fat necks then coming home it was very funny for everyone except Winkie. She was sitting with Charles who seemed as good as gold & just before we got to 14 she diskivered he had been quietly but firmly chewing her tweed skirt to blazes. There was nodink [*sic*] from the hem of it to about a foot from her

151

waist & he was just beginning on her jersey! Luckily dusk was falling & we got her out of the car & sideways into the house on all fours without outraging the decent feelings of the gendarme on sentry opposite.

We then went to bed & Winkie cut the remains of her skirt with nail scissors into 2 intensely dinky bath mats for her & me to stand on after our tubs.

RIP skirt.

It really was frightfully funny & is a new devilment of Charles. He did the same to a scarf of mine.

I got a snice letter from Da – will you thank him please.

Burbidge phoned me, has exchanged Adam & Eve, his 2 pigs, for seven little ones & I must be Godmother. I haven't seen them yet. In fact I've seen hardly anything of the sailors somehow since I've been back.

Goodbye darling & God bless you.

Yr loving Diddles

4th Aug 16

Mother dear – All sorts of excitements here yesterday; George & P of Wales came up to spend day with Teck & to inspect the sailors & give the Bloke, Burbidge, Deb & Ginger their medals that they hadn't had yet at B Palace. It was a very fine affair & all the men mustered in a little review looked very well & were very pleased with themselves. Teck had given me special permission to come, which was nice of him as I was the only non-official onlooker. George came & spoke to me very nicely & said some kind things about my work & my being a good girl & about Da too.

Also Ld Stamfordham [King's Secretary] & Sir Dab Keppel came up & talked about Da, the former is a nice soul.

Altogether a great show & Fritz never threw anything at anyone which was rather disappointing. It would have caused a great sensation to have had a proj [sic] in the middle of the tea party wouldn't it?

Then I was taken up to dine with the sailors. It's only the second time since Xmas I've done so, & I was made to come in honour of the new buttons. Burbidge is going to pawn his to buy a new horse!

Jelly is awfully cantankerous these days & really very hard to get on with. He is half thinking of giving up this work & returning to his hospital. Don't say anything about it please as he may not.

But if he does I am not at all sure it wouldn't be for the best for diverse reasons. I can always go on digging here with Esther & Winkie & working with our people in the day time – as regards my safety – it wouldn't be any the worse & it would make for more peace generally.

Even Winkie who knows the old man well & like myself for auld lang syne & gratitude will stand a great deal is beginning to find it rather trying.

This is only to say that if he should write you he has decided to return do not be alarmed & I think all things considered it would be wisest not to ask him to reconsider his decision but let him go back.

As regard conveniences & that point of view Winkie & I could perfectly well go on here without him.

I know Jelly thinks we can't but I equally know perfectly well I can.

But don't let the possibility, for it is only a possibility, of a change in things out here bother you because I know the pros & cons & know there is no need for your anxiety.

I am sorry Tubby has gone further from me. I shan't ever be able to get to him now – much love from DoDo

4 Aug

Da dear – just think – it's the 3rd year of the war today & the end seems as far away as ever. Thank you for your nice letter I got a few days ago. I love hearing from you although I know the only time you get to write is in your sleep.

I have just heard from the General that he is under orders to leave this beat on Sunday next. He has been given an important command elsewhere, it is too sad, he is such a dear & has been so very kind to me out here. I shall miss him tremendously.

'Big Charles' has been busy again today but I don't know with what result, he has been doing battery work entirely & with fair success. He will doubtless get on to the other job you are so keen he should do, at a later date.

Charles II, my tyke, got lost today & gave me heart failure as I was 'fraid he'd been stolen by some soldiers. But he came to light eventually up at our barracks.

Robert de Broqueville just come in to supper tonight & departed on a motor bike. I hadn't seen him for a long time, he is observer for a Belgian 12" Howitzer & very pleased with it.

It has been baking hot these days & I just sit & ache to go & have a bathe. But the ocean is so stiff with Tommies, 'naked as worms', that there is not means alas.

They seem very full of blessés down at home. Thank heaven Mother has Mrs Annan & the stugs too, those kids are awfully useful.

Went many miles to & fro today with my ambulance today & swallowed much dust. I feel kind of clogged & my brain is foggy in consequence.

Geoffrey Feilding & co all gone to the Somme which is sad. It does away with my chance of having Peter near me when he comes out. I have never had any kind of luck as to having my family in my district have I? They always go as far away as they can.

Goodbye Mr Da dear & God bless you.

Such a big hug from yr loving Diddles

PS The Gen told me a funny yarn yesterday. It appears down at the base town some 20 miles away a large consignment of some 300 English tommies arrived on the beach in lorries. They were lined up very smartly opposite the Villas by the CO & all the local lovely ladies scenting a review of the 'beaux anglais' dashed out in full strength. But the CO merely blew a whistle & before you could say 'Knife' there were 300 tommies stark [naked] in a row, waiting for the next whistle to march solemnly into the sea. There was a yell & a shriek from all the fair ladies, who seized their babies & belongings & fled scandalised to their houses. 'The English really are a curious race,' the General added thoughtfully, 'we Frenchmen would have chosen a spot up the beach not in front of the town!' It happened opposite his present headquarters 2 days ago.

5th Aug 16

Mother darling – I can't quite remember when you have a birthday but believe it is on the 9th so will any how arrange to think much of you when & am writing this as I suppose it will reach you about then. The only present I have to send is a tin of salmon. Would you like it? You could make it into a pretty pendant.

Mother dear, my one wish is that next birthday will see you a little happier & your own at home again with this ghastly shadow of the war lifted at last.

For those whom God keeps in the shadow with Him, we must just always keep the same places for them in our hearts & that won't be very hard will it with our Hughie? There is nothing but love & goodness & happiness to remember him by & that is what he would wish.

I am very sad because Suzanne's father [Hély d'Oissel] has had orders to go to an active part of the line south & is leaving this district tomorrow. He has always been such a very great friend to me out here I shall miss him tremendously & know he was as fond of me as of his own girls & will miss me too; also he has all his own friends here now & is very sorry to leave. Although from an army point of view the work will of course be more interesting. He will have left by the time you get this. If you have a moment send him a line as it would cheer him up. He values your letters so much &

is always so frightfully pleased to hear from you & treasures all your letters as he says yours are the charmingest he has ever read.

He dined here last night & we have had such jolly evenings here with him, like one's own family rather, that it is very sad it is the last. I have said so many lighthearted goodbyes & au revoirs these last 2 years & so many of them for the last time that I have learnt to dread it so now.

Goodbye little Mother & may your next birthday be as happy a one as you deserve –

Your very loving little

Diddles

Je t'aime – tu sais?

5 July 16 [5 August]

Mother dear – I am bitten by moskiters [*sic*] again tonight. There have been perfect plagues of them lately & they drive one silly. Jelly is strafing one now. He hit his chest an awful tonk & of course missed the nit & I expect raised a blister.

Which reminds me, our French Tommy orderly today at our corps barracks told me he had got a boil on his tummy, & it had just burst he was glad to say & would Miss like to look at it?

I suggested he should show it to Monsieur le Docteur instead as a nice treat.

I fear the orderly was rather hurt because I didn't show more interest & I feel sure Jelly wasn't a bit sympathetic.

Winkie is writing pages next to me, she writes 1 inch an hour about & each epistle takes years off her life; she is a dear kid & quite a lot of 'fond' & brain besides the jolliness that strikes one first – we get on splendidly DG.

We have just been looking at a most glorious sunset out over the canal.

Goodbye Mother mine – God bless you always yr loving Diddles

6th [Aug]

Mother darling –

Have been tearing round all day & am rather breathless. Going up after supper in a few minutes to Esther McNeil's who has someone in who apparently plays very well so Winkie & I are going to listen.

Had a ripping ride down the shore in the evening & then supper with Robert on his armoured train. Pa Broqueville wants me to go & see him. Think will do so for 48 hrs at the end of this week. I have him on my conscience as I haven't been there since I went with you & it's rather piggy of me.

Saw Burbidge today & heard a funny story about him. Last Sunday the parson, very priggy, came up from the base for a prayer meeting, all the hands, much against their will, were herded in the mess room, & in the middle of a deathly pause between 2 psalms Burbidge's voice was heard outside the window to yell to one of the hands 'Why the hell aren't you in church!'

At which needless to say the Bloke and co were seized with a bad attack of the giggles inside & the effect was entirely spoilt.

Goodbye dears all. Don't worry to write to me when you are busy. I know it's not because you don't want to. I am glad VAD's aren't so scarce now.

Yr very loving Diddles

9th Aug 16

Mother dearest –

When you send me the [memorial] cards of Hughie's would you please send me half a dozen, as I should like some to give to people like the Gen & those of the sailors here that knew him well.

It is frightfully hot today & I'm boiled having been carpentering hard all the morning.

Winkie gives very funny accounts of her medical advice she is always being asked to give to diverse old ladies of the place who come to Esther's canteen. One yesterday arrived with a quite unmentionable foot, when asked why the hell she didn't wash, said the apothecary had told her 3 months ago, she must on no account let water come near it. Judging by the result at present day she had obeyed his instructions carefully!

Another hysterical old lady came & said she was sure she was dying. Winkie with much pomp gave her a packet of some plain peppermint lozenges telling her to take one twenty minutes after meals. The old soul is completely happy & now cured it appears! Being convinced 'les dames anglaises' had given her a wonderful drug. Such is life – much love DoDo

10 Aug [1916]

Mother darling –

Jelly is going on leave sometime between 23rd Aug & end of the month for 10 days so when he does I will come along too. I am afraid I don't feel I can take longer than that as since the end of March I have been away far more than I have been here, & there are 2 members waiting to take leave until Jelly & I return but even that little bit will please you I hope & you can save up gadgets for me & make me work as hard as ever you like. Tell Peter to come down when I am there if he can. When I know the date for sure I will let you know.

I feel rather guilty at going on leave so soon, but it's better to go when Jelly does as regards the work.

Awful haste – darn it – God bless you.

Yr loving Diddles

No 14
Aug 11th 1916
Flanders

Mother mine –
Isn't this a lovely sheet of paper– it's due to two reasons.

1st that it's your birthday & 2nd that Jelly has been talking hot air at me for an hour & as I wasn't listening to a word he said so had lots of opportunity to draw you pretty piccys.

Charles wishes you a very happy birthday but is depressed. He has a ladyfriend up the road he is frightfully smit with … But this Lizzie is a hot bed of fleas. Yesterday morning I washed Charles & he went straight off to Lizzie & came back crawling again. I gave him a sound belting only unfortunately beat a flea off him onto me. As it alighted nimbly on my arm I saw it & sent it to its doom before it did much damage. He has now been washed again & is sitting very repentant under my chair with a 'till next time' expression.

I must go out now.

Last night Burbidge came to supper. It was rather comic. He & the Bloke had been invited to dine with the Baroness K[nocker]. They looked in here on the way by & Burbidge who hates dining out except here where he can do what he likes, felt his courage oozing out of his boots. He then firmly refused to be dragged to the sacrifice & invited himself to supper & sent the Bloke on alone!

I've got a fine old snuffle in my head – such a time of year to get a cold.

Yr loving Diddles

16th Aug
11pm in bed

Mother dear
I am going back to no14 tomorrow morning. I have written to Moll to ask

her if she can put me up the night of 23rd, if so will go there as it such months since I've seen the old dear properly.

Did you ever get my letter about George & P of Wales reviewing the English sailors & yours truly last week? The censor probably cut it out as I stupidly forgot & wrote you before his visit this side was announced.

Today I've no skin on my stern. Robert & I went for a long ride in the forest to a little village some 15 miles away. We put the gees up for a rest & went to the pub for lunch. Found a Canadian Div just from Hooge there & they dashed out to invite us to lunch with them which we did. They were a nice lot & very interesting. They must have had an awful time poor dears – their Div have been in for 5 months & in all that heavy fighting.

Then we rode back. Great gathering of the Broqueville brothers here: Robert, Pierre, Andre & Jacques all here at once.

The old boy as kind as ever.

Goodnight & ever so much love

Yr Diddles

If you hear of a new member for corps please tell me as one is leaving shortly his 6 months up & he can't stay away longer.

CHAPTER 11

September–December 1916

On 6 September 1916, Dorothie was presented with the Military Medal by the King at Windsor Castle. The Rugby Advertiser *reported on 9 September that Dorothie was the first British woman to receive this award. The Military Medal had been created in March that year solely for acts of bravery in the field under fire and was extended to include women in June. Over the course of the war 115,600 military medals were issued, only 135 of them to women. The King himself had agreed Dorothie should receive this award instead of the Royal Red Cross which was usually awarded to members of the nursing services. This was Dorothie's third award for bravery.*

The initial recommendation for Dorothie's work to be recognized came from Commander Halahan, in the following letter to Alexander of Teck:

Poste de Commandement
Artillerie Anglais NIEUPORT

Sir,

I have the honour to submit for your consideration the services rendered by Lady Dorothie Feilding to the unit under my command, with a view to their adequate recognition. Although your Serene Highness is well aware of the facts it will perhaps be as well to recapitulate the circumstances under which she has been associated with the Naval Siege Guns.

In January 1915 I was sent out in command of three steel barges armed with one heavy gun each for service on the Belgian canals with the Belgian Army.

The unit was later increased by two heavy guns on travelling carriages and one on a railway truck.

As neither a medical officer nor an ambulance were provided arrangements were made with the chief of the Munro Ambulance Corps to provide a doctor and ambulance as required by me, the arrangement being reported to the Admiralty (the Munro Corps is a Red Cross unit attached to the Belgian Field Army and also works for the French in the Nieuport sector).

Dr Henry Jellett volunteered for the duty with us and he, with an ambulance, has attended on us on every occasion of firing from February 1915 to March 1916 when a naval surgeon was appointed. Recently I have been furnished with a naval motor ambulance and this marks the final severance with the Munro Corps.

Lady Dorothie Feilding as a member of this corps has driven the Munro motor ambulance and attended to our wounded during the whole of the aforementioned period.

Dr Jellett's services have already been recognised and I venture to submit that those of Lady Dorothie Feilding should in like manner be rewarded.

The circumstances are peculiar in that, this being an isolated unit, no medical organisation existed for clearing casualties other than this voluntary one and owing to indifferent means of communication etc, it was necessary for the ambulance to be in close touch with the guns when in action. Lady Dorothie Feilding was thus frequently exposed to risks which probably no other woman has undergone.

She has always displayed a devotion to duty and a contempt of danger which has been a source of admiration to all.

I speak only of her work in connection with the Naval Siege Guns but your Serene Highness is also aware of her devoted services to the Belgian Army and to the French – notably to the Brigade de Marins.

I submit that it would be difficult to find a case more thoroughly deserving of recognition and reward.

I can only add that all ranks and ratings in the command would view with the deepest satisfaction a reward in a more concrete form than their heartfelt gratitude, which she already has.

It is indeed impossible to overestimate the moral effect of her courage and self sacrifice and in an official letter it is proving difficult to do justice to either.

I have the honour to be,
Your Serene Highness' obedient servant
Henry C. Halahan Commander Royal Navy

10th Sept 16

Mother darling –
Just got a nice letter written as you left London & thank you very much for its niceness.

Things here much the same, just in from taking a blessé miles away to the big base hospital, if it hadn't been for his tin hat, he wouldn't be alive. The bullet went right through it & a corner only of his pate luckily. Poor man had only just left the very same hospital I took him back to from a previous wound – hard lines.

Ginger & Deb just been given X de Guerre by the French. We are bidden to watch them be kissed at a bally review tomorrow. I do hope they get proper hugged.

Later/
Up to my eyes in gadgets since I got back & accounts, little time to write also had Thérésé de Broqueville here for 2 days & a night to see Robert. As an officer's wife he is not allowed to have her up here so I asked him to dine with me & never told his C.O. she was here. Then at 10pm we rang up & brazenly told him the car was broken down & he couldn't get back till next day!!!

Pure lies – Winkie came in with me in my bed & unlike Squeaker didn't wet it for which I was grateful.

Goo'night very late yrs ever
Much love Diddles

13 Sept 16

Mother dear –
Got your letter & lousy Lucy's enclosure from Charlie, for which thank her very much please, I was much amused there at.

Did I tell you Burbidge is delighted with his policeman & asked me to thank you very much for it. He is going to sit it on 'Mother' when in action & is very proud of it.

He has also just annexed a tame fox to add to his menagerie. The peacock is on its way over, one of the hands had a week's holiday to go & get married in at Market Harboro' & was given an extra day to go to Gravens & collect the peacock!! Sensation when arrival in Flanders avec!

Ginger & Deb just been given X de Guerre for helping to put out fire in French gun pit, while the ammunition was going off. This gun was close to theirs & being heavily strafed.

Winkie is well & full of bounce & sends her love. Have been grubbing with the old car all day, a thoroughly deadly proceeding. It is a pastime one gets very sick of but no sicker than the poor Commandant of hospital gadgets.

I am sorry the new widow VAD sounds rather a fool – poor Mrs Ma
Goo'night & much love
Diddles

14th [Sept] night

I enclose photo with Hun Helmet & one of 3 aeroplane gazers. If the censor grabs strafe the blighter.

Mother dear – life rather scrummy today & such a gale of rain got soaked this afternoon. Some bad blessés at N to take miles away to the big base hospital near D & it poured all the time. Was distributing cigs to the poor blessés down there when a festive Marin in the corner shrieked out 'Meees Dorothee' & I discovered an old friend who swore he had known me since Ghent, we parted the best of friends & he the better off for baccy!

Winkie, Jelly & I were invited to a concert show the French soldiers got up, no end of a kurush [*sic*] & Albert & Elizabeth of Belgium & millions of fat old Generals. The latter behind whom we were sitting gave us giggles. Rows of shiny bald heads beating time to the music!

By the way, a lady pal of Jelly's we saw at Boulogne asked me fatuously what my medal ribbons were for. I assured her one was for putting out a fire in the back garden, 'and the other?' she said, 'Oh another fire in the backyard' I assured her.

'How very interesting. Do you know Lady Dorothie, I tried to put out a little fire at our hospital, but wasn't so fortunate the other day etc etc' so I remained prematurely solemn & bade her adieu. Must really write a pamphlet on fire brigades I think now my fame thereon is sure to spread, as she is the type who would tell it to everyone!!

Ha – Ha

Goodbye little ones

Damn the Huns –

Yr loving Diddles

17th Sept

Mother dear –

I enclose 2 letters, one from the Gen. The other enclosure is from Peter Chalmers of the Lion, will you please give it to Father. I am sorry he couldn't get to see Beatty that time, but suppose it is only postponed.

No letter from NP today but I s'pose you are all still there ok.

Our new member Norton, the one I went to interview at Brinklow just come & the general impression up to date is good. He seems a nice lad & very keen – long may it last.

Somme news excellent these last days & our getting Combles is good. Just rung up to see if any news thro' tonight but no one has heard anything yet.

Goodnight & much love

Diddles

1st Oct

Mother dear – had two nice long letters from you yesterday with enclosures.

Rollo's diary was extraordinary dull! Nothing but Dicksons & Robinsons, tommies & his prospects of leave! That's the worst of these staff bugs. They haven't anything to write about. My letters are much the same too nowadays. Nothing much happens but routine work which may keep you busy enough, but leaves the recipient of the letter stone cold & fed [up] to the teeth!

A plague of flies has come upon us with these sunny days & we had a great 'swot party' this morning with brooms squashing them on the ceiling where they made beastly goo marks. Charles barking madly with excitement & devouring the corpses as they fell. He swears you can't beat them as an hors d'oeuvre.

Just had long letter from HO off to Rollo's vicinity. He says he has a superb lot of men & they are all very pleased at the prospect of having another dig at Fritz ...

Goodbye & much love to everyone
DoDo

No14
6th Oct

Mother dear –
Went to bed at 3am today as we had a little hurrush [sic] last night; our side had a bally gas attack & the devil of a lot of firing all last night. But Fritz was far too wide awake & evidently knew all about it from some of our men he had made prisoners a few days ago, so it all fizzled out & things are 'as you were' which is disappointing very. Very few casualties on our side, I only hope we did some damage but I doubt much beyond teasing them a bit.

The sailors all fired like mad too & the Bloke had rather a hectic time being strafed in a forward observatory which was hit twice.

The 1st birthday at the war, the Boche nearly got me at Ghent. They are determined to keep my birthday on the move.

Many thanks for you people's wire, I call it rather wonderful of you to remember.

Goo'night – off to make up back numbers of sleep.

Yr loving DoDo

Birthdays are hateful things now so full of memories of Hughie, Mother dear. I hate mine.

6th Oct

Mother dear –
A line just to say I am going out & am busy but ok in case you were
worrying because I hadn't written.
Yr very loving DoDo
What a comic birthday I've just been sent another £50. That makes £200
& 2 ambulances I've got in a week – call that nuffink?

9th Oct 16

Mother dear –
Thank you so very much for your nice birthday letter, I meant to write
yesterday but we were awfully busy as there was the devil's own hate on.
Fritz started & looked like attacking, so we gave him hell & then he did give
us hell & so the world keeps going round & round. Dear old N was no
health resort & we trembled for the car one time when we had left it under
an arch while getting blessés at the dressing station. Two fat obus landed
just over the car but luckily both duds & so nothing happened.
Yesterday morning Mr Vaughn, RN (Hughie's friend) turned up
cheerfully here having got 3 days leave to spend in Flanders so he came in
the car with us, got lots for his money so was frightfully pleased at coming
in for a strafe, as are all Cooks conducted tourists! We have given him a
cabin up at our barracks.
Poor Mother is laid up temporarily as a result of yesterday, she had a
very thin time & won't be herself for some time I'm afraid. Burbidge very
fed up.
Thank you ever so much for my birthday fiver. I nearly fell over with
excitement at so much wealth. I will use it for my expenses at 14 & it will
be awfully useful as it takes pretty much all my time to find the pennies, as
I pay more now Winkie is here, as she is extra on my account.
Must go & do my bed – good-bye Mother dear – all quiet & calm today.
Yr very loving
Diddles

10th Oct

Thank you for yr nice long letter I got today. I am so praying the Dunchurch
Dr is too busy & you will be able to close down. Please please do.

Mother mine –

Life is really very odd isn't it? I told you Hughie's friend of the Cornwall, Mr Vaughan RN, you saw in London, turned up here! He got permission through D.I.D. who knows him, to spend 3 days leave out here as he wanted to see me again. He turned up here with the mail on the lorry one day & we put him up at our barracks & Jelly & I took him about in the car with us to show him things & fed him at no14. He is a very nice soul, I like him very much, but was so sorry because before he left he asked if there would be any chance for me to marry him & I had to say I couldn't. Poor soul, he's always had a very lonely time of it through life & was very devoted to his gunner brother who was killed not long ago at Ypres. You remember his writing to me about it when I was home don't you?

I think men are wonderfully brave sometimes at making up their minds don't you? Everything really is very odd these days. The days when things weren't odd seem so far away, almost like a dream.

A lot of blessés the other night. Poor poor devils. But the more one can help them right out here at the pulse of things the more this actual work means to one. I can't describe it, but it's very real, & it means more to me everyday some how.

God bless you dear & goodnight

D

11th Oct

Father honey – I am very bucked, as just got your letter saying you have written Teck about coming out, but you don't say when – soon I hope?

So longing to find out what Teck thought of it, I have just rung up to ask him to dinner tomorrow! He says he'd love to come & he added you have written him & he thought it could be managed & he'd sent you a wire.

Teck forever! That really is nice of him isn't it & I am thrilled to the teeth – what fun it will be having you & won't we raise Cain just.

Things have been very gingery round here just lately, but I expect with your usual luck Fritz will retire for a week's siesta as soon as you arrive.

Very many thanks for the Sapon you say is coming. The powder will be much loved, it's only those soap cakes I think are rotten. The powder proper is A1. For car hands etc.

Brewill's 'Mother' hors de combat from a little gentle persuasion on Fritz part which is sad.

Many thanks too for The Outlook etc, we never see it out here & it's an interesting little rag.

Poor young Capt Field has been wounded in the shoulder by an 'archie', he is in the F Corps now you know. He writes he is home & practically well again. I'm glad it wasn't serious as I can think of nothing more unpleasant than being badly bléssed in the air. He says they lost 13 officers in their one squadron in 3 days – sounds a very high average doesn't it?

The Bloke thanks you for your message & sends you his love in return. The Navy will be very pleased to see you.

Here's a yarn, a Yank in a train with some wounded Tommies said to them about the Somme, 'Some fight'. 'But some don't,' replied a Tommy.

Goodnight Colonel Da, & mind you come out, I am awfully cock a hoop at the idea.

Yrs till hell freezes

Diddles

13th Oct

Well honey – I have just been counting the spoons to see if there are enough to go round, as we have rashly asked Teck, a pal of his & Esther McNeil to supper tonight. He is threatening to get Da out which is very nice of the old boy. He's an awfully kind bird is 'Algy'.

Beastly & wet again today, real wind & I can never think of anything to write on a wet day. A feeling of gloom settles down on one's soul I suppose, hand in hand with the mud on one's toes.

Much love darling DoDo

15th Oct

Mother dear –

The French General here has just left. He has been on the N beat for nearly a year now & on leaving sent us the enclosed. I am sending it you to read & please keep for me. It was rather nice of him.

We now work for the succeeding people who consist of a lot of Zouaves again. Their red Fezs give quite a festive air to old N again, there hadn't been any for a long time. Our work is in no way changed but just the same.

We had a great supper party here for Teck last night. He was in great form & full of beans & made to work & carry the plates as usual!

Tomorrow Pierre de Broqueville is giving me a ride, it being Sunday morning & all. I haven't had any for some time as rather busy.

The last fortnight I have taken between 45 & 50 men in the Fiat – myself only.

Goodnight darling & God bless you
Yr loving
Diddles

15 Oct

Mother mine –
Thank you for your letter & Squeak's enclosure received today. I am on tenterhooks now that you will devise some scheme to keep the hospital on. I here am praying feverishly all the MD will get beri-beri or Brights disease & you will be obliged to close.

Teck is going to English GHQ tomorrow & will see if he can get Da a chit to come out. But it seems still a little doubtful as he says it is frightfully hard to get permission. I do hope it doesn't all fizzle out, Da would be so disappointed & me too.

I mean to come & see you towards the end of Nov if you would like me to or if you are on visits then would come later. That is the earliest I could with decency take more leave I think.

Esther McNeil off to London tomorrow. She has only been on leave once in a year, poor soul. Mrs Taylor better & coming back to the canteen in a few weeks to her & Winkie's sorrow! They much prefer running it themselves!

Lots of love dear & don't think I'm being nearly slain as I'm nothing like it! You seemed afraid 'twas so in your letter today & you mustn't do it there's a dear –
Diddles

17 Oct

Mother honey –
We have been pretty busy these last weeks somehow. My own Fido Fiat has transported 56 people alone since the 1st Oct. One of our new men just come out is as blind as a bat, & we will have to return him on account of his eyesight which is a bore. If you hear of a good driver to suit us let me know. This man just staying on pro tem until we find another. He can't see enough to do any night work at all.

I dined with the sailors last night. The 1st time for a long long while & we had a pleasant peaceful evening all sat round with our feet in the fire & ate chocolates & were nice & truly at peace with the world & nearly forgot there was a war on. Burbidge has added a tame fox to his menagerie – it gets skittish at night & tears round the mess rolling over & over with the dogs.

171

Charles is the only one that can't be friendly with it, memories of going down an earth are too strong for him. He doesn't actually eat 'Bill' the fox but sits 3 inches off glaring at him with all his hair on end! Bill then gives him a playful cuff which adds insult to injury & Charles couldn't bear it any more & looked like trouble so had to be locked up. Caractacus the peacock has been stolen, frightful sorrow but no sign of him, I fear he was boiled in some Frenchman's stock pot, Burbidge swears he has gone over to the enemy lines & was a spy all the time!!

Your policeman was not with B's Mother the day of her trouble which explains the sad tragedy. He lives in the mess & is brought out when wanted. That day they were called up in the devil of a hurry & in the scuffle the poor old policeman got overlooked & Burbidge says he is to blame for everything! He will have to be more careful in future.

I haven't yet heard what GHQ told Teck about Da coming out, but fear the odds are against – all hope not dead yet we must just hope for the best.

Yr very loving
DoDo

17 Oct

Da dear –

Haven't yet heard what GHQ said to Teck about your permit. He wasn't over hopeful about it, but was going to see them yesterday. I expect he has written you direct. I don't like to ring him up again for fear of overdoing it & spoiling the consommé thereby! He has been very nice about it but it is harder & harder to get people out here from home now & there is general ill feeling about in all the staffs. It is forgivable because of course it was so over done by politicians & fools generally from home.

All hope is not yet dead tho' & I think there is quite a sporting chance you may get out. Hope on Horatio!

The French poilu [infantryman] is an impayable gentleman. I was talking to one at N 2 days ago & he was proudly showing me the photos of his wife & family, one of the latter was a pretty little girl, so I politely complimented him on the beauty of his offspring, he merely remarked 'as they should be – considering the trouble entailed in making them!'

I nearly said 'My dear man I think your lady wife has got more to grouse about', but on 2nd thoughts decided I didn't know him well enough so we shook hands warmly & left it at that!

So long Mr Da dear & do come out
Yr very loving
Diddles

19th Oct
Thur

Mother mine –
I had rather an awful afternoon yesterday. Mr de Broqueville, the father, came up to see me at 14 & we had a long talk. It appears his son, Pierre, wants to marry me awfully, & spoke to his father about it many months ago, but was told to wait a little. I don't think you ever met Pierre, he is the one in the 1st Guides Cavalire, the very tall, dark, good looking one, & was in the army before the war. He is an awfully nice boy but just a dear big baby. About 25 I think, but temperamentally a perfect child & I am afraid it could never be for that reason. I wouldn't marry a foreigner unless I cared very very much. I think that is essential to the make up of the racial differences. Pierre is a dear boy, but I really couldn't ever marry him. There is not enough in him to satisfy me I'm afraid. But the Broquevilles have been such perfect dears to me, it is awful not being able to do it, as I am afraid the father was fearfully anxious for it to be & was thinking it would be ok. He wrote to his wife about it already in Brussels & got an answer saying if he was pleased she was too, & was apparently very nice about it, which makes it all worse. It was because he heard Father was coming out here that he came up to see me because he wanted to talk it over with him if I would. I told him that I was very fond of someone who had been killed so that in the hopes it would soften it a little & not make me seem ungrateful & callow for all they have done for me. Will you please write to the father about it & say I told you & thank him very much for all the care & affection he has had for me.
 This never occurred to me, Pierre when quartered near here, often comes now & then & gives me a ride & a gee & I considered it was good for us both to get a good healthy shake up & a change from our respective routines which are both pretty deadly. And now everything is in the consommé!
 I can but repeat what I often tell the sailors that I would like to be a bosun! The B's have been so wonderfully kind to me, I feel it rather.
 I am more fed up than I can say at the new nightmare prospect of your hospice remaining open. I can but hope the HAC day was a frost. That it poured, that no one came & that the only ones who did were few boys who didn't 'part'.
 Much love darling
 DoDo

20 Oct

Da dear –

Teck says your papers re leave here are 'en train' which means wandering about from Bug to Bug with a favourable chit from Teck. He has been awfully good & asked GV [King George V] about it himself in person, otherwise I know it would have been turned down. He says there is quite a good chance of its succeeding & one must just sit & hope for the best & see what happens.

I am up to my neck in oil, doing the oil pumps of the car & just come in to write you this. Oh Da dear I do hope you can come.

Much love from Diddles

20 Oct

Mother mine –

No time for real letter just scrawl for the post to say I am ok & hopes you are de meme [in the same way].

Charles sends his love & says it's damn cold.

Robert de Broq was here yesterday afternoon & went a stroll in the evening. The whole family have been frightfully nice to me & I am glad because it has taken away any feeling of uncomfortableness. I felt at 1st that they might think I had been playing the fool, because they so little understand abroad the way English girls are brought up to be quite natural & pals with men, & that they would think I had meant something by seeing & being good friends with the boy. But I am glad to say there is no question of that, so I am happier about it, because they have been such dears to me all along out here & I would hate to hurt them in any way.

Please return me the enclosed.

Goodbye maman & God bless you.

DoDo

Papa Broq wrote me such a nice letter too yesterday.

24 Oct 16

no14

Mother mine – I got such a nice letter from you yesterday for which very many thanks.

I think your view of Lady Hamilton was quite right. I think women if they wish can help men very very often by using their influence in the right way. At least I know in several cases I have been able to help men over stiles in their lives, whereas if they hadn't been fond of me they would have taken the wrong road. I remember many years ago your telling me 'It can never hurt a man to care for a good woman.' & I have often thought of it since & it has helped me to do the right thing by people. I know if a man looks up to you, he will unconsciously almost do the best that is in him, just because he knows it pleases you to feel he is doing so. Since the war I think women can help men these ways & influence them more than they have ever done before.

Winkie had a birthday party day afore yesterday, & we only remembered it half thro' the day, so hurriedly had a small select supper party to drink her health which was quite fun.

Awfully wet & foggy today. I expect Somme operations held up thereby. Everything here quite quiet today.

Got a letter from Gen HO this morning who says nearly a month ago he was told I was engaged to Pierre de B & he wants to know if it's true. I wrote & said not, it's extraordinary how these yarns get about. I am sorry because it must be beastly for the boy if people go & ask him about it. Foreigners are such awful busybodies.

Am just reading Kipling's articles on the Jutland battle destroyers. I suppose you have seen them. They have the bigness of all his things.

I think you are wonderful keeping the hospital on.

All my love darling

Diddles

Oct 27th 16

Mother mine – Thank you for your letter today about the B's. I had not heard anything from Hughie about his leaving the Defence, & I am sure he would have told us had it been in any way settled. It may have been a rumour & he didn't bother about it as long it was but such, owing to Roberts' unwillingness to change his officers.

Today I got a wire from Da, he is crossing Sat or Sunday. I hope he squares Hall to give him a pass to use a destroyer to D. All the Mission officers always do & it saves a car going 200 kilometres to Boulogne & back. It will be too nice for words having him here & I am just delighted, bless him. These last days I had rather given him up as a bad job.

Yesterday the Zouaves very bucked over the Verdun successes & hung up all sorts of flags out of the trenches with insulting messages to Fritz.

Result today the latter has been on the strafe with his 'minnies' & our people have been busy. A rather expensive joke I'm afraid.

There is an extraordinary regiment here now, composed entirely of French convicts brought back from the colonies & made to fight. They have livened up the district considerably!! When fighting they can't be beaten &

have made a great name for themselves & are always given the dirty jobs. But in billets they are the devil. They have slain 6 Belge gendarmes, 2 old ladies & stolen innumerable hens this last week; diverse of them are shot at dawn at intervals but none of the others seem the least depressed thereby.

One of their officers told me in N the other day that even in the trenches, no sooner is a man knocked out, than all the others are down on him like harpies to bag his watch & rifle his pockets generally.

I think I must send you a few of their blessés to Newnham, just to buck up matron & give her some exercise.

Goodnight dear – I am sleepy tired & wish I was dead ever so much
Yr loving DoDo

31st [Oct]

Mother dear –
It's so nice having Da here & we have had huge fun, but life is simply one damn thing after another & we tore round in circles looking at everything & everybody from Huns to Albert!

Last night a great supper party at the Sailors & Da sang Alouette & Bug a boo. The latter was a huge success & they loved it. Everybody loves Da, he is perfectly priceless when he gets going with an old pianer!

I got such a nice long letter from you last night darling. Will you please keep Papa B's & Pierre's letters for me then? I said send them back because things lie about so at Newnham these days & there is nowhere one can leave anything with any hope of seeing it again.

Must go & do some things. Forgive a dull letter but Da is writing you pages of the gossip.

Yr loving
DoDo

1st Nov

Mother dear – I got the enclosed for you today, but my car took 101 in the month.

Last month our 6 cars took 334 people. We have just been adding up our cases taken the last 8 months. The total is 1,547. You see we don't do nothing & I think our tiny unit pulls its weight & I am justified in keeping it on – our monthly running total expenses average £50 pounds only.

Da went off last night. It was sad seeing him go, we had had such fun together – he is such a lamb that man. Everybody loves him.

Yr loving DoDo

PS Mrs Ma – Do [you] want any more VAD for Newnham? Because there is a Miss Eileen Leader, Classas, Coachford, Co Cork, Ireland who is very anxious to come to Newnham if you want her. Please send her a line direct no or yes & if the latter when. She is 18, a younger sister of Jelly's wife. Winkie says a nice girl & should do. Pretty, rather shy but capable having done things for herself. She could come for a month at least & be prepared to stay longer if wanted. Is strong & since the war passed exam in driving & repair of cars. Could help keeping Sunbeam in order tho' know she wouldn't be allowed to drive.

I believe the Leaders are a good Irish family. Less uncouth than the Jelletts & off the top shelf. So from that point of view she would do, I am writing as I gather you are short of VADs.

She has her name vaguely down for a motor gov job but doesn't really hope to get one as she is young – would pay 10/- a week.

3rd Nov

Mother dear –
I am staying for 2 nights with the Broquevilles as Thérésé is there & Papa has just got back from Paris. I am sorry he missed Col Da, as I should have liked them to have met. Thérésé is coming back to spend the night at 14 with me tomorrow. I then ask Robert to come & supper or to stay & he is let as long as they don't know his wife is there! As soon as it's a question of an officer's wife near the front there's an awful row & shrieks of favouritism. So we arrange it very tactfully & quietly. Thérésé very indignant because she says he is allowed to stay with everyone except his wife & it is most immoral. Such is life.

We had great fun with Da & fairly ran in circles & saw things. I think he enjoyed himself ok. He will tell you all about it.

Burbidge & Mother are going to be at it again on Monday I think, we will be sure & take the policeman this time, having learnt wisdom.

The bit missing out of my letter wasn't important only to say the Boche ammunition had been very bad one particular day when we watched about 18 eleven inch obus come into N & only 3 burst. I said those that did sat on some houses & gave them that same tired look an éclair has after Taffy has sat on it.

The Broquevilles have a new chateau now nearer to me & Dunkerque. Awfully nice, larger & more private than the old one, with a moat round it. Really very snug. They were driven out of the last by the English making a huge depot of munitions & stuff outside their front door & flooding the place with tommies.

Much love dear
DoDo

6 Nov 16

Mother dear –
Thank you for your letter & the cutting about the Yser fighting which was interesting. Nothing strange here – same old routine. Winkie off on leave tomorrow as Esther returns & she wants to fit in with her. W awfully bucked & cock a hoop.

I am dining tonight with old Gen Balfourier who has the corps here now after HO. A dear old bird, with a little white goatee beard, who used to have the famous French 20th Corps, the 'Corps de feu' which has done wonders at Verdun & Somme, his health broke down so he has come here. I enclose you his invitation which keep for me.

He is very kind to us & our cars which I am glad of. Whenever Gens change I keep awfully quiet & hide when I see them till they get accustomed to my being here, in case they said 'Hell! A woman' & get excited at my being here.

I think now tho' I am looked upon as one of the ruins of the sector & will be left in peace.
Much love dear –
Yr loving
DoDo

8 Nov

Mother dear –
Just a line to say it is a motheaten war & I am fati-gued of it. I don't doubt you are too when you have to do all the cooking on a tiny range. You say you have changed the matron. Is the obese one gone? And Night Sister? That poor soul will die of some awful disease if she goes on living like an owl much longer. It is very sad, Ginger has got to leave in a few days to go to sea, as they are short of young naval officers, he came in here to supper last night. I wish he wasn't going he is a nice lad. 'Deb', ie Caswell, the other boy will soon have to go too I am afraid. Soon there will be no one of the old Firm but me in Flanders.

About my leave, instead of coming last week in Nov as I expected, would it be the same to you if I came about the 10th of December & took a long leave of at least 3 weeks & stayed with you over Xmas? I think a longer leave is more satisfactory than little snippets if you don't mind, from all points of view. If I go away too often from here people get the idea I spend my time in Blighty & don't realise when I go often I go only for a short time.

178

Let me know if you mind as if this doesn't suit you as well I could try & fix up something else.

Much love

DoDo

12th Nov

Mother dear –

Before I forget Jelly bids me thank you for the Bower-Colehurst report & also for writing to Eileen Leader, his sister in law. He says he hopes you will like her & be a success. I think mere fact she will be a more or less fixture will be very useful for you. Did Da ever get to the Somme? I never heard. The Bloke just gone off there today again as observer for Bridges, ex of the British Mish here.

A new man for us arrived yesterday, one Kemp, to replace Newall who had to return. He seems nice, but we are sorry to lose Newall who was a very dependable chap & hard worker. He was to take his ambulance with him, but the other day presented it to me, for the corps, as a souvenir of the Mil medal which was nice of him as it saves us getting another car, & it is quite a new one.

If you hear of anyone to suit us let us know as we are hunting for a man to replace a member whose eyesight is too bad for the work out here. He can't drive at night or in the rain in the daylight.

Hélène sends you her love – '& tell Mrs Countess that Charles almost caught a nice little kitten yesterday'

Love DoDo

& 14 Nov

Mother dear – thank you for yours tonight & the bunch of enclosures from Tubby which were very interesting. Taking Da round seems to have given him palpitations somewhat, but he must have been thrilled to the core at seeing a real live tank. It is more than I have, which is a pity as they would roll along beautifully in this country. Jelly made me laugh this afternoon as he took the new member out for a run in the car & made him drive a sort of exam. The poor new man is not a very good motorist yet, very new to it all & easily put in a fuss. So Jelly not finding the high road interesting enough as a test, at once takes him up into N & up byroads where he got proper shelled & the fear of God put in him. All this as Jelly explained carefully was 'just to give him confidence'. Personally I think he will have many nightmares tonight instead & will probably die of fright or the palsy before morning.

My brain is very sluggish tonight & I can think of nothing amusing or interesting to tell you but all the same I love you very deeply.

Yr

Respeckful

Darter

DoDo

16 Nov 1916

Mother dear – there was a lot of noise up at N yesterday so we were out pretty late, when we got back we found that Fritz, to celebrate King Albert's birthday, had had a good old hate at this place, the 1st for ever so long. He cast about 120 but as not a single person or cat was even blesséd it was rather waste of breath on his part. None anywhere near 14 as we are right out of the shelled zone.

Gurney was shook up yesterday at the dressing station. One burst alongside his car & large lumps buzzed by over his steering wheel which did nothing beyond making him sit up.

Somme things seem to be going splendidly & I hear our moral[e] is excellent & the Boche gloomy & our casualties not very heavy, the HAC lost a good many tho' I am afraid. I am told on pretty good authority you need not be anxious about Peter's crowd which I know will please you & Squeaks. I haven't had any news of the lad for a long time – is he still mending roads at Marseilles?

It has got awfully cold here this last two days. The Bloke back from the Somme says observing in a 1st line trench up to your waist in water has its drawbacks & not to be recommended. Awfully impressed with the moral[e] of our infantry but says they are a bloodthirsty crowd & it's extraordinary hearing them talking of things after a scrap; it takes very little to get the veneer off & down to primitive beast man, in spite of everything, doesn't it? Winkie is on leave & returns next week – it's very quiet without her – yr loving DoDo

18 Nov

Mother dear –

Got two letters from you & a nice long one from Da last night. Things are fairly busy here these days one way & another & they threw a few more obus at this place again yesterday but not near 14. Also had us out of bed at 3am on a perishing cold morning with bombs – strafe them. Charles very indignant.

Ginger's brig had a bad time yesterday & won't be able to play for a bit.

I have been spending all the morning making up parcels for soldiers of clothes. It's too appallingly cold for words this week, so it has fallen just the right time. No time for a real letter.

Yes, I will come home about 10th or 12th of Dec & stay over Xmas. I would rather be at home & help all you people, so don't change any plans on my account. The only orgy I ache for is an odd hunt or two. P'raps with suction & the grace of God I may be able to do so. I only had a half day all last season.

A bit 'ard.

Goodbye dears all

Yr loving DoDo

20th Nov

Mother dear –

Mrs Knocker has published a damnable book called 'The Cellar house of Pervyse'. Thank God she has left me out of it practically, but a lot of 'Munco' about it & people will undoubtedly associate one with that type of woman. Get it, read it, see if you don't think it the worst taste you ever saw. It makes one sick of being a woman & I am so sorry she has made little Mairi Chisholm look a fool too.

She should have been held under water for 48hrs when young.

Just been to see the wreck of a little cobbler's house in the town here, absolutely nothing left of it. The old couple were in the tiny cellar at the time & buried under the debris & had to be dug out. This morning they were sitting in the ruins, poor old souls, shivering with cold & shock generally & half crying while they poked about hoping to find some of their belongings in the rubbish. It is so sad to see them & so pitiful.

Yr loving DoDo

Mrs Knocker and Mairi Chisholm published a book of their experiences in 'The Cellar-House of Pervyse' to raise money for Belgian soldiers. Dorothie's opinion is obvious. Peter Chalmers, who had been stationed with the Naval Siege Guns near Nieuport, wrote to Dorothie that:

While in hospital I read Mrs Knocker's book & must confess I was not very impressed. I think the object be very admirable but there seems to me to be a little too much Mrs K & a little too many shells but if it gets them the dollar then it is a good thing ... At the same time I could not help thinking that there were many others of the same sex doing equally valuable work although they did not happen to be in Pervyse. However I had better refrain from further remarks as no doubt your own conclusions are of infinitely greater value than mine.

21st Nov 1916
Flanders

Col Da dear –
I have just received a most compromising wire, which will show the sort of reputation I now have.

'Lady D F etc – Beseech you return my son immediately – Kemp'

I think it is quite priceless & so does everyone else & I am being called a babysnatcher!! Must have caused quite a flutter in the telegraph offices en route. The reason of it all is a youth called Kemp who came to replace Newall & is somewhat a rabbit. He came in for a good few obus at once & Jelly took him up to teach him how to reverse a car under heavy fire at N as he explained 'just to give the lad confidence'. This put the lid on it & the lad wrote home to Papa his nerves & health wouldn't stand it hence frenzied wires from his parent birds – about 3 a day! We explained he was under a military contract for 6 months & must stick it. He is already improved & I think a little hard work & being shot at as often as possible will soon buck him up. Will report progress anyway! Of course, he may pass away under the experiment, but as in this case 'it wouldn't really matter' that great Flanders maxim holds good.

Winkie is enjoying herself so much on leave, she refuses to come back till Sunday – a dirty trick I call it.

Funny old bird with whiskers all over his face, even round his eyes, pranced in here today, & wanted to do a painting of me for the official trench 'Album de Guerre', as he is told off for the purpose, being a distinguished artist. In addition to being in the album I was to have the great privilege to be then sold for 1d on a coloured p.card.

You will be surprised to hear I wasn't taking any, only it took me from 9am to 10.30 to convince Whiskers that I really meant it. He thought it most odd & we eventually parted with many deep bows, & expressions of untold mutual admiration! I quite expect him to be in again tomorrow & go thro' it all over again.

Charles has the itch – but otherwise is as charming as ever.

I am coming home mid Dec for over Xmas. Will you please send this on to Mother as I haven't time to write to both.

Ever so much love Da dear

Yr ever after if somewhat eccentric darter

Diddles

23rd Nov

Mother dear –

I wrote a long yarn to Pa yesterday & asked him to send it to you. Many thanks for all Tubby's letters which are most interesting & I loved Peter's account of the man who had his tail blown off by 'misadventure'!

Last night the Bloke took me down to a place some way away to have supper with Burbidge & his Mother who are off on a stunt & are living in 2 ex cattle trucks. The latter really are fine. He has painted it all & carpentered & put up a cabin & pink curtains & a stove & it's as snug as a bug. We dived about & collected tins of things & had a supper party on nothing which was huge fun & like old days. B's Mother is once more going to take up her strenuous work in a day or two, & I hope she will have an easier time than the last which was bad for her nerves!

I am coming home about 12th of Dec. As 'Tonks' will be with me then, I think I will very likely spend a day or two in London on my way home, instead of at the end of leave, as Tonks doesn't like hunts & I do! Also I want to order some clo' [clothes] for out here & boots which I want in time to take back. Anyway will decide that later. As far I know you can count on having me at Newnham about 14th or 15th Dec & I will stay 3 weeks. Jelly comes home for Xmas for 6 days with his kids in London.

Much love DoDo

24th Nov

Mother dear –

Caswell, ie 'the Deb', Ginger's double out here has got to go to sea in a day or two too. Ginger went last week. It's a pity, they were such a nice couple those two. Real nice healthy, happy, English boys & such good sorts. They have had to go & finish their sea education & have been relieved by others who I believe are nice, but it's sad the old firm breaking up. Bloke, Burbidge & Shoppee will stay on I am glad to say. Deb came here to supper last night to say goodbye & as usual filled his cig case with my nice brown cigs & left me his woodbines instead. But he was fool enough to leave the case behind, so am sending it up today with the cigs out & filled with neat rows of sticks out of the garden – so net result of the transaction I am 2 doz woodbines to the good.

Thank Squeaks for her letter & give her enclosed.

Much love
DoDo

25th Nov

Oh Da dear what fun! I see you have the Order of the Nile, now you will be able to go in procession to the banks of the Nile & wash all your wives & darters in Sapon & make all the other wives furious. Just think how superior you will feel.

Honestly Da though I am delighted. You worked so hard out there it's nice to have it recognised.

We have used all the Sapon powder you sent & Hélène just written you for more – don't send soap as we have lots of it already – much love DoDo

Flanders
25 Nov 16

Mother dear –

Oh dear. No – I'm not blown up by bombs, nor nuffink near it. We had only 1 night's very inferior bombing with no casualties at all, & two days shelling. All excitement is now at an end & life jogs on as before in this salubrious city. The only improvement is that at Sunday Mass we get let off a sermon in Flam. Whatever the reason, suction or grace of God or fear of the Huns' obus I know not, but anyway the result is distinctly good.

You don't say how Miss Leader is doing. I hope she is not a rabbit. I am told she is ghastly shy but very anxious to stick to the job if you are pleased with her.

It is pouring wet again today. Winkie returns tomorrow, having had a macaroni-like fortnight's leave. But as my leave has often been very macaroni too I suppose I mustn't put arsenic in her tea after all – she's a dear kid & we miss her very much.

We have a lot of malade soldiers at times suffering from the acute itch, or as it is politely called in medical circles 'la gale'. I had two of them yesterday up at N to take away; a Zouave standing by was awfully sick at seeing men being evacuated for so small a trouble as he considered & said 'the town I come from near Grenoble has 3,000 inhabitants & over 2,000 of them have la Gale.'

I sympathised, but made a mental note to keep clear of the neighbourhood of Grenoble!

Squeaker would like it I feel sure – Matron would have too!

I am delighted night sister is such a success & Piper is better.

Much love DoDo

27th Nov 16
Flanders

Mother mine – Frightful flutter here at Furnes yesterday. I went up to see Esther McNeil & take her for a walk but she wasn't taking any walks having just got engaged to a cousin of hers, one Col McNeil, & as they had only just fixed it up I was much de trop [one too many], so tore out of the other door & fled. He seems a nice soul, though a good bit older than her. She then came down to supper & as we had nothing to drink her health in we made some Birds Custard & drank it in that!

Winkie is back again full of buck & having had the devil of a time in London with her people, the twin is going to be married in Jan, by the way Esther is going to get married in about a month too, but is staying on here. Her hubby is in Indian cavalry regiment & therefore she would be able to see much more of him by being this side of the water than at home. I am glad she won't be going off.

Mustn't it be nice to go on being McNeil & not have to re-mark your vests & pants!

Yr loving DoDo

30th Nov 1916

Mother dear –
Jelly is prancing round in circles in the kitchen, finding fault with the porridge, the bacon, me, Charles, Winkie, Hélène, the war so I have come in to write to you – so it has done someone a good turn anyway!

How go things with you? I got your copy of the review of Mrs K's book last night. Reviewers are odd people, it is impossible to know what they will praise or crab. Get the book yourself & read it & tell me how it strikes you as a casual reader? I of course may be prejudiced, but the whole tone of it disgusts me.

I am going up to see Mairi Chisholm today, so will see what she thinks of it. How is Eileen Leader getting on? Is she an emmet or worthy?

Yr loving DoDo

2nd Dec [1916]

Mother dear –
I would rather cross on the 12th because Tonks will be with me next day, as I have clo' to get in London I don't mind his coming shopping & doing gadgets with me, whereas I should be awfully bored if he came to stay in

the middle of my time at home to interfere with a golden letter day of a hunt! Of course it's very selfish to want to hunt, but I am just aching for one. I missed them all last year & am feeling depraved at this moment & panting for one!

We had 2 generals to supper here last night: the corps & div French Gen. Nice old birds both. They enjoyed themselves muchly & the old boy Balfourier brought us some heavenly carnations & mimosa which give a most depraved look to the 'salon' in Flanders, war time & all!

It really is very simple being English out here. If French people ask Gens to dinner & make them fetch the soup & wash their spoons between the soup & the pudding it is rude! If you're English it is 'original et amusant'.

Burbidge has gone home on leave for a fortnight.

My own car took 106 men during the month of Nov from N about the same as the month before.

Goodbye & much love dear

DoDo

Although Dorothie's attention was now focussed on her first Christmas break at Newnham since the war began, there was still vicious fighting going on. The Times *of 4 December 1916 reported: 'An artillery duel is in progress in the Dixmude region, to the north of that town, together with violent trench-mortar fighting.'*

6th Dec

Eileen Leader wrote Jelly she loves being at Newnham & you are awfully kind to her.

Ma dear –

I am awfully bucked. Burbidge is on leave & hunting & has practically bought another gee to bring out here for the Navy. If he does so, instead of taking it back on the 11th with him, he offers to lend it me to hunt while I am home. I am thrilled to the teeth as you can imagine. Have asked the Heaths if they will let me stable the gee with them as a 'paying guest'. Panting to hear if they will, otherwise I shall have to bring it & keep it in my bed at NP. As my bed is generally your bed on leave, I expect you to take a great interest in the Heaths' decision.

The Bloke goes on leave on the 12th when Burbidge gets back & has offered me a lift to Boulogne which is decent of him. He hasn't had leave for years. They get awfully little the poor sailors. I think Tubby is the limit, he gets leave most weekends as far as I can make out. That's 2 or 3 isn't it since I was home? – dirty dog.

I am glad you are fed up with Mrs K's book as I think it's a rotten shame on all other women working out here, as it will tar them all with the same brush.

Winkie is learning to type so I am suggesting she practice on you. She's getting quite excited because she can address an envelope now in under 25 minutes.

Hélène sends her love & Charles too.

Yr loving

Diddles

It's so nice to see you all soon

38 Cadogan place, SW

Tuesday night [12 Dec]

Oh Mother mine –

It's very nice to be in Blighty, indeed it is. I've had a lovely hot bath, have a fire in my room, am writing snug as a bug in bed with a Jim, linen sheets and a loverley [sic] pink ribbon in a nifty nightie.

In fact the war seems very far away – I wish it was really.

It was very nice to hear your voice on the phone tonight Mother dear. Father rang me up just after to say he will be in London on Thursday night & he is very anxious for me to spend that evening with him as he won't be able to get down to Newnham – he is wiring me his plans tomorrow. If he wd like me to I will try & arrange & come down early Friday morning instead of Thurs aft as I'd intended.

That rotten Tonks hasn't arrived yet I am furious as I asked him on purpose to come & shop with me!

Ever so much love darling

A great big hug from Diddles

CHAPTER 12

January–February 1917

Dorothie returned to Furnes after her Christmas break into the worst winter Europe had seen for years. War diaries of this time all comment on the conditions: 'The cold was intense, which, combined with a biting wind, made life almost unendurable.'

6 Jan

Mother dear – a little scrawl by this morning's post to tell you I am at 14 again & very nicely too, sitting up & taking nourishment. We had a good crossing. Poor Winkie has a perfectly awful cold & has been feeling rather rotten. She is going home for a few days tomorrow for Brownie's wedding & I am doing her work at the canteen all lunch time. It's lucky I didn't put off my return any longer, as Mrs Taylor is still very very ill in hospital & couldn't let Winkie go if there was no one to superintend. So this fits in all right, I do her job half the day & mine the other half.

Must run now – ever so much love & a big hug from yr loving Diddles

Jan 7th 17
Flanders

Mother dear – bustled Winkie off this morning, to her twin's wedding, she wants a change too as she had a flu while I was away & was feeling rather rotten with an awful cough so I am glad I was back in time to do the canteen job & release her.

Yesterday quite a strafe up at N, a powerful lot of noise but luckily very little result. We got in late in consequence, a poor little arab nag belonging to some Zouaves was tethered in one of the buried homes that was getting a bad time. 3 obus came into the building & knocked the walls about & filled the place with smoke & the poor old gee whinnied & was in a great fuss. Luckily the owner turned up soon & removed it. It hadn't any business to be there to start with – but wasn't hurt a bit.

Everything here much the same.

Mrs Taylor terribly ill in hospital with 105 erratic temperatures at intervals & awful abscesses. I don't think the poor woman will ever be right again.

I hope Squeaks & Peter had some real good hunts, our last day all together was such fun. I enjoyed it more than I've enjoyed anything for ages. Saw Burbidge today who's very pleased with himself. I hear the Navy nag arrived safely at Dover without any trouble. They got a govt order to box it but it's held up there a few days waiting for a transport.

Yr loving Diddles

8th Jan 17

Mother dear – am scribbling this at the canteen between cutting 450 treacle sandwiches & getting the kids' dinners – treacle days are a joy of stick as you can imagine!

Yesterday at our barracks, George the orderly (soldier) dashed out in a great state of excitement & congratulated me on the naissance [birth] of my 'petite fille' [little girl]. I declined the honour gracefully & when he was calmer found it was his petite fille that had just blown in & he wanted his 5 days leave. He then explained that he had now 3 living & 2 dead & added 'isn't it sickening those 2 died, or else I should be at the arrière [away from the front]'. Because you know all French soldiers having 5 kids are now given base jobs. What amused me was his utter indifference to the kids being gone until he found it entailed his doing more work. But as he philosophically remarked with a shrug 'I do not have a chance!'

I do Winkie's job till lunchtime & then my usual run in the afternoon.

Torrents of rain the last 2 days & nights & everything a sea of mud. It's today Peter goes back I do hope he got a bit of an extension. It seems ages ago since I was at home, just as when I get back home, Flanders seems at the Antipodes.

The Belge C in C General Wilkins just died suddenly. He was a nice old boy but absolute putty. The new man is a much more competent soldier & I hope will give the boot to many at GHQ. The Belge staff is a collection of awful slackers who have pulled strings for a soft job & do as little work as possible. Their army will never be 1st rate on account of its bad officers.

Charles sends his love & me too.

Diddles

I expect George's wife will have to work double time now to produce twins before the war is over so that he can get a base job. Votes for women!

Wed night
10th Jan

Father dear – it was awfully nice of you to hurry up to London to spend the evening & to come & see me off, & I was glad I didn't have to cross while you were doing your course.

It has poured with rain, every blessed day since I've been back & the roads are in a grand state of old slop. In fact Flanders in top winter form. I am working double time these days as I do canteen from brekker to lunch for Winkie so that she could slip back for a few days to her twin's wedding in London. Then in the afternoons we go down to the far off hospital near the base practically every day now & don't get in till after dark. There is nothing very new or exciting to tell you. Been one or two little hates up at N since I've been back. My friends, the convict regiment, seemed to have quieted down & not committed any enormities lately which is dull of them. They are leaving too which is sad.

Hélène is still blessing her bon poudre Sapon & gets very indignant when I give it away to the others. She looks on it as entirely her property. The sailor's gee I had at the Heaths has arrived here safely, but not without humour. The gee had to wait a few days in England for a transport so the groom came over. Then the transport officer wired the Mish that '2 cases of Perrier for the King Albert & the horse' were arriving at once so Teck pattered out at 11pm to wake the groom & say there was a horse arrived for the King & he must go & get it so a minion had to go & fetch it & put it in the Royal stables. Then the sailors heard what had happened & Burbidge went down to claim the nag. The groom said it was H.M's & refused to give it up or believe Burbidge or even give him his own horse-rugs! Little B frothed at the mouth with indignation & had to spend the whole forenoon seeing a general & Col etc before he could have the nag. All of which has amused everyone except Burbidge, who as you know loathes all Belges & is always ready for a scrap even with HM.

It's late & I will turn in & am tired. Goodnight Mr Da – forgive a dull letter, & write me the back chat when you have time.

Yr loving Diddles

11 Jan 1917

Mother dear – I've just got your letter from London. You & P & Squeaks seem to be having the devil of a spree. Mrs K is away on leave so I had supper with Mairi the other day which was fun. She is a dear kid & is growing so pretty too.

I see Winkie's twin was safely married & Winkie was present.

Delighted Taffy had such a jolly hunt, but expect the grey will die in the night!

I have pinched some awfully good photos of N off the Bloke. You will have to wait to see them till next leave. The little Gen who came to call in yellow gloves just before dinner has gone, & the same people come back that were here a few months ago. We never expected to see them turn up here again. One is so accustomed to having to say goodbye to people just as you get to know & like them, that it's an unusual sensation to find them coming back unexpectedly. They are a nice lot but less pugnacious than our convict pals.

A great concert going on in the café next door & Jelly blowing the most nauseating bubbly noises up his pipe, so I will close. Hoping this finds you in the pink as it leaves me at present.

Diddles

'Yesterday (Monday) evening an enemy party attacked one of our advanced trenches to the south of Dixmude. He was completely repulsed by our rifle and grenade fire. One of our chaser airmen brought down a German machine, which fell in the neighbourhood of Beerst (north of Dixmude)' – The Times, *13 January 1917.*

Jan 15th, Flanders

Mother dear – a scrummy day today. All sorts of excitements on at the canteen which I am running pro tem as Esther still honeymooning, so I couldn't go to N today. I've been trailing round all day, & of course Tonks would come along too, he always enjoys anything like that so! As I'm on my way to bed, forgive a dull letter.

Poor little Burbidge down with appendicitis which is sickening for him. He is down at the base hospital but they hope by starving him to get him over to Blighty in a few days to get him operated on there instead of here. The Bloke & he very sick as they are afraid someone might get sent out here instead of him if he takes a long time getting well. I hope he doesn't get moved on – it would be sickening. Do you remember our last new member, one Kemp of 'Beseech you return my son' fame? He & Gurney were in one of the cars yesterday & a 11 inch neatly removed all trace of what a second before was a more or less complete house. As it took place alongside their car, it ought to teach him to be neurasthenic. He's getting on quite well tho' except he still drives abominably.

Good night Mrs Ma & such a lot of love & thank you for your letter from Harrow.

Yr loving DoDo

17th Jan 1917

Mother dear –
Poor Winkie wires she is in bed with an awful cold & rheumatic pains & not allowed to cross yet. She has had bad luck for her leave poor child.

Today I was asked to lend a comfy car to take a Belge officer to La Panne. When I suggested the ambulance I was told 'oh but I don't like to suggest his going in an ambulance – why, he belongs to the nobility.'

When I said the nobility had to do a lot of comic things these days & the sooner he realised it the better, I fear I was looked upon as unsympathetic!

Went to see Burbidge this afternoon at his hospice after depositing my blessés. He's looking rather seedy, poor little man.

Delighted to hear you have a pet of a night sister to excite Da – it's an ill wind etc, & now he can have his 'comfortable little nurse' at last.

Lots of love – awful busy.
DoDo

18 Jan 17

Mother darling –
I have just had a circular from General Booth, Salvation Army (perhaps you have heard of it? Yes? I continue) He is very keen on immigration to Canada as a job for superfluous women in England. He apparently considers I am one & is awfully bucked for me to go to Canada & ginger up the birth rate. Isn't it sweet of him to take so much trouble over me? Shall I tell him to mind his own blinking business or shall I hustle off & get a ticket? Perhaps the latter cos then I could probably mail you a brace of twins bi-monthly to give you something to do at home, instead of wasting your time at the Denbigh Arms in the scandalous way you do.

Snow all day here & rain alternately. Perfectly loathly out. I got a nice letter from P today & am glad to hear he isn't being given an active job 'up' yet. They have more sense than I gave them credit for.

Lots of love darling
Yr ever
DoDo
Teck just been in & full of chat. He's an awfully kind old boy.

Jan 19th

Mother dear – you'll be glad to hear I have just washed my hair, you should have seen the little nippers nip, lovely ad for Earl of Denbigh's Sapon powder.

Must go & do cars, we have got a lot down for repairs all at once as usual. If one car goes in dock there is always a collection at once.

It's bitterly cold & beastly here now. Winkie wires laid up with flu & rheumatic pains & doctor won't let her cross for a fortnight. Poor kid it's bad luck. Bar the one day she got up for the wedding she has been in bed all the time. I miss her awfully, but am glad for her sake, tho' not mine, she is laid up at home – she'll get better much quicker. This is an awful place for shaking anything off. I don't know why, but it is & everyone finds the same.

Esther just got back, full of vim & honeymoons seem to agree with her.

Lots of love, forgive mouldy letter but great hurry & I have got a frightful 'blight' so would write a stupid letter anyway.

Yr comic

DoDo

Jan 19th 17

Mother dear –

Just got your letter of 15th saying only one letter from me & Peter since we left. I am so sorry letters are taking so long getting thro' as I've written nearly every day. Tell me do you prefer scrappy letters & often, or longer ones when one happens to have time? I go on the supposition you prefer them often, tell me if I'm wrong.

One of the dear nuns said to Esther 'Oh, I am so cold, although I have nine petticoats on.'

Esther – 'I have none on & I am quite warm although there's snow.'

Nun – 'Ah, but then you wash all over & that is so fortifiant.'

Things the same here – Fritz quieter again for the moment. He has been rather lively since my return this time. It's funny to see all our old friends of the Div that used to be HO back again. They had got rather sick of Flanders I think & were not entirely excited & pleased at seeing it again for another winter. I wonder how snowy places like the Vosges compare with these flat muddy countries as regards discomfort for the men in the trenches. Today the 1st day since I'm back, it hasn't rained or snowed, but there was a bitter wind to make up & snow still lying. You poor people in the dark, I do hope the carbide has turned up ok.

Yesterday going into N an apparently new sentry dashed out at the car, waved his bayonet excitedly & said to me 'Êtes vous Mees Dorothie?' I agreed I was & he then said condescendingly 'Alors allez'.

He had been warned I gather I wasn't worth bayoneting which was lucky, as he was full of vim & time seemed no object to him.

It's very late & I am tired. Had a long day & have the pip.
Goodnight & bless you all
Yr loving DoDo

22 Jan 17
Flanders

Dearest Ma – I haven't heard from any of you for several days, I expect you are all exhausted from crawling about & cooking tripe in the dark. God knows what Squeaker may have deceived you into eating for supper these dark nights, & as for the Light Diets I expect they are dropping off like flies.

Went for a ride yesterday with the Bloke down the seashore on Brewill's nag, which was very pleasant to have one again & given me some good colour, thereby improving temper considerably. Am scribbling this between chewing at lunch so look out for bits of margarine & sardines.

Poor Winkie still tied by the heels in bed, but she hopes to get up soon now. She has had bad flu with pains in her chest much as I had here last winter & the doctor won't let her cross yet. She was to have been back over a week ago poor child.

Must fly to dear old N – Stupid letter this & I quite realise it but néanmoins [nevertheless] I lof [*sic*] my ma.

DoDo

23 Jan 17 Flanders

Dearest Mother – such hard frost here & we are all having awful trouble to stop cars freezing up. However much you empty the radiator there is always a small deceptive bit of water lurking in some bit of pipe that succeeds in freezing up & doing you in the eye in the morning.

I dined with the sailors last night for the 1st time since Da was here & had a very merry evening. There is a sailor, one Adams, now with them who is one of the corniest cusses I've ever met; a rough diamond who has done everything from Navy to S Pole with Shackleton, then chucked Navy & did absolutely everything for a few years & joined terrier artillery (Lord FitzWilliams) at beginning of war. Got awfully bored with them all, so just got into a train, went away to Admiral Hood at Dover & joined up with him in the Navy again. The gunners want to courtmarshal him for desertion after the war! But he tells the most priceless yarns in quite the funniest & most solemn way. All the others love him & last night I laughed so much, I couldn't manage to do any eating as I nearly choked whenever I tried. He's a great asset to the stagnation of Flanders.

Here Jelly comes in to say another bit of pipe being discovered frozen – quell hell – must go & help.

Lots of love DoDo

25 Jan 17

Mother dear –

Still the blackest of black frosts & we are all frozen to everything but it's much better than mud & the tommies prefer it too.

Shoppee told me a nice yarn yesterday about Gen Bridges of the 'Mish' in the early days here in 1915. It appears Bridges, Shoppee & one Major Thompson (also Mish) went out to a place where Germans had been driven back in the night, to collect papers off Boches that might be of interest. At one spot Thompson stayed behind while the other two went exploring up a trench. Here there was an old wounded sheep among the dead Boches, so Bridges used his revolver to kill the poor beast, on returning Thompson anxiously asked what the firing had been.

'Oh,' Bridges bluntly remarked, 'it was only a wounded German in that trench. He was damn rude to me so I shot him.'

Thompson was perfectly furious & refused to speak to Bridges for days, & then was madder still when he found it was all invention. T being a great Socialist & always explaining what nice kind creatures the Germans really were.

I must go & do my bed & then some work.

Adieu kind friends adieu.

Yr loving

Diddles

Jan 26th 17

My dear Mr Da –

It seems ages since I wrote you & do you know you've been a pig & not written to me since Feb 1903? So pull up your socks & write to darter no 2 in Flanders.

We had a hate today up at N & they made a nasty mess of the road, & a lot of noise generally. But as so often happens more noise than results.

The Bloke's toys are now most beautifully housed in the 'dernier in' manner & they are very proud of them. They really are dashed fine. I was looking at the last new one this afternoon & they would interest you.

Such a black bitter frost out here, much nicer than mud except that it gives endless bother with the cars however much you run the water out

195

something always manages to freeze up in some strange way. Little bits lurking in queer pipes do you in all the same.

There is a great concert going on in the pub next door & a be-oootiful solo being sung by a beery tenor. As he stops every bar to apparently cough up a cork (as a concert) it is rather disjointed.

It makes it hard to write to a Col, when you feel that any remark you may make, may end the war in the Huns favour with a snap!

Such lots of things I want to tell you about that would interest you.

Mother has burst out into vulgar stories at last!! She sent me 2 very choice ones yesterday which delighted me.

Lots of love dear Mr Da

Yr loving

Diddles

Sunday 28 Jan 17 Flanders

Mrs Ma dear – I am expecting to be assured into heaven at least as a reward for my piety; it was an awful effort getting up to go to mass this morning so cold & all. Such tremendous frost as we are having here, 22 degrees a few nights ago, at least so they told me, the lie is not mine & I know you wouldn't believe it!

I had all sorts of exciting things to tell you & now they have simply wandered from my brain.

Kaiser's birthday yesterday & Fritz showed his excitement in many ways, one of them being casting 400 little presents to one of the Bloke's toys who are rather fed up about these little attentions which get monotonous after a while.

Charles has been washed & is feeling kittenish as a result so insists on sitting on my knee & putting his paw on the paper which is so helpful.

Lots of love

DoDo

29th January 1917

Dearest Mother –

Shrieks of excitement in Flanders because Da is sending along some sloe gin to keep the circulation going this cold weather. I won't be really happy till I get it though for fear he should play me the same dastardly trick as he played Rollo at Xmas, ie such as counterordering the patient's stimulant if a thaw should set in.

Have you heard from Peter lately? I haven't since he wrote he wasn't taking an active part in the war for the present.

I've just been given a ripping bowl of violets that smell lovely & enclose a sample to make your mouth water.

Got a long letter from Taffy yesterday full of yarns. Midge seems to have given her lots of exercise catching him lately & probably reduced Taff's waist measurement considerably thereby.

Please give enclosed to Squeaker.

Yr loving DoDo

A good many blessés yesterday – still the aftermath of Kaiser's birthday.

29th Jan 17

Mother dear –

My fingers are frozen absolutely stiff & I cannot write you a sparkling letter in consequence for I am much too cross.

All the canals here are frozen the most amazing thickness & I go sliding in the evenings when we come in, until the ends of my toes are all blistered. I shall have to give over for a day or two. It annoys me when I slide 10 yds & sit down hard to see a tiny Flam in vast sabots slide some 500 yds all out.

Lots of love

DoDo

31st Jan 17

Well Ma – since you like 'em 'often' here's another! Many thanks for your letters & the yarns of Rasputin & George Armstrong.

The most tremendous heavy firing last night & we were afraid it was the Boche making a stunt across the ice as the inundations are of course frozen. However they keep it broken every day with field guns enough to stop any serious advance over it. The noise turned out to be of the Belgians making however as they were ousting Fritz from a forward position you saw in the communiqué he had captured a few days ago.

We had practically no casualties tho' the noise was terrific, of course at night things always sound exaggerated & the flash of guns make everything light up. Hope Fritz was bored by the proceeding though I imagine he holds that part of the line as thinly as he possibly can, an old concierge every half mile or so & I bet they are wily old birds to get with an obus.

I've just been talking to Mairi Chisholm whose farm is close by there & she says the old house was proper on the shake all night from the firing, so was no14.

197

It's awfully odd the way sound carries further inside a house. Mean often here when there is heavy firing going on a long way away 30 miles or so you hear & feel it awfully plainly in the house. You then go outside to listen & you can hear nothing.

The vibration I suppose up the walls of the foundation in the ground.

Goodbye darling

Yr loving

Diddles

Philip Gibbs described the incessant noise from artillery:

'round Nieuport, Dixmude, Pervyse ... one could see the stabbing flashes from enemy's guns and a loud and unceasing roar came from them with regular rolls of thunderous noise interrupted by sudden and terrific shocks, which shattered into one's brains and shook one's body with a kind of disintegrating tumult. High above this deep toned concussion came the cry of the shells – that long carrying buzz – like a monstrous, angry bee ... which rises into a shrill singing note before ending and bursting into the final boom which scatters death.'

By this stage Dorothie had lived with this noise on and off for almost three years.

Feb 7th 17 Flanders

Tres cher monsieur le Colonel –

My letter to you complaining of your absence of epistles crossed the 1st of yours & since then letters from you have been pouring in. It's most nice of you to write me so often & very many thanks for all the news. No, the sloe gin hasn't yet come. It may possibly be that parcels are being hung up at Dover as they sometimes are, or again the DNTO [Dover Naval Transport Office] may have succumbed to the charms of your sloe gin.

I spent two days at Etaples during the time Rollo came last weekend & it was great fun. It's too far away to get to as a rule but this time Jelly had to go to Boulogne & I stretched a point & got him to drop me there Sat night & pick me up early Mon. It was so nice seeing Tubby again & we had a cheery time.

The drive back from there to no 14 was hectic to a degree. The snow had come down very heavily in the night & where it had been swept on the hills had just become a sheet of ice & the car wheels couldn't grip. Eventually, whenever we stuck, by beseeching the aid of any passing members of the British Army, I persuaded them to help push the pram up the hills. Then home here late that evening & most amazing cold – today I have a dirty cough & a throat & am feeling fed up & most shop soiled.

Timed my return just right because yesterday (Tues) we had a strafe on here up at N, no end of a tea party, artillery & infantry. All our cars were on the road all day, & we only got in late so I hadn't time to write to Mother. P'raps you will please send this on to her. The frost is bad here as everywhere & been to below zero often lately at nights. Even the edges of the sea are frozen which I believe hardly ever happens. I didn't know it ever did anywhere near England or France. The bombing season is quite over here now I am glad to say & I have invested in another 7 francs worth of glass for my bedroom window which bores me. The place here where we keep our reserve cars had the door knocked cock eye by the explosion of one. Last time they shelled too one hit the next house to the garage some 10yds away, so our cars seem lucky. Nothing ever comes near no14 so you mustn't be fussed.

I am turning in early tonight to boil my cold, so am neglecting my sainted Ma p'raps you'd send her on this & she won't be so fed up.

Good night & much love

Diddles

CHAPTER 13

March–May 1917

In March, Dorothie travelled to Switzerland to visit her younger sister, Marjie, whose husband Dudley had been captured in May 1915 and, after a year's imprisonment in Germany, had been sent to Switzerland as part of a prisoner exchange. For Dorothie the break was a welcome respite from the ugliness of the war.

Chateau d'Oex
March 30th

Mother dearest –
We are having great fun here. All the English colony sit & grouse & hate at Switzerland, till I feel it's as much as my life is worth to mention that I am loving every minute of it, whether it's snowing or blowing or sunning.

Of course it's very different for them after a year's captivity in a little village till they get to hate the very mountains they loved too at the beginning; it's the having nothing to do that wearies them all most. The Swiss are swines to the men here. Our Gov't pay them for hospital treatment of the men. The Swiss just herd them into a big building, feed them abominably, give them the minimum of doctoring & absolutely no nursing or care. Not even a single nurse or orderly or attendant in the whole building. The men just look after each other & everything is beastly. Some of the men go 2 & 3 weeks without having their beds turned or made. All the officers' wives here imploring to be allowed in as VAD & to run the place & look after the men, but the Swiss won't hear of it. They aren't even allowed to visit the men there. The reason is the Swiss doctors bag half the money for themselves that should be spent on the men & don't want to be interfered with.

I can't tell you what a revelation it is to me. I thought they were as well looked after as at home.

Today Marjie & I have hired 2 nags to ride. Great excitement. We are going out in Dudley's breaks so of course he has to go to bed for the afternoon.

The Earls here are a delightful couple & so good to Dudley & Marj. He is much better than I expected. The depression he suffered from has practically gone & he is very cheerful, of course he won't be fit for a good long while. He is rather generally seedy, but I think nothing permanent as I feared.

　　Much love
　　DoDo

4th April

Chateau d' Oex

Mother dearest – we are just off on an expedish down the valley for the day to a place called Gruyere, & it's sunning fit to burst itself & everything looks lovely & the war so far away.

　　I forgot what I told you about Dudley so we possibly will repeat. I thought his skull had been chipped. It apparently never was but the bullet depressed the skull with a result it presses slightly on the brain. This gives him often headaches & general mental depression. Then if he takes any violent exercise or overtaxes his brain the blood pressure resulting increases the pressure of the brain on the skull & gives him bad heads. The specialist at Montreux has dieted him etc & says to give it a good chance to respond to treatment as he hopes the brain may adapt itself in time to the skull pressure & cease to react. If this doesn't happen later on when he returns to England he may have to be trepanned & the skull raised.

　　Meanwhile there is nothing for him to do but wait. He is pretty fit himself. The chief trouble is he gets so awfully sick of this little place, since he is cooped up & has nothing to do. I think England would of course cure him quicker than anything. Generally speaking he is much better than I expected to find him. It's the fact he gets so bored & hipped here with endless days with nothing to do, which are the worst for him. Marjie is looking better than I have seen her look for 3 or 4 years. More like her old self & fatter, not such a thin run down little rake.

10pm – later
Couldn't post this today after all. We had a gorgeous day & only got in at 8.30. A really lovely little valley & God sent day. The sunset on the mountains was a dream. All the snow lit up with orange pink lights. In fact the nicest day I've spent for many months. Really lovely things to look at on all sides, which made one feel good inside.

　　Quite a lot of wild flowers down there, as the valley being wider than here gets more sun. Crowds of 'snowflakes', fat snow drops with yellow patches. I enclose you one to see.

Goodnight & lots of love.
Yr weary but vastly pleased darter
Diddles

Flanders April 10th 1917

Mother dearest – I got back here ok after the most awful journey from Switzerland – it takes 3 days each way from here to Chateau d'Oex. I was lucky enough to get a lift back from Paris in a little Belgian lady's car, on the way we stopped at Amiens to lunch with a Belge, Grisan of the big nose, Evy's pal who had been to NP. Walking thro' the restaurant there was suddenly a yell & my arm was grabbed by someone at a table who turned out to be Peter in there for a 24hrs jolly for Easter. Sensation! So I went & lunched with him & we had huge fun. He is out of the line for the moment making roads & being due for 3 or 4 days Paris leave is coming to spend them with me here instead. Grisan is coming up here himself next Thursday & is bringing Peter up in the car with him.

He is one of the few members of my family who have never visited the 'Chateau Mees' at no 14 & it will be great fun.

... I had the strangest journey coming back from Switzerland. Even more of a scrum than going down. One has to change about 8 times from Chateau d'Oex to Paris & never gets any sleep as all through the night you have to keep climbing out of trains & waiting hours for the next. At Dijon I had to wait 3 hrs on the platform at 1am. A seething mass of soldiers returning from leave everywhere & nowhere for a nit to wriggle even on the platform, whereas all waiting rooms out of the question. Getting weary I proceeded to sit on my suitcase in the middle of the mob. In the dark a fat French Tommy some 3yds square falls right over me & nearly squashes me flat & leaves me for dead. He got up & said 'Mon Dieu, I have almost run over a small animal!' & proceeded to pick me up & apologise & we departed the best of friends. Of course no sooner had I sat down again than someone else fell over me, so I gave it up! I shared supper with a nice little Zouave who hadn't any, & the dear thing in consequence carted my suitcase for me for the rest of the journey & so it was a true case of bread upon the waters. He had come from St Quentin & had a hectic time of it.

Then at last a train arrived & we got off, all the places full of course. Then arrived 3 Tommies & said they were permissionaires & might they squeeze in too – so they did. But then they saw their pals: George & Joseph & Alfonse & Jules & Robert & le sergeant on the platform & brought all them in too. Then Alfonse & Jules & the sergeant sat on me & proceeded to have supper. Alfonse was the underneathest but one (which was me) & proceed[ed] to try & extricate a string of sausages from his pocket. This sort like they have here. Greenish sausages on a string & each sausage tied round & round with string too. I suppose to try & localise the explosion. Of course Alfonse was so squashed he couldn't get the sausage out of his pocket & everyone had to come & do a tug of war. At last it came out with a rush & was cut up & distributed. I was offered some & had to think of all sorts of reasons why I couldn't eat sausage so as not to hurt their feelings. An old French lady in the carriage was very stuffy & scornful about it.

Of course at least half of the company were genteelly tight. It's the 1st time in my life I have seen anyone tight & was not disgusted. Here were these poor devils, all going back to Verdun, all good soldiers & pals & just been spending their leave as they liked, after all there was no merit in my not being tight, just because I hate it; my form of leave was to see my family & see something lovely & mountains. Theirs was to see their families & have a drink. After all we each had what we were hankering for hadn't we? Why should I have it & not they?

Much love darling
Yr after
DoDo

10th April
Flanders

Dearest Mr Da – it seems ages since I wrote you but I have been on a great beano to Switzerland & only got back on Sunday. I had a fortnight's leave & it takes over 3 days each way on the journey! But the time I had there was huge fun. I wrote Mother about Dudley & s'pose she showed it you. He is pretty well physically – it's more he gets awfully depressed & down in his luck. This is of course all a result of his head. Marjie is looking better than I have seen her for a long time. It was such a long time since she'd seen any of her family she was feeling rather homesick & lonely & was awfully glad to see me. I just loved a real rest in getting right away from war & hospital things for the 1st time for over a year. The country is perfectly gorgeous there after the monotony & dreariness of these everlasting plains. I had some fine weather there & some snowy days, but enjoyed them all. I found my watch here from you when I returned. It is most awfully kind of you to have seen to one for me & it goes very well indeed, I am wearing it now & it will defy the wear & tear which used to be too much for my little gold one. But I am afraid I am awfully greedy as I now want something else! Namely my rubber collapsible bath is worn out & beginning to leak, one can't buy any out here. Do you use the one you had in Egypt? If not do you think you could lend it to me? The green canvas ones leak so after a little, they are only usable in tents, the rubber ones are the best for out here. If you are using yours after all at Brentwood, p'raps you'd be a saint & ask Moll or someone to choose one in London would you please? Then I promise that's the last thing I'll want for ages & ages!!

Peter is coming here on Thursday to spend his leave with me for 2 or 3 days. Not home leave but what is known as Paris or local leave & Grisan, Evy's pal, is going to bring him up which is very decent of him – he was coming anyway in his car.

Lots of love Mr Da
Yr loving DoDo

Friday 13th April

Mother dear –
Peter never turned up yesterday which is very sad. I've heard nothing so suppose he just couldn't squeeze a few days leave he hoped for out of the OC. But Grisan will, I know, always give him a lift up, so next time he can get away I hope to see him instead. It's sad tho' because I was looking forward to having him here awfully.

Charles is sitting on my tummy which makes it hard to write & I am dead with sleep from the wind & will turn in. Such bitter cold gales blowing over these perishing plains, sleet & hail most days since I've been back. When you get a really bitter N wind you can't beat this for a climate as there is nothing between here & the N Pole but the N Sea to stop the gales.

Dined with Teck t'other night, everyone here very pleased over the advance but there's been some terribly hard fighting I'm afraid.

The Colonel of the _____ Regt was killed today in the street up at N poor old boy. I just knew him & he was a good sort & very popular with his men. I am very sorry.

Good night & much love – DoDo

April 15th

Mother dearest –
The world is a very sad place – I have just been spending today busy up at N which is active, but mostly on our part, & last night with Mairi Chisholm at P in the old cellar house where she is now. The Baroness was away & she was all alone poor kiddie & very unhappy as the boy she had just got engaged to, young Jack Petre, our cousin in the RNAS [Royal Naval Air Service] was killed 2 days ago in his machine on the Somme. They were only engaged privately so don't talk about it but I am so sorry for the poor little kid – she feels it dreadfully – all the more because she is a very quiet

reserved little soul, & as charming as the Baroness is 3rd rate which is saying a lot.

I am dreadfully sorry about it, he was such a nice boy & had a brilliant career. His machine came down like a stone through engine trouble while flying over the aerodrome & he was killed at once. He had been in the RNAS squadron up here a long time.

There is just a chance the Bloke may be able to fetch Peter in a day or two. He is taking some engineers down to the Somme & is going to try & hike P back on the way back. I hope it comes off.

Love from Diddles

19th April 17

Mother dear – such fun – Peter blew in here late last night as that saint Bloke went & picked him up on the way back from his Canadian job, & this time, owing to a pass from the Mish, all went well. He is here till Sunday & today we have been pottering round & showing him the sights & all & tonight are having a binge in his honour at 14 & some of the sailors to dine – great excitement because we have a tin of real cream, a tin of raspberries & a tinned duck we have been saving up in case he came, so won't we all have tummy aches tomorrow morning my word. Tomorrow, Prince Alexander has bidden me drag him to dine at the Mish. I can but hope he won't disgrace me by blowing bubbles in his soup.

Mairi Chisholm was sleeping in my bed last night, so Peter was dumped in a camp bed in the dining room. I went in to call him this morning & you never saw such a mess, on the table he had got: 2 bottles of beer, a whisky & soda, a slice of cake, 2 prs filthy Somme mud boots, braces, collar studs & a collection of horrible & unknown smells in an old haversack.

I tidied out the room & everything without his turning a hair or waking up.

Love
DoDo

Telegram – Furnes 24 April 17 – To Denbigh Rugby – All well Dorothie Feilding

26th April 17

At no14

My dear Colonel –

Things have been moving here just lately but I haven't had time to write you much about them, also I was waiting till the events had been duly recited in the communiqué before writing about them, as it is always wisest.

This having been done I will now tell you more about it, also the rubber bath has come before I forget to thank you for it. It is a dashed fine one & I am very grateful to Mr Da.

On the 23rd about four am, Fritz suddenly started launching gas at us from the local metropolis up at N. The wind wasn't very good for him, too much to the N with the result the gas came diagonally back from the lines & we here at no 14 got a very bad go of it. Jelly smelt it & woke up which was most intelligent of him; we all got up & threw on a few garments & of course hadn't a gas mask in the house as ours were in the car, which that night happened to be in the other garage down in the town. There was the limousine here however & Jelly started that & then he went off with the ambulance up to the lines & the gas being very bad by then here I evacuated Winkie & Hélène & the girl next door up to a hospital a few miles up the road. There I borrowed some gas masks & a spare driver as I was feeling rather faint & thought it best to have two drivers in the car. I left Winks & co there & tore back to no14 to find the gas had cleared away very quickly from there, as a matter of fact it had been following the road we took to the left & we were in it for 3 or 4 miles & so by bad luck got much more than the people who stayed here. By this time I was quite sure the Boche had overrun the sector as I couldn't imagine our having it so bad & the lines being still tenable. As a matter of fact, the waves were very local & came in gusts. For instance, the main part of the town here got none. It just travelled down in long columns. I rushed up to our barracks & was awfully relieved to find them all ok. They had had very good masks & the main gas column had passed to the right of them & on our way.

Then we just worked like navvies all day till dark. Simply never an engine stopped all day & we were all pretty beat at the end of it. At the beginning, Boche had rushed our lines but we drove them out again as the communiqué said & things are exactly as they were before now which is very satisfactory. The sector was very lucky to get off with the line in the old place.

It's a dirty business gas & rather frightening; comes in great foggy waves & makes you cough your head off. Those poor, poor devils of men. I can't tell you what it's like to see them all lying about unconscious & in the most awful states. Much worse than blessés in a way because there is so desperately little you can do for them. In many cases they are alright for 12 to 24 hrs & then go down like logs. The Boche had a lot of casualties from our fire & we got some prisoners too.

I felt quite (fairly) alright the day itself after the 1st hour. Just rather cut. It didn't work on me till 24hrs after when, at about 5am, I couldn't breathe except like a scared rabbit & went down to get a drink & then felt awfully faint. This kept coming on at intervals all that day, so I went to bed in the afternoon & have been there ever since. I am quite all right again now & am getting up again now as I haven't had a proper go of it since yesterday. It's a beastly feeling – you can't get a proper deep breath.

Winkie it affected quite differently. It made her cough awfully for 2 days. She is pretty right again too. Charles was awful fed up. He wheezed & was proper sorry for himself for several days. Jelly didn't feel it after the moment & all our people are ok. So would we have been if we had been able to get at our masks. All the Bloke's party ok. This is a long scrawl isn't it? Peter just missed the smell by a day which was lucky – yr Diddles

26th April 1917 Flanders

Mother dearest –

Have written Da an account of the fighting here & asked him to send on to you. I haven't had much time for writing lately & while Peter was here it was such fun having him & such a breathless life of one damn thing after another that letters slid then too. The boy was looking awfully well & in great spirits. He is making roads near Sully Sallisie where the Boche went back from 2 months ago & where he spent the winter in the trenches. Rather nice now to able to walk about & take the air where before one had to go on all fours!

I have been spending a day & a half in bed as the damn gas started working on me 24hrs after. We were all very lucky to get out of it so lightly & Fritz is no better off than he was before. I sent you a wire 'All well' in case you got anxious as a result of communiqués.

End

Sunday [29 April]

Mother dearest –

It's so nice & sunny today I am writing in the garden after brekker. Charles is full of fleas & awfully affectionate. Got a long letter from Marjie yesterday, they are down at Lausanne for 3 weeks leave which will do them both good. She seems to be getting over her bilious attack poor child.

Went to see old Ronarc'h yesterday who had just been having a few obus in his house. I think he was secretly rather pleased as now he sees so few obus he feels quite lonely! Such a mess as his drawing room was in after one had burst in his drawing room.

It had come in via a gilt consul table & he showed us with pride a bit of gilt cement about this size O which was absolutely all that was left of it! A large chunk had gone thro' his study door & made a dent in a picture of poor old Poincaré on the wall! Ronarc'h was in bed at the time so no one was any the worse.

The Bloke has just had one of his officers & 3 men killed in action here & several wounded, a very bad business & a case of sheer bad luck. A very nice chap too called Donovan who hadn't been here very long.

Lots of love DoDo

1 May 17

Mother dearest –
I've just been gardening after supper & planting radishes & sweetpea, in a faint hope of gingering up the great offensive. Nothing like making yourself comfortable to get moved.

The forget-me-nots we put in this year are going to be a failure. They didn't like the gas any more than I did & are quite yellow. I'm afraid it will put them out of their step pretty permanently.

Was at the Mish this afternoon where that arch fool, Major O'Connor, Da loves so, is being replaced by a Lord Vivian, a very nice bloke, who says he met Da a lot in Egypt & the other day in Blighty. I think he will be a distinct asset to the Mish.

A certain Hunnish activity today but nothing much, a lovely sunny day & I am beginning to hate my scratchy combinations & long for a chemise.

The dust is once more what Staley Johnson would call chronic.

Am awful sleepy today & feeling too uninteresting for words so bonsoir madam.

I wonder how French hospitals will affect Newnham – lower your no of blessés I trust.

Mrs Ma dear I want to ask you to be a good Samaritan. Next time I come on leave may I suggest to Mairi Chisholm that if she can get away (which is rather doubtful) she should come to Newnham with me for 1 or 2 weeks? She badly needs a complete change, & she has not got a single member of her family to go & stay with & so won't go on leave. Jack Petre's death she has felt dreadfully & it's so nice May on at NP. It would do her good, she could share my room whenever you liked & be no trouble. It would be sweet of you if I may suggest it her. Let me have an answer as soon as you get this, will you please?

Yr loving DoDo

3rd May 1917

Mother dearest –

Sailors just given me a great armful of little wild daffies that grow out in the dune. They are lovely & remind me so of Newnham, but I expect yours aren't out yet.

We had another gas alarm yesterday about dinner time & all dragged out our masks & waited for it – but nothing happened! Taut mieux [all the better].

You ask me if we had many passengers t'other day. Between six & seven hundred.

I see in my passbook an item in my private account: Feb 9th. Countess of Denbigh £10.

Was this a Xmas present or anything from you to me, or is merely it should have been paid into my no2 Ambulance account in joint names yourself & me? Would you be a saint & let me know please as if it's ambulance money I must transfer it.

Am praying it's not as I am overdrawn as a result of going to Switzerland so until I hear the worst am being an optimist for once & hoping for the best!

Love DoDo

4 May 1917

Mother dearest –

Lovely peaceful day yesterday & everybody decided not to fight which was very pleasant.

Thérésé de Broqueville is staying with the minister for a few days & came up to have supper with us. She had come to see Robert, who is with his gun near Vimy, but he was recalled in a hurry & so she hardly saw him & was very depressed. He seems to have had a most interesting time there. During the advance when their gun was being moved up again he had nothing to do, he used to follow up behind the English infantry & amuse himself collecting Hun prisoners hiding in the dug outs. He saw the English cavalry in action there at the beginning of the offensive. Apparently one of the reasons they lost so many was because the cavalry officers did not know the ground. Why they weren't acquainted with it thoroughly from opt. [observation post] etc before the action I can't think.

The French are having an awfully stiff time of it down Rheims way owing to the Boche having chosen the same ground for a counter offensive. Had a short scrawl from Zette's Pa in the thick of it there. He says it is desperately hard fighting & a case of hand to hand fighting over every inch of ground to be won; artillery preparation useless there as the Boche has so much massed too & countershoots. Losses desperately heavy & things pretty well stalemate on both sides. It's a pity & a waste of effort. I don't know what will be the next move now that has failed.

Poor France, she has been sadly 'éprouvée' [tested] in the war. Her losses compared to the population are overwhelming compared to ours. Down there this offensive alone they have already had over 86,000 casualties.

Of course the Boche must have lost a lot too, but not so many there as in front of the English.

Peter writes they show no sign of moving them which is a good thing isn't it? I must tell you when I come on leave as to how I took him back there, a most interesting day but I can't write about it now. Much the same scenery as Da saw with Tubby only of course under different conditions now & all the more interesting really on that account.

I took some groups when Peter was on leave with me one day we were riding with the sailors. I am telling Seaman to send you some as they are quite good of the lad.

Lots of love Mrs Ma & Gott strafe Tonks

Yr loving

DoDo

Wed 9th [May 1917]

Mother dearest –

Came down here to spend the night with Thérésé & Papa Broqueville who, poor dear, is laid up with very bad sciatica so I came down to cheer him up & pass the time of day. Am just on my way back to no 14 with huge armfuls of heavenly Azaleas, pale yellow & cherry blossom & nice copper beech branches etc it's so nice to see flowers again. I hope the daffies will be nice when I come on the 17th & not too over. I haven't heard yet if I may bring Mairi Chisholm. Will wire you if there's no letter for me at 14 as she will need a little warning. I hope you can have her poor kid, she has nowhere to go & it would do her such a lot of good.

Lots of love

DoDo

CHAPTER 14

June–July 1917

When Dorothie's letters start again following her leave, she is engaged to be married to Captain Charles Joseph Henry O'Hara Moore, Irish Guards. Their engagement was announced in the Daily Mirror *on 12 June and seems to have happened quite suddenly, catching even some of her friends and family by surprise. Dorothie was happy, though, having found the big, strong man she had joked about marrying in October 1914.*

Thurs [7 June]

Dearest Mr Da – I am just off to Flanders for a bit to settle things there & I was so sorry not to see you again.

Mr Da dear, it's so wonderful to feel perfect peace & happiness again it seems almost another life since I have felt really happy.

I was scared to death the 1st day wondering if everything would be all right but now I am quite quite sure of it. As for Charles he is sure enough for six!

Goodbye Da darling – I'll be back soon – you have been such a saint to all us kids always & spoilt us so, we can never thank you enough.

Charles is going to put the 'fiasco' in the paper on Monday.

All my love

Diddles

8th June

Mother dearest –

Had a perfect crossing yesterday & got here about 9pm. The mail is going early today & I am only having time for a scrawl. I began this hours ago, but the navy has been firmly planted on the doorstep in successive deputations since dawn! I am threatened with every form of death from gas to crucifixion & Burbidge is strafed because they tell him if he hadn't given me the bad example I'd never have thought of it.

I am very glad I came now as there are changes on & it is just the right moment.

I missed a repetition by 24hrs of that [gas] stunt that made me seedy a month ago. It wasn't so bad & didn't come to no 14 this time. But the Tommies had a grim time, it's a ghastly business always, I wish I had been able to help them just once more. We are getting spliced at Newnham early in July, Mrs Ma, if possible in the cellar or on the flag staff. The padre chaplain in Charles battalion if he can get leave.

Mother darling I am very happy. I think Tom & Edie [Charles's sister] & Hughie saw & wanted to help me. The last few months have been awful & it's so wonderful to be at peace. Especially in this country so full of memories of sorrow & pain.

Goodbye Mother dearest

Diddles

June 9th Sat

Mother mine – I've had the most lovely day. I had plotted with that long suffering man the Bloke, to go & hunt up Tubby & Peter today as they are quite close. It was all settled when at 8am this morning they suddenly blew in here, bursting with excitement & awfully pleased with themselves. We had the greatest fun & in the afternoon begged an array of nags off the sailors & Mish & all went nagging down the beach & dunes. Then to tea with the sailors & then they went off about six. It was a joy having them & they are both looking frightfully well. Peter said he was due for a drop of leave about July & would try his best to be at Newnham to 'see me pass away' so if we can fix it up for 1st week in July that ought to suit everybody.

 Mother dearest, I feel it's almost wrong to be so happy these days. I wish I could bring some happiness into you too to make up for your dear Hughie. Will you be glad I'm not in Flanders getting potted at any more? Mairi Chisholm ran in this morning, looking worlds better, she was so touched at your having her at Newnham & I never thanked you half enough. It was because I know that awful desolation that sweeps over every corner of one's soul & being that I wanted so to help her a little. It was so awfully nice of you to have her, & thank you so much dearest.

Goodnight & all my love

Yr funny Diddles

In this letter, Dorothie explains how the men in her life impacted on her work with the Corps.

12 Juin Flanders

Mother my darling – I got your sad letter last night, & I have been a selfish beast. It seemed so wonderful to feel at peace & a desire to live once more that I have left you thinking all the help I have been to you these years is at an end. Mother dearest, my being happy won't come between us for 'a daughter is your daughter all her life' & our sympathy is too deep for anything to change it.

At times I have wished I hadn't the power to feel things deeply & that the superficial beings are the happiest. But it's not so – God gives you a bigger soul in exchange for pain & the power to be capable things.

Some time before the war Charles & I were very near caring for each other. Then, for no particular reason, we drifted away imperceptibly back to just friendship. I think it was then I first began to think a great deal of Tom [Fitzherbert Brockholes]. Then Tom went to India & I never saw him again as I went straight to France. But we wrote to each other & in so doing had both felt a deeper & newer affection growing out of our old camaraderie. We weren't engaged but I know we should have been had we met again – we both always thought we would meet again quite soon. Then he died just as my love for him was beginning to waken & the bottom seemed to have fallen out of my life. I didn't care whether I lived or not so you see it wasn't very meritorious to be brave. I just threw myself heart & soul into the work out here & I got to love my soldiers like my children. It was a positive need to me, to share the life & dangers of this war with them. My whole soul cried out for it & no other kind of work would have helped me one fraction as much; out here right at the heart & pulse of things one finds realities & greatness. The best of everyone comes out. But the sadness of it all worked its way into my very soul. Of all these men who cared for me, it only made it harder & the last 6 months I had got into a sort of mental stupor. I can't describe it. Just a great ache & loneliness. You see, God by teaching me suffering had given me a bigger soul capable of far deeper feeling, but had given me nothing else as yet to make up for the suffering.

I used to try & force myself sometimes to care for people I saw who sincerely loved & needed me, so that I might make them happy. But then at the last minute there was never anything but bare friendship & it couldn't suffice me & I was afraid to marry with only that.

When I met Charles the other day & he told me how he cared, I felt for the 1st time, that he could awaken my power to love (which I thought had died in me) if he loved me strongly & enough. At the very beginning I was afraid perhaps my loneliness was influencing me unduly & that I had not yet found the real thing. But so very soon I was quite, quite sure everything was right. The big things in Charles had not been stirred before the war. He was inclined to be idle & drift through life without being properly alive. The army & war generally has done to him what it has done to many people including myself. He loves me so much, Mother dearest, & so deeply that he has made me love him; it is not just a wild wave of sentimentality, it is [a] real thing which grows greater every day & is coupled with an infinite trust & confidence in him & in what the future will bring. Please God, he will be some months at home, before all the mental 'angoisse' [anguish] begins again. I am feeling so small & stormtossed, I couldn't bear any more just yet. I need just a little bit of peace & happiness so badly Mother dearest. I could keep going before without it Mother darling. Now I seem just to have crumpled up & I couldn't stand any more just for a little while.

I must see about some clothes I suppose – my dress bill has certainly been small enough for 3 years!

All my love dearest & thank God for you & all you have meant to us kiddies. I fear I could never be one-tenth the mother that you have been the way you have cared for us all.

Yr loving

Diddles

When Rollo & Peter came to see me & were so glad to see me happy again it gave me such an ache for our Hughie. I think he would be glad it's Charles don't you?

13 June Flanders

Mother dearest –

I am returning on Saturday unless anything odd happens to prevent me. Then to Newnham. There's an awful lot of things to see to & do before pushing off & life is one damn thing after another. Got a good obussing up at N yesterday for the last time. I'll feel very lonely without it but I've been good as gold as I said I would; yesterday I sat for ages in a dugout as if butter wouldn't melt in my mouth instead of investigating the bursts. I don't think I could keep it up for long.

Must fly & do chores. Went out for a really heavenly ride down the beach with the Bloke before breakfast, colours of the sea & dunes too lovely.

Winkie & I had a farewell supper party at the sailors which was too sad. They have represented home to me out here & been such dears to me. They got up one by one & drank my health & wished me happiness so sincerely & said such nice things if it had gone on another minute I should have sat down & howled!

So to cheer us up we then took Winkie on a joy ride to N where of course she had never been; a perfectly peaceful evening & very creepy in the moonlight. She was so excited she nearly burst! We felt as she was leaving she might as well commit an enormity!

All my love Mother dearest
Yr loving DoDo
Who needs you as much as ever.

Sat 10pm in train from Folkestone [16 June]

Mother dearest –
You can't think what a scrum life has been out yonder these 10 days. There was a lot of corps business to do as the English are taking over from the sea to Pervyse including Nieuport, only don't repeat this at present of course. There is going to be the devil to pay up that way soon & big fighting. Furnes I expect will be wiped out in a few months, poor little place. Our cars are working temporarily for the English during the changeover & then follow the same French corps we have been with all along & which will be somewhere between Ypres & no14 instead of at Nieuport. The corps is going on – of course future months may change it. It's rather extraordinary all this happening as I got back, for as far as I can see my active work with the corps would have been at an end as they will be working in an English area which puts the lid on poor me too. So I feel less of a rat leaving a sinking ship than I did when I returned – it never rains but it pours does it & just think how miserable I should have been at having to chuck the work like that.

Winkie, at the last minute, refused to come home! She is staying on for some weeks anyway & possibly for the summer to work at her canteen. Rather comic after making me swear I would bring her back with me & not desert her in Flanders! No 14 is being kept as a depot & Hélène coming to be my minion in July.

You ask about Tonks which might come & see me about 26th. Hun apart I would like to get spliced 1st week in July & at Newnham. I would hate & loathe a London wedding unless Charles & Binkie [his mother] have damn good reasons I'm not taking any at all at all.

I want to go & see something nice in the way of country for a change. There is an idea of our honeymooning at the Kenmore's place nr Killarney & getting a car to go motoring there & the W coast of Ireland which I believe is so lovely.

Mother darling I am very very happy & love you beaucoup beaucoup
Diddles

Mon Ritz hotel London [18 June]

Mother darling –
We have decided Thursday 5th not the 3rd after all for the funeral if that suits you.

Could you put up Binkie, Charles & best man? His regimental pals, one or two as really want to come, could come by Irish mail to Rugby. I've asked Mellins to let Billy & David be pages. I'm getting a little plain white frock & veil, no train or bridesmaids or fuss, but would love those stugs as minute guardsmen with their white clothes & guards belts.

Any immediate relations of Charles who insist on coming we intend billeting on Aunt A at Holthorpe but haven't broken it to her yet!!! She could bring them over that morning.

I couldn't bear the thought of being cremated in London for the amusement of Tit Bits, Mothers Home & Pigeon World.

Thank you so much for your dear letter, Mother darling. Yes, you & I understand each other pretty well, I love you so much & will always need you you know, so don't imagine you are going to be let off lightly for 2 years.

Feeling sick as a dog after too many strawberries & cream.

Yr loving
DoDo

Her letters for the rest of June are full of wedding preparations. Dorothie was determined to have the last laugh and sent the following telegram to Newnham from Rugby railway station on the morning of her wedding day:

5th July 17

To Commandant Newnham Paddox Monks Kirby

Got cold feet decided take single ticket to Skegness

Diddles

Dorothie and Charles were married at Newnham Paddox on 5 July 1917. Photos of the wedding appeared on the front page of the Daily Sketch *and show her and Charles posing with the soldiers who were convalescing at Newnham.*

CHAPTER 15

July–December 1917

Dorothie and Charles honeymooned in Ireland, travelling around Killarney and spending time at Charles's home, Mooresfort. Dorothie was desperately trying to rediscover the beauty in life after her experiences, although she always kept one eye on the war. She also continued to write to her mother throughout her honeymoon.

Waterville 12th July [1917]

Mother dearest –This country is just too beautiful. It really is. The most lovely 'purple' evenings rather like Granada that I sit & gloat over. The car is great fun but we are now running out of petrol & will I expect have to go to Mooresfort by train. But who cares, it's not ours so we can leave it in a ditch somewhere.

I am most awfully distressed to see the bad communiqué about Nieuport. It means the whole div the other side of the Yser was killed or taken prisoner & they have got right up to the locks which is the important ground the French have always worked so hard to keep. I hope all my friends there are ok & the sailors & all, but it's beastly & I can't get it out of my head.

Lots of love darling

Yr always

DoDo

The following day:

I haven't heard anything new from Nieuport beyond what is in the papers. It's a bad business isn't it? It must have been pretty ghastly there the day of the big attack. I'm worried.

When does Peter go back? I hope to see him in London with luck on his way back.

Charles sends his love & we haven't fought yet. Positively uninteresting in fact ... He gets slightly more unhinged every day. I really must try & grow a bit to compete better.

Lots of love & I am so glad you have P back.
Yr loving stug
DoDo

She was back in England by the end of July, missing her brother Henry who had been home on leave.

Ladies Imperial Club
1 Aug pm

Mother dear –
We have been trying to get news of Peter's whereabouts for you & Squeaks, & Charles has seen diverse guards people, one just back. The rumour they were at Nieuport is wrong. The Guards attacked directly opposite Boesinghe marching on the right of the French. The latter had very light casualties. Guards casualties unknown as yet – Irish G were in the 1st attacking lot. The Guards were divided into 3 brigades for the stunt to go on in turn. Peter's was the third to go if needed. So that means his people only went if badly needed which is unlikely & Da tells me P was down to stay back as 2nd in com for the 1st shove, so I think this will make you less anxious. The guards threw bridges over the river & got over with little difficulty I believe because the Boche 1st line on other side was knocked to blazes & practically not held at all by the Boche who had taken his men back to the next line after the destruction of the prelim bombardment.

If I hear any more I will of course tell you as I know you will be anxious these days. This weather is bad for them all poor souls. Just seen the 'best man' of ours who says he had a great theatre party with the cook [Clare] & enjoyed himself muchly.

Just dining with Da & then back home ... Lots of love Mother dear I am praying hard you may not have too much anxiety over Peter these days but so far it has been so lucky the way everything has turned out – DoDo

Warley 3rd Aug

Mother dear –
No news to be got as yet from beyond for you. I fear everything is hung up. I got a letter from Peter of the 29th saying 'I'm not taking a leading part in this hunt, more of a scene shifter than anything else.' If I hear anything I will tell you at once. This wet weather is awful for things out yonder ...

... Charles was vetted yesterday in London by his doctor who says there is still a certain amount of adhesion after his pleurisy. He still feels it you know at times. The Dr says he wouldn't consider him fit for abroad for about 2 months as until it has cleared off entirely exposure or a bad chill would go to the lung again. He now has to go for a regular board again with the Dr chit & so I hope it will mean he is here for about 2 months for sure yet. Of course if they should be hard up for officers after this push he would go & chance it.

Still thank God for adhesions & long may it adhere!

Love DoDo

Warley
5th Aug

Mother dear – this awful weather seems to be holding everything up in Flanders. I haven't any news to give you as there is none. I wired you Charles went up to London to see the orderly room & they said Peter was alright as they had the unofficial list of casualties & no mention of him.

The Irish Guards have lost a good lot of officers. They led you know. Poor Charles is awfully low because his 3 best friends were all killed that day. Col Eric Greer (married Pam Fitzgerald), Sir John Dyer & Father Knapps who was to have married us. All 3 were with him all the while in France & are about the only ones of his old lot still out there.

Lots of love Ma dear
Diddles
It will be so nice seeing you all some day.

This latest offensive was the 3rd Battle of Ypres, more commonly referred to as Passchendaele. Dorothie and Charles used their contacts in Flanders to try and keep track of Peter's movements. Halahan wired Dorothie whenever he had definite news:

17th Aug 17

To Denbigh Rugby
Bloke wires Peter still out
Dorothie

Charles had a stud at Mooresfort and Dorothie, a keen rider in the hunt, embraced the world of racing. On 28 September she wrote her mother a triumphant letter:

Had a most amusing 2 days at the Curragh & I enjoyed myself disgustingly, our 2 little nags ran awfully well. 'Sister Barry' won her race but was dead heated by another gee owing to her fool jockey making a mistake. But that was good anyway. Then 'Judea', the one we pin all our hopes on was a close second in the big race the turf Cub Cup. I got so excited I nearly burst & am all of a dither still.

Unfortunately tragedy was just around the corner. Dorothie had missed Henry [Peter] when he was last home on leave and so had not seen him since that June.

Henry was wounded in action near Broembeek, Belgium, whilst leading No. 2 Company, 2nd Coldstream Guards on 9 October 1917. The Battalion War Diary described how the men struggled through a muddy morass following incessant rain. Henry died just after midnight on 11 October. General Follett, Henry's commanding officer, wrote to the Earl the following day:

> I am most awfully sorry to have to write & tell you that Henry Feilding was wounded on 9th and died of his wounds yesterday. He was commanding the company on the right of the assault and got into a heavy German barrage.
>
> I cannot tell you what a loss he is both as a friend and a soldier. It was the first time that he commanded a company in action, and he was doing so well. He was full of enthusiasm for this first attack and I only wish he could have seen the successful ending of such a great day for the regiment, but all the officers of his company fell wounded before reaching the final objective.

He was buried at Dozinghem Military Cemetery; he was twenty-three years old.

Following the loss of her youngest son, the Countess decided to close Newnham as a hospital. On 31 October, Dorothie wrote to her mother:

> I know so well how absolutely down & out you are. Thank God the hospital is closing & it won't be so hard in London away from the dreadful memories of Newnham. Mother dearest I would so willingly have given myself to keep one of your two dear lads. But God did not seem to will it so. The poor mothers have so much, so much more to bear than anyone these dreadful days.

The conflict had certainly taken its toll on the Countess, who passed away on 8 December 1919. The inscription on her grave simply states: 'Worn out by her hospital work, and the strain of the war. She has gone to join her two sons.'

In Belgium, Dorothie felt she had been surrounded by brave men fighting for their country; being back in England she despaired:

> The shreds of beauty that the war brings out are like a gleam of gold in all the darkness & sorrow of grim realities out there.
>
> It's only out there you come upon the beautiful moral side of it all I think.

The mentality of the country here at home & the corruption of politics & on all sides are very sad to see; war is, I suppose, sent as a purifier to the world but the longer it goes on the more all the sordidness of 'powers that be' at home & live only to pull the strings for their own ends, drown the heroism & self sacrifice of the fighting men.

For that reason the end seems further & further away each month.

In France one didn't realise what a rotten state the core of the Mother country was in.

All the best & bravest have gone & oh Mother darling I have seen so much of it, that fears for the future haunts me as much as sorrows we have met already.

Epilogue

Little did Dorothie know but 1918 would bring the longed-for end of the war, although she would lose more precious friends. Captain Field of the Royal Flying Corps went missing in action on 9 January and later was officially declared killed on that date.

The Bloke – about whom Dorothie said, 'He was the best friend I had' – was killed leading an assault party from HMS *Vindictive* during the attack at Zeebrugge on St George's Day. He was buried at sea and is memorialized on the Chatham Naval Memorial. He had written 'Write to 64 Pont St' (Dorothie's London address) on the reverse of his ID tag.

While she had enjoyed a lady's leisurely life in the first months of her marriage, Dorothie was not one to be idle for long and had soon found familiar employment driving ambulances for a London military hospital. 'I am busy driving Fido Fiat & like the work very much – lots to do so one feels refreshingly useful again – I had got tired of being merely ornamental.'

Much to Dorothie's consternation, Charles was passed as fit for overseas service on 28 March. She wrote to her mother that evening: 'I had been so afraid of this these last days – oh Mother darling pray hard – I am so afraid.' He rejoined the 2nd Battalion, Irish Guards on the Western Front shortly after this but was wounded on 16 April during an action near the forest of Nieppe. He wrote a quick note to her before being shipped back to hospital in London:

18/4/18

Dearest
I am safely in hospital at Etaples with a small wound in my thigh, so I expect to see you soon, bad luck isn't it? ... I got here this a.m. I was only hit about 11.30a.m. yesterday so I have been quick. I don't know when I will be sent over but I expect soon – Char.

Charles had not been at the front for long, but long enough to be awarded the Military Cross. The citation in the *London Gazette* on 16 September reads:

For conspicuous gallantry and devotion to duty. In a situation of extreme gravity, when the troops on the right had been forced out of their trenches by the intensity of the fire, this officer collected them, leading them back through a heavy barrage to the original line, when he stayed with them, walking down the line under sniping and machine-gun fire, until their confidence had returned. His courage and coolness were an example to all.

When the war finally came to an end on 11 November 1918, for Dorothie, as for many others, it was a bitter-sweet moment. She wrote to her mother:

I couldn't bear to hear the people laughing & clapping yesterday. One was so haunted by the memories of those dear boys who have gone. But Mother dear thank God that supreme sacrifice was not for nothing as I have often feared it would be.

Bibliography

PRIMARY SOURCES

All of the following are located in Warwickshire County Record Office:

CR 2017/C580 /1-61 Dorothie Feilding Letters Home 1914; CR 2017/ C581/1-189 Dorothie Feilding Letters Home 1915; CR 2017/C582/1-109 Dorothie Feilding Letters Home 1916; CR 2017/C583/1-85 Dorothie Feilding Letters Home 1917; CR 2017/C584/1-50 Dorothie Feilding Letters Home 1918; CR 2017/ C585/1-14 Lady Dorothie Letters 1915–18; unaddressed and undated. CR 2017/ C875/ 1-5 Letters from Dr Henry Jellett to Lady Denbigh re Dorothie's health. CR2017/C1078/1-24 Original bundle of letters to Lady Dorothie marked 'mostly letters on my engagement'. CR 2017/ C1079/1-6 Letters to Dorothie offering comfort upon the death of her brother Hughie KIA 1916. CR2017/C1141/1-28 Letters to Dorothie Feilding from her husband Charles Moore. CR2017/C1280/4 Copy letter from Commander Henry C. Halahan of RN in Nieuport to Brigadier General H.S.H. Prince Alexander of Teck of the British Military Mission to the Belgian Army submitting Lady Dorothie's name for recognition, 1916. CR2017/C1307 Letters Henry C. Halahan to Cecilia, Countess of Denbigh on the death of her son Henry. CR2017/F236 Dorothie Feilding's account of the 1st Yser Battle, October 1915. C2017/F238/1-12 Lady Dorothie's Flanders Reminiscences 1914–15. CR 2017/ F246/1-492 All formerly in envelope marked 'Dorothie's Photos'. CR 2017/ F200/ 1-238 Photos of Rudolph Visc Feilding. CR 2017/ X31 Newspapers 1916 relating to her wedding.

NEWSPAPERS

Rugby Observer

Rugby Advertiser

War Illustrated, vols 1–9

BOOKS

The Naval Who's Who 1917, J.B. Hayward & Son, 1981

De T'Serclaes, Baroness and Chisholm, Mairi, *The Cellar-House of Pervyse*, London, A & C Black Ltd, 1917

De T'Serclaes, Baroness E., *Flanders and Other Fields*, London, George G. Harrap & Co. Ltd, 1964

Foster, R. and Cluley C., *Warwickshire Women*, Warwick, Warwickshire Publications, 2000

Gibbs, Philip, *The Soul of War*, William Heinemann, 1915

Gleason, Arthur and Gleason Hayes, Helen, *The Golden Lads*, Toronto, McClelland, Goodchild & Stewart Ltd, 1916

Lomas, David, *First Ypres 1914*, Oxford, Osprey Publishing, 1998

Macdonald, Lyn, *1914: The Days of Hope*, London, Penguin, 1989

Mussell, John W., [names of co-authors], *Medal Yearbook 2009*, Honiton, Token Publishing, 2009

Nason, Anne (ed.), *For Love and Courage: The Letters of Lieutenant Colonel E.W. Hermon*, London, Preface, 2008

Raitt, Suzanne, 'May Sinclair and the First World War', *Ideas*, vol. 6, No. 2, 1999; digital copy at: http://nationalhumanitiescenter.org/ideasv62/raitt.htm

Steel, Nigel and Hart, Peter, *Jutland 1916: Death in the Grey Wastes*, London, Cassell, 2004

INTERNET

London Gazette: http://www.london-gazette.co.uk/

Daily Mirror Archive: http://www.ukpressonline.co.uk/ukpressonline/

The Times Archive: http://archive.timesonline.co.uk/tol/archive/

National Archive: http://www.nationalarchives.gov.uk/documentsonline –

Medal Index Cards

Coldstream Guards War diaries 2nd Battalion WO/95/1215; 3rd Battalion WO/95/1342

Prisoner of War interview Capt E.W. Hanly WO/161/95/28: http://www.greatwardifferent.com/Great_War/index.htm

Ancestry: http://www.ancestry.co.uk – Medal Index Cards

New York Times: www.query.nytimes.com/search/archive.html

Kipling, Rudyard, *The Irish Guards in the Great War*, vol. 2: http://www.di2.nu/files/kipling/IrishGuardsv2.html

A War Nurses Diary: http://www.greatwardifferent.com/Great_War/Furnes/Furnes_Nurse_01.htm